SCOTLAND:
the new future

GEORGE T. MURRAY

Published by SCOTTISH TELEVISION LIMITED *Theatre Royal, Hope Street, Glasgow and* BLACKIE & SON LTD. *Bishopbriggs, Glasgow*

Filmset and printed in Great Britain by THOMSON LITHO *East Kilbride Scotland*

First published August 1973

Foreword

THIS IS THE THIRD survey of Scotland's economy published by Scottish Television. As its title implies it is a book of wider scope than its predecessors, not only because of our brief to the author, but also because Scotland's horizons themselves have broadened immeasurably since *Scotland—A New Look* was written in 1969.

Three major influences are shaping Scotland's future. The first stems from the enlightened and visionary work of such bodies as the Scottish Council, and others who are dedicated to the Nation's progress. The second will be Scotland's part in the development of the European Economic Community. The third is the immense impact of the discovery of North Sea Oil off Britain's eastern seaboard.

At last plans are becoming projects and dreams reality; this book shows that those who prophesied a bleak future for Scotland are being proved wrong. An immense amount of effort is needed still, and traditional skills will have to be applied to take advantage of the new situation. But Scotland is poised to offer a stable and prosperous economy, a quality of life and an environment which could be unique.

This book is intended for the Scot who wishes to participate in the Nation's future, for the Briton who sees in Scotland a prosperous and challenging market and for those from overseas who realise that Scotland will soon take an increasingly important role in European and World trade.

Many individuals and organisations have helped in the preparation of this book. We should like to record our sincere thanks to them all for making a contribution to the extension of knowledge about Scotland's new future.

James Coltart
CHAIRMAN
SCOTTISH TELEVISION

V

Author's note

THE COVERAGE ATTEMPTED BY this book is deliberately wide, so wide in fact for a volume of its length as to invite accusations of superficiality. Such accusations are in themselves well-founded, but they misinterpret the purpose of the book, which is to impart a perspective and a useful level of general information over the range of subjects covered for those less familiar with Scotland, coupled with highly specific reference material for use by the student, analyst or businessman.

By describing the general framework of the Scottish economy, and indicating—where practicable—the sources both of the data shown and of further more intensive or specific information, the book is also designed as a stepping-stone towards the enquiries which by their nature the reader in pursuit of deeper knowledge must make for himself.

Despite its breadth, the book's coverage remains highly selective, and whole areas of Scottish life and institutions have been excluded. The Scottish educational and legal systems, for instance, receive the barest of mentions, whilst the entire subject of the Arts, in its broadest sense, has with regret been judged beyond the scope of what is fundamentally a handbook with scant pretensions to literature. The brief appearance of history is a concession to perspective and by its brevity a cultural impertinence. A justification is the rich and varied treatment of these aspects in other works to which ready access can be had.

The assistance of the Scottish Council (Development and Industry) in throwing open its own information resources is gratefully acknowledged, as is the valuable help given by the Scottish Office in verifying details of the Scottish administrative structure and clarifying policy aspects of the North Sea oil discoveries. An earlier volume, *Scotland—A New Look* (1969) of which the present writer was co-author, has also been a source of inspiration and reference.

A list of those bodies which have constituted the principal sources of 'live' information is given as an Appendix; the complete list is much longer, and thanks for their willing co-operation are extended to all.

Contents

1 Topography and vital statistics

An introduction to Scotland

The image of Scotland as a remote northern land, rich in scenic grandeur and gaunt relics of bygone ages, but far from the mainstream of contemporary economic growth, is still widely held. Without doubt Scotland is a land of great beauty and abundant in natural resources; but it is a land too of great contrasts—above all between the lonely Highlands and Islands and the highly concentrated, industrialised central belt which encompasses Scotland's two principal cities and four-fifths of its people, in only one-seventh of the total land area.

Scotland extends to 29,798 square miles (77,176sq.km.) excluding inland water areas totalling 616 square miles (1,595sq.km.). Scotland is thus of a size comparable to that of Portugal or Austria, nearly twice the size of Switzerland or Denmark, and two-and-a-half times the size of Belgium. It is 247 miles (441km.) from Cape Wrath in Sutherland, to the Mull of Galloway in south west Scotland, and 154 miles (248km.) from Buchan Ness, near Peterhead in the east, to Applecross in Wester Ross. The heavily indented coastline has a total length of 2,300 miles (3,700km.).

Overall, the region is relatively lightly populated, but again sharp contrasts are met with (population density in the central corridor is as high as 1,200 persons per square mile, compared with an average of 175 for the whole region) and Scotland's population of $5\frac{1}{4}$ million considerably exceeds that of Denmark or Norway, and is only one million less than that of Switzerland.

History

Although in modern times an integral part of the United Kingdom, Scotland's proud and distinctive personality stems from centuries of independence as a nation, many of them spent in bitter conflict with the English and in alliance with England's enemies.

1

The Roman occupation of Scotland was short-lived and largely unsuccessful. There followed centuries of internal tribal warfare between the Celtic Picts (north of the Forth and Clyde) the Scots, also Celtic, immigrants from northern Ireland, in the west, the Britons south of the Firth of Clyde in the region known as Strathclyde, and the Angles, Teutonic invaders from north of the Elbe, who occupied the area between Strathclyde and the south coast of the Firth of Forth.

The earliest Viking invasions date from before the year AD 800, with the conquest by the Norsemen of the northern part of Scotland and the Islands. Common faith and the need for unity against aggression brought Pict and Scot together in AD 844. By the 11th century, the basis of the Scottish Kingdom had been created. In the 12th and 13th centuries, Scotland became a feudal state and entered the orbit of western civilisation.

In AD 1290 Edward I of England asserted feudal rights over Scotland, and it was the rebellion of the ill-fated John Balliol which led to the Anglo-Scottish alliance which lasted over 260 years. The battle of Bannockburn routed the English near Stirling in 1314 and finally led once more in 1328 to English recognition of Scotland's independence, the most glorious achievement of Robert Bruce, confirming the existence of Scotland as a separate State.

Scotland became heavily influenced by French culture and institutions, and the 'Auld Alliance' is still at the root of sentimental ties between the two countries. When Henry VIII invaded France James IV of Scotland, true to the alliance, marched against England and fell at the still commemorated disaster of Flodden in 1513.

On James's death Henry VIII renewed the claim of overlordship of Scotland and the infant Mary Stuart, daughter of James's second marriage to Mary of Lorraine, was sent to France for protection while her mother ruled as Regent. Mary was betrothed to the Dauphin, who reigned briefly as Francois II of France from November 1558 until his death in December the following year. Soon afterwards, and following the death of her mother, Mary returned to Scotland in the face of the enmity of Catherine de Medicis (acting as Regent for the infant Charles IX of France) and at the invitation of her Scottish nobles.

It was the refusal of Elizabeth I to recognize Mary as her

successor to the English throne which finally led to the tragedy of the famous Queen of Scots. Mary's uncontrollable passions and driving ambition to oust Elizabeth from the throne of England were her undoing; she was finally executed at Fotheringay Castle in 1587 after 18 years' imprisonment.

Earlier, her mother's Regency had only succeeded in replacing hatred of England by dread of French domination. The Scottish reformation, under the inspiration of John Knox, came to a head and the Treaty of Edinburgh (1560) severed connections with Rome and brought the 'Auld Alliance' with France to an end. The way then became clear for her son James VI who succeeded his exiled mother in 1567 to realise the ambition which had lain beyond her reach, and inherit the English throne on the death of Elizabeth in 1603, thus uniting the two kingdoms. The union was purely personal, however, and Scotland remained a separate State until economic pressures on Scotland's part and political necessity on that of England brought the Act of Union in 1707.

During the preceding 17th century there was no free trade between Scotland and England and Scotland was also excluded from trading with the British colonies. Scots became mercenaries in the armies of France and the Scandinavian countries, and traded with northern Europe and the Baltic lands.

Attempts to reinstate the Scottish crown continued until the final defeat of Prince Charles Edward Stuart (the 'Bonnie Prince' of legend and song) at Culloden Moor near Inverness in 1746—the last battle fought on British soil—but Union marks the beginning of modern Scotland.

Language

The Gaelic language is still spoken in parts of northern Scotland, but amongst dwindling numbers—the numbers speaking only Gaelic halved between the two censuses of 1951 and 1961 and are now less than a thousand, while the 1961 numbers speaking both English and Gaelic totalled 75,508—one-and-a-half per cent of the population.

Geography

The physical characteristics of Scotland have to a large extent dictated the modern pattern of population and activity. The three principal sub-regions are the *Highlands and Islands,* the most northerly and sparsely populated area, the *Central Lowlands,* the smallest but most densely populated part of the regions, and the *Southern Uplands* which border with England.

The Highlands and Islands

The central part of this area, the Great Glen, is bisected by a connecting system of lochs and canals (the Caledonian Canal) of which the largest and best known is Loch Ness, 24 miles in length and of great depth. To the south of this chain are the Grampian Hills, whose highest peak Ben Nevis, 4,406 ft. (1,323m.) is the highest point in the British Isles. The most isolated parts of the mainland are in the North West Highlands, the heatherclad land of glens and lochs, steep valleys and rivers, home of the Scottish crofter.

The six-mile span of the Pentland Firth separates the northern Caithness coast from the Orkneys, an archipelago of 90 islands (of which only one-third are inhabited); 50 miles further north are the Shetland islands, around 100 in all, of which only one-fifth are inhabited, famous for the knitwear bearing their name, and as close to Norway as to mainland Scotland. Both Orkneys and Shetlands were under Danish suzerainty until AD1590.

To the west of Scotland, between Sutherland and Argyll, are some 500 islands, the Hebrides, of which around 100 are inhabited, but whose topography permits only some 300 square miles out of a total of 2,812 square miles to be cultivated. The Hebrides were ceded to the Scottish king Alexander III by Magnus of Norway in 1266. The Outer Hebrides include the Island of Lewis with Harris, home of the celebrated tweeds, while among the Inner Hebrides are the picturesque and much-sung islands of Skye, Mull, and Islay.

The Central Lowlands

This area, sometimes called the Midland Valley, is the most prosperous agricultural region of Scotland and the principal industrial centre. It contains the valleys and estuaries of the rivers Tay, Forth and Clyde, and the two cities of Edinburgh and Glasgow. The latter is Scotland's principal commercial centre and seaport, while Edinburgh, the capital, is both a city of great beauty and a cultural centre of international standing. To the north of Glasgow is Loch Lomond, Scotland's (and Britain's) largest stretch of inland water (24 miles long).

The origins of Scottish industry lie in the presence of coal in large quantities amongst the carboniferous rocks of Central Scotland, while Scotland's development as a trading nation owes much to the narrowness of the land corridor separating the Forth and Clyde estuaries (a mere 25 miles) and to the consequent development of inland ports. The two cities themselves are less than 50 miles apart.

The Southern Uplands

This southernmost part of Scotland, although rising at places to nearly 2,800 ft. (848m.), consists chiefly of open moorland country. Once glaciated, it contains deep valleys or dales which provide natural routes from south to north, and rich farming soils in the Border country. Farming activity centres around cattle in the south-western Galloway region, while in the east the Tweed basin has become the major sheepfarming area of Britain.

The long (96 miles) Tweed valley is the centre of Scotland's woollen goods industry. A natural barrier between Scotland and England is formed by the Cheviot Hills, which rise to 2,676 ft. (804m.), although the remnants of the wall constructed by the Roman emperor Hadrian in the second century lie further south, along a line from the Solway Firth to the river Tyne at Newcastle.

Climate

Although Scotland's northerly position in the British Isles is inevitably reflected in unfavourable comparisons of climatic and other meteorological averages, Scotland's weather presents contrasts as great as its other characteristics. The rich, glowing colours of spring and autumn, with heatherclad hills blending with multi-hued foliage and matching blues of sky and loch or burn, are part of Scotland's legendary attraction, while the summer sun not so infrequently outshines that of England, and the snow-clad Highland ranges have made Scotland a winter playground rivalling traditional resorts.

today the figure is 12·3 per cent. Females, with naturally greater longevity, greatly outnumber males among the over-65s, and begin to preponderate from age 35 upwards.

The age/sex structure of the Scottish population today is shown in the following two tables.

DISTRIBUTION OF THE SCOTTISH POPULATION 1972
1. Sex distribution by age group

Age	Males %	Females %
0–14	50·8	49·2
15–19	50·8	49·2
20–24	50·3	49·7
25–34	49·8	50·2
35–44	48·8	51·2
45–64	47·1	52·9
Over 65	38·0	62·0
Total	48·1	51·9
	(2,504,500)	(2,706,200)

Source: Registrar General for Scotland.
Annual Estimates of the Population 1972.

2. Age distribution by sex

Age	Males %	Females %	Total %
0–14	27·5	24·1	25·8
15–19	8·1	7·3	7·7
20–24	7·5	6·9	7·1
25–34	12·7	11·8	12·2
35–44	11·7	11·4	11·6
45–64	22·6	23·5	23·0
Over 65	9·9	15·0	12·6
Total	100·0	100·0	100·0
	(2,504,500)	(2,706,200)	(5,210,700)

Source: Registrar General for Scotland.
Annual Estimates of the Population 1972.

Birth and Death Rates

Historically, the birth-rate in Scotland has been higher than the average for Great Britain, and this is still so, although the difference is narrowing. As the table below shows, Scotland's birth-rate has been falling faster than that for the country as a whole, since the change of trend in the mid-nineteen sixties.

BIRTH RATES IN SCOTLAND AND GREAT BRITAIN
(live births per 1,000 population)

Year	Scotland Birth-rate	Index (1961 = 100)	Great Britain Birth-rate	Index (1961 = 100)
1961	19·5	100·0	17·8	100·0
1962	20·1	102·9	18·2	102·2
1963	19·7	101·1	18·5	103·9
1964	20·0	102·7	18·7	105·1
1965	19·3	99·1	18·3	102·8
1966	18·6	95 3	17·8	100·0
1967	18·6	95·1	17·5	98·3
1968	18·3	93·6	17·1	96·1
1969	17·4	89·1	16·1	93·3
1970	16·8	86·0	16·2	91·0
1971	16·6	85·1	16·1	90·4
1972	15·1	77·4	14·8	83·1

Source: Central Statistical Office: Annual Abstract of Statistics 1972.
Registrar General for Scotland.
Annual Report 1972.

Regional Distribution

For statistical purposes, Scotland is divided into four regional divisions (although the whole of Scotland constitutes a single Economic Planning Region of the United Kingdom). These divisions are illustrated in the maps which appear on pages 11 and 12. It will be seen that if the two central divisions are added together, the resultant grouping corresponds approximately to the physical divisions already discussed. The population grouping is as follows.

REGIONAL DISTRIBUTION OF
THE POPULATION OF SCOTLAND
(30 June 1971)

Area	Population	Per cent of total
Northern	971,943	18·6
East Central	1,528,002	29·3
West Central	2,478,669	47·5
Southern	238,786	4·6
All Scotland	5,217,400	100·0

Source: Registrar General for Scotland.
Annual Estimates of the Population 1971.

Scotland is also divided for economic planning purposes into a total of eight regions, whose boundaries (which differ from the basic regional divisions discussed above) are illustrated in the map on page 12. The populations of these eight planning regions are as follows:

SCOTLAND'S EIGHT PLANNING SUB-REGIONS

Region	Population June 1971
Greater Glasgow	2,498,607
Falkirk/Stirling	250,653
Greater Edinburgh	1,034,374
Tayside	452,556
Borders	100,822
South-West	149,478
North-East	451,298
Highlands	279,612

Source: Registrar General for Scotland.
Annual Estimates of the Population 1971

The constitution of these planning sub-regions in terms of counties—for those who wish to perform further calculations—is set out in Appendix 4.

Major changes in the organisation of local government in Scotland will take effect within the next few years and will render these divisions obsolete. The changes and the system to which they will lead are discussed in the next chapter.

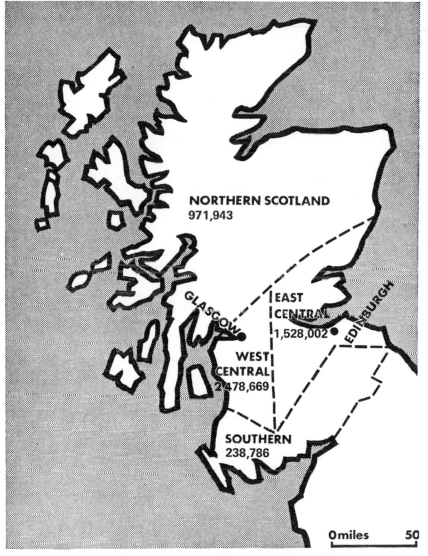

NORTHERN SCOTLAND
971,943

GLASGOW

EAST
CENTRAL
1,528,002

EDINBURGH

WEST
CENTRAL
2,478,669

SOUTHERN
238,786

0 miles   50

Regional distribution of population

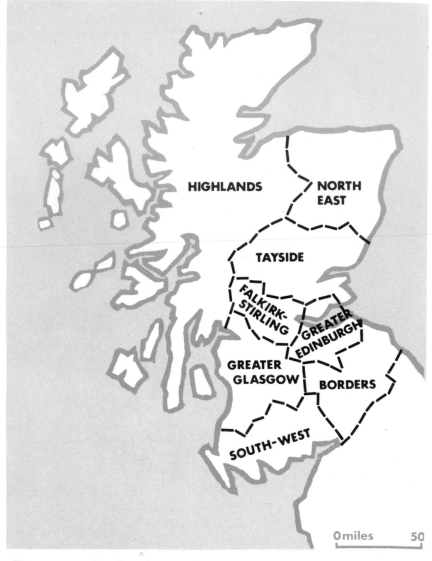

The economic planning regions

The Central Region

This region, in which over three-quarters (76·8 per cent of the Scottish population reside, also largely coincides with the boundaries of the Central Scotland Independent Television Area (STV), the larger (in market terms) of the two elements making up the STAGS Marketing Area. The STV area in fact contains Scotland's three largest cities—Glasgow, Edinburgh and Dundee. Dundee itself falls in the area where STV and its northern partner, Grampian TV, overlap, the two largest cities in the Grampian area being Dundee and Aberdeen, though the latter falls outside the Central Region and is instead the largest town of northern Scotland.

Dominant in the Central Region is Clydeside, Scotland's only urban area ranking as a conurbation, at the heart of which is the City of Glasgow. A map of the conurbation appears below.

The Clydeside conurbation

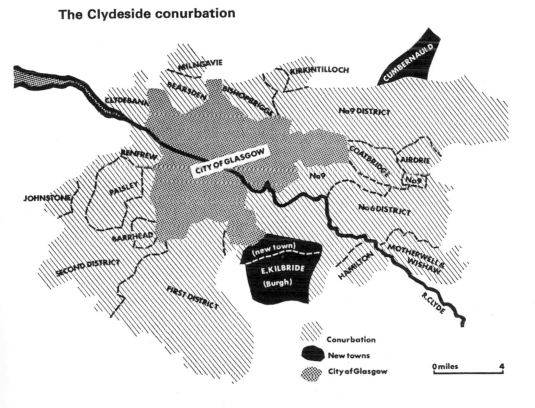

The conurbation has (1971) a population of 1,722,558 and Glasgow City itself numbers 893,790. The administrative areas making up the conurbation are shown below with their status and 1971 populations.

Administrative areas	Status	Population
Dunbarton County (part)		
Bearsden	Small Burgh	24,654
Clydebank	Large Burgh	48,170
Kirkintilloch	Small Burgh	25,237
Milngavie	Small Burgh	10,634
Lanark County (part)		
Glasgow	County of City	893,790
Airdrie	Large Burgh	37,744
Bishopbriggs	Small Burgh	21,299
Coatbridge	Large Burgh	51,985
East Kilbride	Large Burgh	63,456
Hamilton	Large Burgh	46,376
Motherwell & Wishaw	Large Burgh	74,038
Rutherglen	Large Burgh	24,829
6th District of County	Landward District	67,866
8th District of County	Landward District	52,589
9th District of County	Landward District	59,974
Renfrew County (part)		
Barrhead	Small Burgh	18,348
Johnstone	Small Burgh	22,743
Paisley	Large Burgh	95,067
Renfrew	Small Burgh	18,573
1st District of County	Landward District	49,414
2nd District of County	Landward District	15,682

Source: *Registrar General for Scotland.*
Annual Estimates of the Population 1971.

The numbers living in both Glasgow itself and the conurbation have been falling, the former at about twice the rate of the latter (by about 15 per cent since 1964) in consequence of slum clearance schemes and the development of new towns on green field sites. Edinburgh's population too has been falling, though more slowly.

Nevertheless it is striking that the Clydeside conurbation, Edinburgh and Dundee between them account for nearly 60 per cent of the total Central Region population; hence these cities remain separated by large tracts of open land largely unspoiled by urban sprawl. Clydeside alone accomodates 43 per cent of the Central Region's inhabitants.

A complete list is given below of all cities and towns in Scotland with 1971 populations of over 20,000.

Cities

Glasgow	893,790	Dundee	182,930
Edinburgh	435,025	Aberdeen	181,785

Burghs and New Towns

Paisley	95,067	Falkirk	37,489
Motherwell &		Cumbernauld	32,600
Wishaw	74,038	Inverness	31,426
Greenock	69,171	Stirling	29,788
East Kilbride	64,150	Dumfries	28,963
Coatbridge	51,985	Glenrothes	27,700
Dunfermline	51,738	Dumbarton	25,357
Kirkcaldy	50,091	Kirkintilloch	25,237
Kilmarnock	48,992	Rutherglen	24,829
Clydebank	48,170	Bearsden	24,654
Ayr	48,021	Grangemouth	24,228
Hamilton	46,376	Arbroath	22,764
Perth	42,438	Johnstone	22,743
Irvine	42,300	Port Glasgow	22,482
Airdrie	37,744	Bishopbriggs	21,299

Of these, only Dumfries, in the southern border country, does not fall within the area covered by STAGS.

Urban/Rural Balance

As indicated in the foregoing, the central area of Scotland is highly urbanised. Over the whole of Scotland, though, more than two-thirds of the population live in either cities, 'large burghs', or 'small burghs'. Even this does not give an accurate impression of the extent of urbanisation, since many of the 'landward districts' in which the remainder of the population live contain large

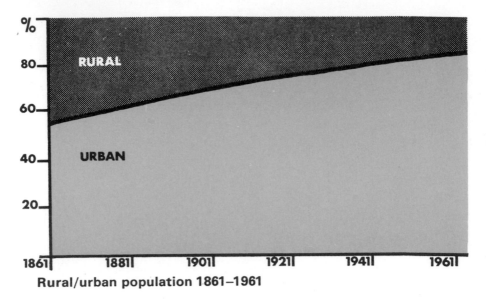

Rural/urban population 1861–1961

communities—up to 60,000 in some cases. Recent estimates by the
Registrar General for Scotland treat all burghs and non-burghal
towns and villages with populations of 1,000 or more as 'urban',
and those under 1,000 as 'rural'. This division is recognized as
being arbitrary, but is useful for international as well as national
comparisons in assessing urban populations.

Calculations on this principle based on the 1961 Census of
Population show that only 14·5 per cent of Scotland's population
could be classed as 'rural', with the remaining 85·5 per cent as
'urban'. Figures for the main regional divisions are shown in chart
form below. It is probable that the urbanisation process has
continued still further since these measurements were taken.

The trend towards urbanisation has been a slightly more significant feature of population development in Scotland during the
last century than for Great Britain as a whole. The trend is
illustrated overleaf, using again the '1,000 inhabitants' criterion.

The New Towns
Four of the towns listed on page 19—East Kilbride, Irvine,
Glenrothes and Cumbernauld, plus a fifth, Livingstone (pop.
14,300)—are New Towns. Since 1945, urban overspill and the

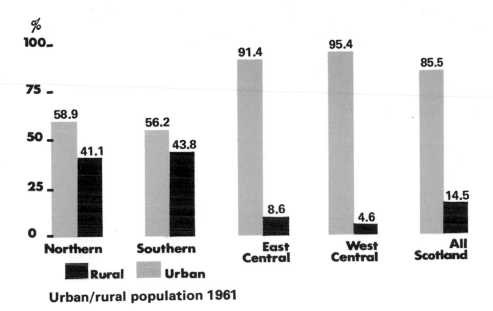

%
100
75
58.9
56.2
50
41.1 43.8
25
0
91.4 95.4 85.5
8.6 4.6 14.5

Northern **Southern** **East Central** **West Central** **All Scotland**

■ Rural ▨ Urban

Urban/rural population 1961

need to resettle populations from old, substandard urban accommodation in Glasgow and elsewhere, coupled with the urge to
create an environment fit to attract new industry to the area, have
given rise to a New Town development programme impressive by
any standards and positively dynamic in its Scottish context. The
five New Towns within the relatively small central valley have
already transformed the area and brought a modern, spaciously-
planned urban environment within the reach of thousands who
previously knew only grimy Glasgow tenements, with corresponding improvements in health and affluence, and far greater
opportunities for home ownership.

The growth already achieved by these New Towns, and planned
for the future, is indicated in the table overleaf.

Both East Kilbride and Cumbernauld were designed to cater for
Glasgow overspill; both embody advanced principles of town-
planning, and Cumbernauld in particular has attracted much
attention for its outstanding design. Glenrothes, on the other hand,
was established to create new jobs in an area suffering from the
decline of coal-mining, and has become a centre for the
electronics industry. Livingston is at an earlier stage of development but has already attracted a mixture of public and private

DEVELOPMENT OF THE SCOTTISH NEW TOWNS

New Town	Started	Location	Population 1971	Population Target
East Kilbride	1947	9 miles South of Glasgow	64,150	82,000
Cumbernauld	1955	14 miles East of Glasgow	32,600	70,000
Glenrothes	1948	Fife, North of Kirkcaldy	27,700	55,000
Livingstone	1962	Midlothian/West Lothian border, 15 miles West of Edinburgh	14,300	70,000
Irvine	1966 [1]	Ayrshire coast, 30 miles South-west of Glasgow	42,300	95,000

[1] Irvine's existing population was some 30,000 before New Town status was conferred.

industries. Irvine, in a different category since it already existed as a town of some 30,000 people, is designed to aid the further industrialisation of the relevant part of Ayrshire.

All the Scottish New Towns have increased their population and employment targets since inception, and a sixth New Town, at Stonehouse, Lanarkshire, 18 miles south-east of Glasgow, and with an existing population of 5,000, has been designated.

2 Infrastructure One: Organisation and supplies

Status

Since the year AD 1707, Scotland has remained united with the rest of Great Britain and its modern status is that of a single Economic Planning Region within the United Kingdom. However, Scotland enjoys a greater degree of autonomy than other regions of mainland Britain. Overall administration since 1885 has been vested in the Secretary of State for Scotland, who is a member of the Cabinet. He is assisted at Ministerial level by a Minister of State and three Parliamentary Under-Secretaries of State.

The Scottish Office is the collective name given to the four administrative departments responsible to the Secretary of State. These are listed below, with their principal functions.

Scottish Development Department	Land Use, Planning, Housing, Roads, Water, Electricity, Local Government
Scottish Home and Health Department	Health and Welfare Services, Police, Prisons
Department of Agriculture and Fisheries	Promotion and development of agricultural and fishing industries in Scotland
Scottish Education Department	Administration of all forms of public education in Scotland

The Scottish Office is located at St. Andrew's House, Edinburgh EH1 3DQ.

The Secretary of State has an overall interest in questions affecting the economic and industrial welfare of Scotland. Within the overall framework of national policy, the Secretary of State is responsible for the formulation of plans for Scottish development, and for co-ordinating their execution (in which he has the support of the Regional Development Division run by a Permanent

Secretary). Being a member of the Cabinet of the Government of the day, the Secretary of State is among the senior policymakers in the national administration and is also able to speak for Scotland in Parliament at Westminster (as of course are other elected Members of Parliament representing Scottish constituencies).

The responsibilities of certain British Government Departments extend to Scotland. These include the Department of Trade and Industry, the Department of Employment, the Treasury, and H.M. Customs and Excise. The organization and functions of the National Health Service are fully operational in Scotland through the Scottish Home and Health Department. As implied by the organization of the Scottish Office, education in Scotland has continued to develop independently of the English system, and retains its distinctive structure, together with its own examination system (the Scottish Certificate of Education corresponds to the Ordinary level of the General Certificate of Education). The universities however (of which there are eight in Scotland out of a total of 44 in the United Kingdom) fall outside the administration of the Scottish Education Department.

It is appropriate here to include a brief note on the important distinctions which exist between the legal systems of Scotland and England. Whereas statutory provisions of law apply to Scotland equally as to England, the system of courts and organization of the legal profession are different. In particular, solicitors in Scotland offer a wider range of services than is usual elsewhere, extending to accountancy and property matters as well as specifically legal advice and representation.

The system of land tenure is also different in Scotland, being a direct descendant of the feudal system, under which the 'feuar' or tenant pays 'feu duty' to the landowner, thereby earning a permanent and unassailable right to the use of the land. The 'subject to contract' procedure customary in England does not apply in Scotland, and an offer in writing, once accepted, becomes a binding contract. Scottish Law Commission is the statutory body concerned with the Scottish legal system while the Law Society of Scotland represents the interests of the profession.

Local Government
Scotland is divided into *counties, burghs,* and *districts,* with a local

authority structure similar to that of England and Wales. Scotland has a total of 33 counties, including Orkney and Shetland (Zetland), which are both separate counties. For certain administrative purposes the counties of Perth and Kinross, and Moray and Nairn are combined.

The county councils are responsible for local government within the county apart from the Large Burghs, which are independent of the county except for matters of valuation, electoral registration, education, and the police. In the four 'Counties of Cities' (Edinburgh, Glasgow, Dundee and Aberdeen) the councils are all-purpose authorities similar to the County Borough councils in England and Wales and are presided over by a Lord Provost. Here, the County Council has no jurisdiction. Elsewhere, town councils consist of a Provost, Baillies (the equivalent of Aldermen in England) and councillors. The Provost and Baillies hold office for three years and perform the duties of magistrates of the Burgh.

The present administrative structure of Scotland is summarised below, and a map of the present county boundaries is shown on page 24.

Counties of Cities	4
Other Large Burghs	21
Small Burghs	176
District Councils	196

Local Government Reform

Proposals presently under consideration will abolish these county boundaries and with them the existing administrative structure, radically altering the organization of local government in Scotland. The recommendations of the Royal Commission on Local Government in Scotland (the Wheatley Commission) were substantially accepted by the present Government, and the basis for change was set out in a White Paper published in February 1971 (Reform of Local Government in Scotland. Cmnd. 4583).

Although part of an overall reform of local government in Great Britain, the changes proposed for Scotland will be more fundamental and far-reaching than elsewhere in Britain, and their

c

SCOTLAND

ZETLAND
(Shetland)

ORKNEY

CAITHNESS

LEWIS

SUTHERLAND

ROSS &
CROMARTY

MORAY

SKYE

NAIRN

BANFF

ABERDEEN

INVERNESS

KINCARDINE

ANGUS

PERTH

MULL

FIFE

ARGYLL

STIRLING

EAST
LOTHIAN

RENFREW

MIDLOTHIAN

BERWICK

LANARK

PEEBLES

AYR

SELKIRK

ROXBURGH

DUMFRIES

KIRKCUDBRIGHT

WIGTOWN

Reprinted by kind permission of
John Bartholomew & Son

debate has consequently aroused more passion. The Local Government (Scotland) Bill, when it left the House of Commons in June 1973 provided, subject to any further amendments in the House of Lords, for nine regional councils and forty-nine district councils with most-purpose status for three new Islands councils for Orkney, Shetland and the Western Isles. The regions proposed, with their 1971 populations, are as follows:

Borders	99,000
Lothian	742,000
Highland	175,000
Grampian	437,000
Tayside	397,000
Fife	328,000
Central	263,000
Strathclyde	2,578,000
Dumfries and Galloway	143,000

The main departures from the Wheatley report are an increase in the number of proposed regions from seven to nine (the Borders and Fife), the separate status for Orkney, Shetland and the Western Isles, and an increase in the number of districts from 35 to 49. However, most of Argyllshire will be included in the Strathclyde region in a separate Argyll District rather than the Highlands, Kincardineshire will be placed in the Grampian region rather than being divided between Tayside and Grampian.

Under the proposals, the four cities will cease to be all-purpose authorities and with their surrounding areas will constitute district authorities within the regions in which they fall, thus losing a substantial part of their present powers. The proposals notably avoid a 'metropolitan' solution for the West of Scotland and redistribute responsibility for housing and certain other services in favour of the district authorities.

This reorganization is the first reform of local government in Scotland for over forty years. It entails sweeping changes, not least the abolition of many of the existing county names with their historical and sometimes hallowed associations. The difficulties of imposing a new, modern structure are reflected in the huge, sparsely-populated area still to be covered by the Highland region (stretching from John O'Groats to Ardnamurchan) in contrast to the two-and-a-half million population of the Strathclyde region (nearly half of Scotland's total).

This size imbalance has been a natural target for criticism by opponents of the concept; however the boundaries of the Strathclyde region correspond broadly to the area encompassing the homes and workplaces of a distinct population, and any subdivision would represent a fatal weakening of administrative cohesion. At the same time, without undermining the power of the regional authorities, the districts outside the cities have been much strengthened and made more attractive bodies for public service by elected representatives and full-time officials.

In relation to this last aspect, the question of financing the new system poses special problems, and the financial aspects of local government reform in relation to the whole country have been the subject of a Green (preliminary) Paper published in July 1971 (The Future Shape of Local Government Finance, Cmnd. 4741).

The Bill at present before Parliament is expected to become law in 1973. It is intended that the new system will be functioning alongside the old in 1974 and will supersede it in 1975.

Plànning and Development Authorities

The 'supreme' planning authority for Scotland is the Government at Westminster, with overall regional responsibility in the hands of the Secretary of State for Scotland, operating through the Scottish Development Department.

Changes in Government structure in the mid-1960s led to the setting up of a series of Regional Economic Planning Boards and Development Councils. The Scottish Economic Development Council is an advisory body with members individually appointed by the Government and drawn from different spheres of Scottish life, under the Chairmanship of the Secretary of State. The Scottish Economic Planning Board is made up of senior civil servants and is the executive body representing those Government departments whose responsibilities in Scotland are not handled by the Scottish Office. It is thus unique as a meeting point for the Departments concerned.

As noted above (p. 22) the functions of the Department of Trade and Industry extend directly to Scotland, and the recently formed Scottish Industrial Development Office has generally strengthened DTI involvement and the channelling of financial assistance. The activities of the Development Commission for Scotland, which works in close collaboration with the Scottish Development Department and with the various local and regional authorities, lie chiefly in financing schemes of benefit to rural areas. The Commissioners are appointed by Royal Warrant and report directly to the Government. Research for the various divisions within the Scottish Development Department is undertaken by the Scottish Office Central Planning Research Unit, and in 1972 a Planning Exchange was set up in Glasgow to interchange and integrate projected planning developments.

The evolution of the modern framework of Scottish planning is outlined below. Scottish development has been part of regional policies in Britain since 1945. The various Distribution of Industry Acts governed regional development until 1960, and were administered by the then Board of Trade, using a variety of methods to attract industry to the 'development' regions. In Scotland, these originally comprised the Clyde Basin, including Glasgow, plus Dundee and the Inverness/Dingwall area around the Moray and Cromarty Firths. Between 1945 and 1950, 49 million square feet (4·5 million sq.m.) of new space for manufacturing industries was completed in Scotland, of which 11 million sq. ft. (1·02 million sq.m.) was financed by the Government.

The Local Employment Act of 1960 designated certain districts suffering from chronically high unemployment rates. Later, in 1963, the provisions of this Act were extended to encompass a number of growth areas regardless of the level of unemployment. Eight such areas were designated in Central Scotland: the five New Towns (themselves a product of the original Distribution of Industry Act) the Vale of Leven, North Lanarkshire, and Falkirk/ Grangemouth.

This legislation was in turn replaced by the Industrial Development Act of 1966 which, while altering only slightly the overall value of incentives in the Development Areas, scheduled the whole of Scotland as a Development Area, with the exception of Edinburgh and the adjoining districts of Leith and Portobello. This remains the present situation, with the exception that Greater Glasgow, Dunbarton, parts of the counties of Renfrew, Lanark, Ayr and Stirling, and small areas of Fife and Dumfriesshire have been upgraded to Special Development Areas. The five New Towns are also Special Development Areas, or have equivalent incentives for approved projects. Edinburgh (with Leith and Portobello) now have 'intermediate' area status. An outline of the various forms of assistance available for industrial development in these areas is given later in this chapter.

In the private sector, the main planning impetus at the central level is provided by the Scottish Council (Development and Industry). This was formed in 1946 by the merger of the Scottish Development Council and the Scottish Council on Industry. It is financed voluntarily by Local Authorities, industrial companies, banks, Chambers of Commerce, Trade Unions, and other corporate bodies all of whom are represented on the Executive Committee.

The Council has the broad aim of promoting the industrial and social development of Scotland; its main activities are thus promotional in character, including the publication of numerous surveys and development studies, sponsoring of trade missions, symposia and the like. The Council also plays an active part, however, in seeking to procure new industrial investment in Scotland and in providing specific assistance to firms in matters such as location, power supplies, finance, labour, and even markets.

The Scottish Council (Development and Industry) was the sponsor of the Committee of Enquiry into the Scottish Economy (the Toothill Committee) whose report in 1961 set out the requirements for an extensive and integrated programme of investment in communications, power and social services, to provide the basis for a modern Scottish economy. The main elements of infrastructure proposed were subsequently adopted as part of official Government policy towards the region, finding expression in the White Paper 'The Scottish Economy 1965–1970: A Plan for Expansion' (Cmnd. 2864) produced by the then Scottish Economic Planning Council.

Another major Scottish Council planning contribution has been the concept of 'Oceanspan',* suggesting that the natural deep water off the West Coast of Scotland could be exploited to create a major new port, thus overcoming the congestion and shallow water making the English Channel increasingly less suitable for the passage of ever-larger ships. By linking this development to expanding port facilities in the East of Scotland, industrial development would be stimulated and a valuable 'land-bridge' for onward shipment to and from European ports provided.

Now, with the pressing need to reassess Scotland's long term pattern of economic growth in the light of the new oil and natural gas discoveries in the North Sea, and Britain's entry to the European Economic Community, the Scottish Council has initiated a new Industrial Growth Strategy Study designed to show in a new light the possibilities for Scotland if the deep-water potential, oil resources, and other energy-generating potential, manufacturing capacity and environmental resources available to the region are developed in proper relationship to each other. Publication of this new study is expected in 1973/4.

1973 should also see completion of the first phase of the West Central Scotland Plan, produced under the direction of a Steering Committee appointed in October 1970 by the Secretary of State and jointly financed by the Scottish Office and the Local Authorities in the Clyde Valley area. This is the largest and most important planning exercise among several conducted in Scotland in recent years (others including Tayside and the Borders) and its task is no less than the construction of a complete physical and economic plan for West Central Scotland up to the year 1991.

The coverage includes housing, industry, employment, social services, transport, recreation and other aspects of community and private life. The work of the study team is expected to be substantially accepted as a basis for action by the new Regional Authority, which will represent roughly the same interests as the present Steering Committee.

In a more direct 'development' sense, a number of regional bodies also exist with the objective of fostering the industrial

*'Oceanspan': A Maritime-based Development Strategy for a European Scotland', February 1970.
'Oceanspan 2': A Study of Port and Industrial Development in Western Europe. October 1971.

development of the area in question. Most of these are formed by groups of local authorities (they also include some individual local authorities and county councils) and are evidence of the change in attitude in local government towards a direct involvement in promoting economic growth. The principal ones are the following:

Eastern Borders Development Authority
Highlands & Islands Development Board
North East Scotland Development Authority
Tayside Development Authority
South West Scotland Development Authority
Scotland West Industrial Promotion Group
South East Scotland Development Authority

The odd man out is the Highlands & Islands Development Board, which is a statutory body responsible to the Secretary of State. The Highland Board administers a budget of some £4 million a year, and has played a central part in the growth of local industry, publicising the area and researching its potential.

It is inevitable that some lack of co-ordination is present among the efforts of these bodies and the consequence has on occasion been poor understanding of Scotland's industrial potential and resources among target 'clients' and even unfavourable publicity where promotion has been the objective.

To overcome these dangers and avoid duplication of effort, and also to provide a common front for the presentation of a concensus viewpoint to Government, a Consultative Committee has now been established under the Chairmanship of Lord Clydesmuir, Chairman of the Scottish Council. This includes all the bodies listed above, the New Town Development Corporations, the Scottish Chamber of Commerce, and (in the capacity of assessors) the Scottish Development Department and the Department of Trade & Industry. It is intended that a gradual unifying of effort should follow, especially in the promotion of Scotland abroad.

Significantly, the areas covered by the regional development bodies correspond roughly to the projected Regional structure of local government in Scotland and (with the exception of the Highland Board) it is likely that they will be assimilated into the new structure, thus gaining for the first time direct executive powers.

Co-ordination is already at an advanced level regarding exports from Scotland. The Scottish Export Committee, established in 1966 (again replacing an earlier body) consists of 19 members nominated by the participating bodies, which include the Scottish Council, the Scottish Chamber of Commerce, the Confederation of British Industry, the Scottish Office, Committee of Scottish Bank General Managers and the Scottish Trades Union Congress. Outgoing trade missions are a major activity organized by the Committee. A 'Europe in Scotland' Committee has also been formed.

Industrial Development: Facilities and Incentives

The Development Area status enjoyed by almost the whole of Scotland means that a wide range of privileges and inducements are available to industry wishing to relocate or expand in Scotland and (to a lesser extent) to Scottish firms planning extensions. It does not fall within the scope of this book to give a detailed description of these, which are in any case subject to periodic change in response to Government policy. The actual benefits vary according to the status of the individual locality and, as noted above, three different levels currently apply to Scotland.

At all three levels, Regional Development Grants are available towards capital expenditure on premises, and in the Special Development and Development Areas (the whole of Scotland but for the Edinburgh area) these Grants also apply to new plant and machinery. Changes introduced under the Industry Act 1972 (which made free depreciation available nationwide on plant and machinery, with a 40 per cent initial allowance on buildings) increased the Regional Development Grant to 20 per cent on both plant and buildings, with a rate of 22 per cent for most categories of plant in the Special Development Areas.

A number of other changes of particular benefit to Scotland were also introduced in 1972. Firstly, the new Grants are not deducted from a firm's capital expenditure in calculating its eligibility for depreciation allowances. Secondly, the grants paid on buildings are no longer linked to the creation of new employment. The average value of recoveries on typical projects is now over 50 per cent, and the new system is to be maintained at least until the start of 1978. A new system of aid to shipbuilding in the form of a three-year tapered production grant was also introduced in 1972.

Relocation privileges available through the Department of Trade and Industry in Development or Special Development Areas are as follows:

> Factories for sale or rent
> Building Grants
> Operational Grants
> Low interest Loans
> Removal Grants

In the Special Development Areas, rent-free periods for as long as five years plus operational grants of 30 per cent of labour costs are in some cases obtainable. This applies only to new projects brought into the area, and existing plants are not eligible.

In addition, a variety of employment incentives are in force, notably a Regional Employment Premium of £1·50 (lower for women and juveniles) weekly for employees in manufacturing or scientific research. This Premium will be available up to September 1974 although there are pressures for it to be extended. The Department of Employment also makes direct grants for the training and re-training of labour. A network of Employment Offices in all cities and main towns of Scotland is maintained and has recently been strengthened and regrouped so as to correspond to the principal labour market areas. There are 10 Government Training Centres in Scotland, with about 1,400 places, and instructors can also be provided to train labour for semi-skilled jobs at the work-bench.

Much new industry in Scotland has been attracted by the ready availability of 'advance' factories in suitable locations. The principal agency for the construction of these is the Scottish Industrial Estates Corporation. This was set up in 1937 and now functions as agent for the Department of Trade and Industry. The Corporation has so far provided a total of 29 million sq. ft. (2·7 million sq.m.) of new factory space for over 400 companies, both on its own estates and on individual sites elsewhere. This is

FINANCIAL ASSISTANCE TO SCOTLAND UNDER THE LOCAL EMPLOYMENT ACTS 1966/67–1970/71

	1966/67	1967/68	1968/69	1969/70	1970/71[3]	Eleven years 1960/61–1970/71 Cumulative	Yrly. avg.
S.I.E.C. Factory Approvals (No.)	36	28	30	41	21	300	27
Estimated cost £000	3,858	4,520	2,913	6,684	2,146	36,681	3,335
Grants/Loans (general purposes or operational) No. of projects	45	65	58	60	33	429	39
Assistance offered £000	9,552	10,150	15,400	9,278	19,296	141,910	12,901
Grants (provision or extension[1] of premises) No. of projects	605	714	904	648	547	4,129	375
Grants offered £000	8,231	7,249	6,617	7,057	6,969	48,638	4,422
Grants (towards cost of plant and machinery)[2] No. of projects	329	35	9	4	2	1,637	149
Grants offered £000	2,678	799	134	30	195	7,596	691
Total Assistance offered £000	19,543	17,643	17,364	18,410	18,958	163,870	14,897
Scotland as percentage of Great Britain	35·3	38·0	31·6	22·0	27·1	36·2	—

Source: *Department of Trade & Industry.*
1 From 1966/67 also under the Industrial Development Act 1966.
2 Superseded by Investment Grants from 1966/67, payments of which to end March 1970 totalled £170 million.
3 1970/71 figures relate only to Development Areas, and do not include intermediate Areas.

in addition, of course, to developments by New Towns and other local authorities, and to the activities of private developers, which are a growing force.

All in all, the incentives, aid, and facilities available to new industry in Scotland compare well with those offered in development regions elsewhere in Europe. Over the eleven years 1960/61 to 1970/71, Scotland attracted well over one-third (36·2 per cent) of total regional assistance offered in Great Britain. The trend is shown in the table on p. 33.

While some details may change, it is unlikely that Britain's entry to the European Economic Community will lead to any radical alteration in existing regional policies. Indeed the British system may well serve as a model for future Community policy. The Special Regional Fund to be established will in any event ensure that the full weight of Community resources and authority are available for regional development programmes. The appointment of a former Scottish Member of Parliament, and one of Britain's two Common Market Commissioners, to the E.E.C. Regional Development portfolio is a fitting one.

Power Generation and Distribution

Electricity

Electrical power is generated and distributed by two separate organizations, the South of Scotland Electricity Board and the North of Scotland Hydro-Electric Board. Both are responsible to the Secretary of State for Scotland. The two Boards operate a joint generating account so that resources can be pooled, and there is considerable interconnection capacity with supplies in England and Wales.

The Boards are markedly different, however, in the nature of the areas they serve, and their sources of power generation. The northern 'Hydro' Board serves a population of $1\frac{1}{4}$ million in an area of almost 22,000 sq. miles (57,000 sq.km.) lying west and north of a line from the southern end of Loch Lomond to the Firth of Tay, and including the Islands, while the South Board serves the remainder of Scotland, consisting of just over 8,000 sq. miles (20,700 sq.km.) with a population of four million, and including of course the central industrial belt.

The northern Hydro Board makes use of the water power resources of the Highland area to supply most of its generating capacity.

	Installed capacity 1971/72 (kw)
Hydro (conventional)	1,051,938
Pumped storage—Generated	400,000
—Pumped	(436,000)
Steam—oil-fired	307,000
Diesel	62,329
Total capacity	1,821,267

Diesel generating stations are used in the Islands and in remote areas or for standby purposes. The last coal-fired capacity was closed down early in 1972, and converted to oil-firing. The Board's main oil-fired station at Dundee has the highest thermal efficiency of any station in the United Kingdom. The pumped water storage station at Cruachan at the head of Loch Awe in Argyllshire offers a special flexibility and helped to stabilise frequency on the national grid system during the power crisis of early 1972. Another 300 MW pumped storage station at Foyers, on Loch Ness, is due to come into operation in 1974.

The particular nature of the Hydro Board's area means that new industrial investment very often requires new electricity supply lines and possibly new generating capacity. The British Aluminium Company's new smelter complex at Invergordon consumes about as much power as a city the size of Dundee, and the ready availability of electrical power on this scale was a decisive factor in the selection of this site.

As Government incentives and the promotional work of bodies like the Scottish Council and the North-East Scotland Development Authority (and the Hydro Board itself) bring industry further north, the Board's generating capacity is geared to keep in step. Major new installations clearly require consultations with the Board's officers at the earliest possible stage, however, and a full time staff is now maintained to deal with enquiries connected with North Sea oil exploration.

In contrast, the South of Scotland Board has for a decade been the largest customer for Scottish coal and now consumes over half of all coal mined in Scotland (six million tons in 1971/72). The escalating cost of coal has placed the Board at a constant disadvantage and the Board has frequently complained of its lack of flexibility in planning future fuel requirements. The South Board's dependence on coal is illustrated below.

	Installed capacity 1971/72 (kW)
Coal-fired	4,242,000
Oil-fired	539,000
Hydro-electric	123,000
Nuclear	300,000
Gas turbine	195,000
Total capacity	5,399,000

Massive changes are now under way in the structure of power generation. After the completion of the two gigantic new coal-fired stations at Cockenzie (1,200 MW) and Longannet (where the fourth unit, now in operation, brings capacity to a huge 2,400 MW) it is expected that the use of coal will level off. An oil-fired station at Inverkip on the Firth of Clyde is being built with an eventual capacity equal to that of Longannet. The first generator is scheduled for service in 1975. Before this, however, in 1973, the new nuclear plant at Hunterston, Hunterston 'B', which is an advanced gas-cooled reactor will join the existing Hunterston 'A'. This is a 1,320 MW station, over four times the capacity of the earlier nuclear plant. Already, over £100 million has been spent on this project, which will produce electricity at a cost 14 per cent below the most advanced coal-fired station.

Since 1945, the demand for electrical power in Scotland has more than doubled every ten years. The two Boards have increasingly collaborated in matters of new generating plant, and this has become steadily more important in the light of new developments now foreseen for Scotland.

In addition to the massive investment programme described above, a contract has been negotiated for the purchase from the

Atomic Energy Authority of the whole of the output of the 250 MW prototype fast reactor at Dounreay, on the Caithness coast, which should be commissioned in 1973. However, Government permission has been refused for the construction of a further nuclear station of 2 × 630 MW capacity envisaged for Stake Ness in Banffshire, and an oil- and gas-fired station of 1320 MW capacity near Peterhead is being built instead.

A summary of operations over the 1961–71 period is shown on page 38.

Gas

Production and distribution of gas is the responsibility of the Scottish Gas Board. Gas, like electricity, has been subject to fundamental changes in fuel sources, and has made a major effort to respond to the needs of modern industry. The Scottish Gas Board now has over 4,000 industrial customers and there are many recent recorded cases of changeovers of heating and boiler plant to gas.

At the root of this progress is natural gas. Whereas by 1967/68 over 70 per cent of the gas made in Scotland was oil-based, having begun the switchover from coal in 1958, Scotland is now in the midst of conversion, in step with the rest of the country, to the use of natural gas, originally brought in tankers from Algeria, but increasingly from the new North Sea fields. Some 20 per cent of domestic consumers have now had their appliances converted, and over 40 per cent of supplies to industrial customers are now of natural gas.

The domestic conversion programme is moving ahead at a rate of 2,000 households per week, and by 1976 all supplies should be of natural gas. The conversion of domestic customers in the Glasgow area is due to start in August 1973. Already, because the network of main pipelines is virtually complete, any commercial or industrial customer can be connected to natural gas without delay, including the laying of a spur main where the load is large enough to justify this. The price advantage compared to manufactured town gas, too, is substantial in the case of large users. A technical advisory service for industry is available for free consultation.

The year 1971/72, with conversion in full spate, saw an increase of 24 per cent in sales of gas to industrial customers, including

SCOTTISH ELECTRICITY—SUMMARY OF OPERATIONS 1960/61 TO 1970/71

	North Scotland		South Scotland		All Scotland	
	1960/61	1970/71	1960/61	1970/71	1960/61	1970/71
Consumers (thousands)	395	473	1,363	1,513	1,758	1,986
Units billed[1] (millions)	1,672	4,143	7,414	16,239	9,086	20,381
Revenue[1] (£ million)	12	33	51	116	63	149
Peak Load[1] (MW)	585	1,082	2,036	3,748	2,682	4,830

Source: *North of Scotland Hydro-Electric Board.*
South of Scotland Electricity Board.
[1] Excludes interchange of electricity between Boards.

an agreement with the British Steel Corporation to supply up to 30 million therms of gas annually to British Steel's Ravenscraig works, constituting the largest single load ever connected in Scotland. Growth in the domestic sector has been similarly rapid, and over 60 per cent of new houses built in Scotland are now equipped with gas central heating, though for some reason average consumption rates in Scottish homes remain lower than elsewhere.

Natural gas, of course, needs no 'gasworks' to generate supplies for local communities. However, a storage centre for liquefied gas is now operational at Glenmavis, near Coatbridge, Lanarkshire. This site is at the end of the Gas Council's transmission line to Scotland, at the point where supplies are received into the high pressure grid main of the Scottish Gas Board. As the major visible structure embodied by the new gas era in Scotland Glenmavis is impressive. It represents an investment of £3½ million; the plant's storage tank, which is 150 ft. high and 150 ft. in diameter, holds 20,000 tons of liquefied natural gas (or 1,000 million cubic ft. of gas—LNG occupies only one six-hundredth of the basic fuel's volume) or sufficient to satisfy Scotland's present fuel requirements for a week. Already the largest storage tank in Europe, the capacity of Glenmavis is now being doubled.

Oil

All the major oil companies are active or represented in Scotland. Major distribution depots are located at strategic points, and technical advisory services for industrial customers are provided in the usual way.

The major oil refinery at Grangemouth is owned by BP Chemicals (UK) and has an existing capacity of nine million tons per annum. Plans are in existence to double this capacity at a cost of £30 million, and make the refinery one of the largest in Europe, although at present these are in abeyance pending an appraisal of overall needs for refinery capacity.

The refinery is integrated with a major and fast-growing petrochemical complex, based mainly on ethylene and propylene production and the derivatives ethanol and isopropanol. Growth of the petrochemicals plant has been led by the expanding demands of the plastics industry.

D

Crude oil is imported to Grangemouth via pipeline from the ocean terminal at Finnart on Loch Long. Tankers of over 200,000 tons can already berth at Finnart and there is the potential for increasing the size limit to 500,000 tons. However, by 1974 crude from the new wells in the North Sea will probably start to form part of the refinery's input.

These North Sea developments, which are discussed fully in Chapter 4 have already initiated new activity in regard to refining capacity in Scotland, and are the start of a completely new era in Scotland's oil industry.

Water

Water supplies in Scotland are under the administration of the Central Scotland Water Development Board and 13 Water Boards. The abundant water resources of Scotland ensure plentiful supplies, but important new schemes have been needed to harness these to the requirements of industry in the forseeable future.

These will increase available supplies in Central Scotland by more than 200 million gallons per day (Loch Lomond alone can provide up to 100 million gallons per day). In the North East, improvements in supplies to the Fraserburgh area and much of Aberdeenshire have been completed or are under way, while the Loch Glass scheme in the Highlands has been designed to supply 20 million gallons per day for the new industrial centre at Invergordon and can be expanded still further as requirements grow.

Pollution Control

The discharge of smoke and gases into the atmosphere is regulated in Scotland as in the rest of Great Britain by the Alkali Acts, reinforced by the Clean Air Acts of 1956 and 1958. Both, in the case of Scotland, are administered by the Scottish Development Department, and are chiefly concerned with the reduction and control of smoke emissions, defining in the case of the Alkali Acts, a large number of industrial processes and emissions subject to control. The Factory Inspectorate, which forms part of the Department of Employment, is on the other hand concerned with pollution levels and possible toxicity of the air inside industrial plants.

Particular concern arises in Scotland—because of its long, indented coastline, rivers, and large areas of inland water—regarding the disposal of effluents into sea, rivers, or lochs. Local authorities in Scotland are handling an increasing proportion of industrial effluents, which are disposed of through the general sewerage system and discharged after treatment into rivers and sea. Pre-treatment is sometimes necessary before effluents can be accepted into local authority systems.

At present, local authorities are under only limited obligation to accept industrial effluents; this position will change somewhat as and when the Sewerage (Scotland) Act 1968 is brought into force, giving manufacturers the right to discharge effluents into local authority sewers provided the consent of the authority is obtained.

Regulations govern discharges to rivers and, to some extent, into tidal waters. No consent is needed for uninhabited stretches of coastline, but in a total of 36 areas, comprising the major estuaries and parts of the coast, discharges are controlled. For rivers, consent must be obtained from the appropriate River Purification Authority under the Rivers (Prevention of Pollution (Scotland)) Acts, and conditions are usually imposed.

As an example of power for industry with due regard to conservation, the North of Scotland Hydro-Electric Board maintains counts of ascending salmon and grilse at its main fish passes and participates directly in conservation activities and research work. A model fish pass of the type developed by the Board was exhibited in the British Pavilion at the World Exhibition of Hunting Game Management and Conservation in Budapest, and was seen by an estimated one million people. The Board's power stations and dams are now among the tourist attractions in the Highlands.

Housing and Housing Policy

There are fundamental differences in the organization of housing policy between Scotland and the rest of Britain. Home ownership has a less strongly marked tradition (due to an historically low rent structure) and the proportion of houses built by Local Authorities is much higher. This is clearly shown in the table on page 42, which also indicates Scotland's importance in total UK housing programmes.

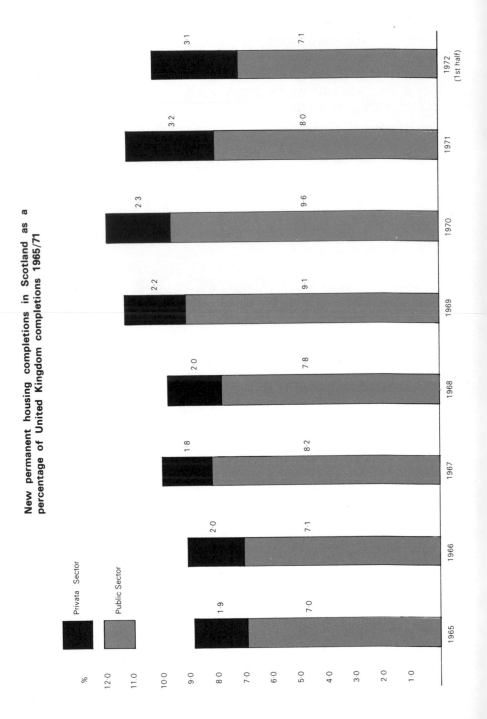

New permanent housing completions in Scotland as a percentage of United Kingdom completions 1965/71

In the aggregate, new Scottish housebuilding (the term being taken to include also flats and apartment building) is currently running at a slightly above-average per capita rate (11·9 per cent of total UK completions in 1970 and 11·2 per cent in 1971). This represents a return to the post-war position up to 1960, whereas in the early '60s the rate lagged for a while below the national average.

Scotland's housing programme has had two main objectives: to rehouse populations in slum and other substandard accommodation, and to meet the needs of new industries in the New Towns as well as in existing centres. The careful co-ordination required is another reason for the continuing dominance of local authority-financed construction (some two-thirds of total new houses built). An additional public sector body, the Scottish Special Housing Association (which has no equivalent in England) has the special responsibility of providing housing where new industrial development is taking place or is in prospect. The SSHA currently builds approximately 3,000 new houses a year.

The structure of new housebuilding in Scotland by type of 'agency' is more fully set out in the table on page 44. The urgency of the rehousing problem is underlined by the continuing high rate of closures and demolitions, which at around 20 per cent of the UK total, reflect over twice the average national rate expressed in per capita terms.

Postal and Telephone Services

Postal services in Scotland are integrated with those of the rest of Great Britain, and services are generally excellent even in the Islands and remote areas. Postage rates by air or surface mail to other countries are the same as from other regions. Concessionary rates are granted by the Post Office for large mailings, and special services (now being extended abroad) are available for the conveying of computer data, etc. The Post Office also offers a wide range of methods of transmitting cash or credit.

Scotland also forms part of the national Post Office telephone network of automatic Subscriber Trunk Dialling (STD) services, and the Scottish cities and most important towns can be dialled direct from London and vice versa. Over the whole country, in

NEW HOUSES COMPLETED (BY AGENCY) IN SCOTLAND 1966/67 AND DEMOLITIONS

	1945/1965 yearly avg.	1966	1967	1968	1969	1970	1971
Local Authorities	18,960	21,343	27,092	26,756	27,497	28,086	23,086
as % of total	70·6	59·2	65·3	63·7	64·5	65·1	56·7
New Towns	1,028	3,870	3,941	3,207	3,656	2,790	2,394
as % of total	3·8	10·7	9·5	7·6	8·6	6·5	5·9
S.S.H.A.	2,617	2,302	2,189	2,048	2,779	3,525	3,058
as % of total	9·7	6·4	5·3	4·9	6·5	8·2	7·5
Housing Associations	89	118	181	288	183	244	332
as % of total	0·3	0·3	0·4	0·7	0·4	0·6	0·8
Government Departments	502	526	557	970	187	302	260
as % of total	1·9	1·5	1·3	2·3	0·4	0·7	0·6
Private Sector	3,667	7,870	7,498	8,719	8,327	8,220	11,614
as % of total	13·7	21·8	18·1	20·8	19·5	19·0	28·5
Total New Houses	26,863	36,029	41,458	41,988	42,629	43,167	40,744
Demolitions and Closures	12,695[1]	16,650	19,087	18,768	17,847	17,345	20,554
as % of completions	—	46·2	46·0	44·7	41·9	40·2	50·4
as % of Great Britain	—	20·0	21·2	20·8	20·5	20·4	22·7

Source: Scottish Development Department.
[1] 1955/1965 period only.

the year ending 31st March 1972, 81·3 per cent of trunk calls were subscriber-dialled. The equivalent percentage for calls made from within Scotland was 75·2, and it can be assumed that roughly the same figure would apply for calls made *into* Scotland.

Services by landline are now supplemented by microwave links between a national network of 100 towers, handling about half of all calls between major centres. The Post Office has embarked on a massive investment programme to double the size of the telephone system in less than a decade at a cost of £4,400 million. Virtually all long-distance calls will be self-dialled by 1978, and by 1980 two-thirds of British homes will have 'phones.

Comparable statistics for private and business installations in Scotland and the United Kingdom are shown below:

Telephones and Telex:
Exchange Connections at 31st March 1972

	Scotland	United Kingdom
Residential	670,545	7,218,282
(Per thousand households	38·8	40·8)
Business	203,522	2,628,934
(Per cent of U.K.	7·7	100·0)
Telex lines	3,024	37,774
(Per cent of U.K.	8·0	100·0)

Source: *Post Office (Telecommunications Div.).*

The Post Office is now in the process of setting up a series of Regional Boards in an attempt to ensure more consideration for local circumstances and needs in future planning, and hence to improve the quality of service. The formation of both Postal and Telecommunications Boards for Scotland was announced in November 1972. The Boards include representatives of Trades Unions and users of Post Office services as well as of the business community.

3 Industry and employment

Patterns of Employment

Whatever the future results of the incentive and aid schemes outlined in the previous chapter, and however far-reaching the implications of the oil and gas discoveries beneath the North Sea, the indispensable key to Scotland's future growth and prosperity is labour. Much has been made of the cumulative problems caused by emigration and declining industries, and an examination of the recent past and of the present situation is essential to an appreciation both of these problems and of the future potential of the region.

With a virtually static population, there has clearly been little scope for an increase in the working population of Scotland. However, an analysis of even the last decade shows that important trends are concealed within the total picture. The male labour force has shown a persistent decline since the mid-nineteen sixties, while the female labour force has grown steadily (see page 48).

While the drop in male workers may be due to some small extent to increases in the numbers of self-employed, a recent shrinkage in the male working population (amounting to close on 100,000) has undoubtedly also taken place. The main contributory factor to this is emigration amongst younger workers. This has only partly been compensated by larger numbers of women and girls available for employment, with the result that the whole labour force has marginally shrunk over the period. The overall effect is illustrated on page 49.

The actual number of employees in employment is a function of the combined factors mentioned in the previous paragraph together with the extent of unemployment. Whereas during the mid-'sixties the growth of female labour (principally in Scotland's new light engineering industries) coupled with relatively stable unemployment figures—apart from 1963—kept the labour force steady, for the last five years a declining male labour pool and

47

increasingly high levels of unemployment, mainly affecting males, have led to shrinking numbers actually in employment. This is the contemporary measure of Scotland's economic transition in human terms.

WORKING POPULATION[1] AND EMPLOYEES IN EMPLOYMENT, 1961/71

Year	Males	Females	Total	Employees in Employment[3]
	(000's)	(000's)	(000's)	(000's)
1961	1,437	782	2,220	2,116
1962	1,450	796	2,247	2,134
1963	1,438	798	2,236	2,102
1964[2]	1,433	806	2,239	2,127
1965	1,422	815	2,236	2,139
1966	1,409	826	2,235	2,143
1967	1,397	819	2,216	2,100
1968	1,375	825	2,200	2,086
1969[2]	1,370	835	2,205	2,098
1970	1,361	836	2,196	2,077
1971	1,347	834	2,181	2,018

Source: *Scottish Abstract of Statistics.*
Scottish Economic Bulletin.
[1] Includes H.M. Forces and Women's Services. Excludes employers and self-employed.
[2] Change of classification: figure shown represents average of old and new systems.
[3] Averages for second quarter in each year.

The word transition is deliberately used; the disposition of Scottish employees over the range of the Standard Industrial Classification differs substantially (as indeed do those of other regions) from the national average and the changes brought about by 'natural' forces and official measures are by no means at an end. The position in 1971 is shown on page 50.

The differences between the Scottish and national patterns— which appear small in terms of percentages of the totals—can more easily be appreciated by taking the percentage figure for Great Britain in each case as a 'norm', and comparing the Scottish figure percentage-wise with this. It is reasonable to take a range of within 15 per cent either side of the 'norm' as approximating to

PERCENTAGE CHANGE
IN SCOTLAND'S WORKING POPULATION, 1962/1971
(1961=100)

the national pattern, and to identify industrial occupations falling respectively above, below, and within this limit.

WORKING POPULATION[1] IN SCOTLAND 1961/71

	Males (000's)	Females (000's)	Total (000's)
1961	1,437	782	2,220
1962	1,450	796	2,247
1963	1,438	798	2,236
1964[2]	1,433	806	2,239
1965	1,422	815	2,236
1966	1,409	826	2,235
1967	1,397	819	2,216
1968	1,375	825	2,200
1969[2]	1,370	835	2,205
1970	1,361	836	2,196
1971	1,347	834	2,181

Source: *Scottish Abstract of Statistics.*
[1] Includes H.M. Forces and Women's Services. Excludes employers and self-employed.
[2] Change of classification: figure shown represents average of old and new systems.

EMPLOYEES IN EMPLOYMENT BY INDUSTRIAL CATEGORY, SCOTLAND AND GREAT BRITAIN 1971

	Scotland		Great Britain	
	Number (000's)	Per cent of total	Number (000's)	Per cent of total
TOTAL EMPLOYMENT	2,018	100·0	22,027	100·0
Agriculture, Forestry, Fishing	55·3	2·7	344·5	1·6
Mining & Quarrying	40·2	2·0	401·3	1·8
Manufacturing Industries:				
Food, Drink & Tobacco	108·3	5·4	837·4	3·8
Coal & Petroleum Products	3·3	0·2	57·6	0·3
Chemicals & Allied Industries	28·3	1·4	466·1	2·1
Metal Manufacture	45·8	2·3	554·8	2·5
Mechanical Engineering	101·6	5·0	1,142·3	5·2

Instrument Engineering	18·9	0·9	157·4	0·7
Electrical Engineering	50·2	2·5	880·5	4·0
Shipbuilding & Marine Engineering	44·8	2·2	191·8	0·9
Vehicles	37·1	1·8	812·9	3·7
Metal Goods n.e.s.	29·1	1·5	614·2	2·8
Textiles	76·0	3·8	612·3	2·8
Leather, Clothing & Footwear	37·0	1·8	524·7	2·4
Bricks, Pottery, Glass, Cement etc.	22·5	1·1	324·9	1·4
Timber, Furniture etc.	25·7	1·3	293·3	1·3
Paper, Printing & Publishing	54·0	2·7	617·8	2·8
Other Manufacturing Industries	16·2	0·8	343·6	1·6
Construction	158 7	7·9	1,248·6	5·7
Gas, Electricity & Water	30·1	1·5	368·8	1·7
Transport & Communication	140·2	6·9	1,564·0	7·1
Distributive Trades	242·3	12·0	2,582·2	11·7
Insurance, Banking, Finance & Business Services	66·3	3·3	971·3	4·4
Professional & Scientific Services	291·5	14 5	2,903·8	13·2
Miscellaneous Services	166·4	8·2	1,794·0	8·1
Public Administration & Defence	128·1	6·3	1,416 3	6·4

Source: *Scottish Economic Bulletin.*

Sectors where Scottish Employment is more than 15 per cent above the national average:

	% difference
Agriculture, Forestry, Fishing	+69
Food, Drink & Tobacco	+42
Instrument Engineering	+29
Shipbuilding & Marine Engineering	+144
Textiles	+38
Construction	+39

Sectors where Scottish Employment is more than 15 per cent below the national average:

	% difference
Coal & Petroleum Products	−33
Chemicals & Allied Industries	−33
Electrical Engineering	−37
Vehicles	−51
Metal Goods n.e.s.	−46
Leather, Clothing & Footwear	−25
Bricks, Pottery, Glass, Cement etc.	−21
Other Manufacturing Industries	−50
Insurance, Banking, Finance & Business Services	−25

Sectors where Scottish Employment is within 15 per cent of the national average:

	% difference
Mining & Quarrying	+11
Metal Manufacture	−8
Mechanical Engineering	−4
Timber, Furniture etc.	—
Paper, Printing & Publishing	−4
Gas, Electricity & Water	−12
Transport & Communication	−3
Distributive Trades	+3
Professional & Scientific Services	+10
Miscellaneous Services	+1
Public Administration & Defence	−2

To some extent these results already reflect the new industrial structure in Scotland—the above average weighting in instrument engineering, for instance. But this is only a fraction of total employment, and the weighting of Scottish labour towards ship-building (representing 23 per cent of the *national* labour force) is particularly marked, while Scotland is far from 'parity' with newer industries such as chemicals, vehicle manufacture, and electrical engineering.

A measure of the rate of change in employment patterns in Scotland is provided by the chart opposite, which shows the actual number of jobs gained or lost in each category by sex over three recent periods. It is pointed out by the compilers* that the latest of the three periods (1969–71), being only two years, cannot be compared fully with the earlier four- or five-year periods, but it is clear that most of the decline in traditional sectors (mining and quarrying, metals, agriculture) took place during the earlier periods (early to mid-sixties), while the growth of employment in financial services and public administration has accelerated recently. In female employment, the recent reduction in growth in the professional and scientific services sector is marked (though this sector has produced more new jobs for women since 1960 than any other).

Employment changes 1960/64, 1964/69 and 1969/71

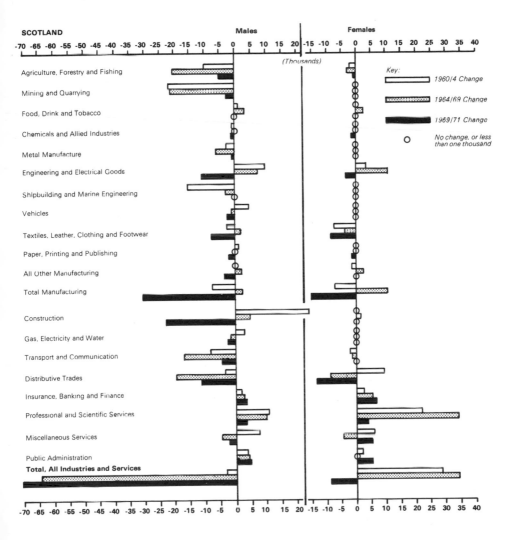

Source: *Scottish Economic Bulletin.*

Industrial Production

These changes in employment patterns mirror (allowing for automation and technical change) the emphasis of industrial production
itself. We will examine the overall pattern first, in comparison
with the U.K. as a whole:

INDEX OF INDUSTRIAL PRODUCTION (ALL INDUSTRIES)

	1963	1964	1965	1966	1967	1968	1969	1970	1971
Scotland	100	108	112	114	112	116	118	118	116
United Kingdom	100	108	112	113	114	120	123	124	125

Source: *Scottish Abstract of Statistics.*
Annual Abstract & Monthly Digest of Statistics.

From 1968, the failure of growth in Scottish output to keep
pace with that of the economy in general is most evident. This
comparatively recent illustration, however, masks important
underlying trends. Scotland's marked growth in the mid-sixties
was largely the result of regional economic policies initiated in
1960 (see Chapter 2). Earlier, though, output in Scotland grew
by 29 per cent overall between 1948 and 1957, compared with
38 per cent for the whole U.K. Between 1957 and 1960, the
relative position further deteriorated. The main reason was
Scotland's legacy of declining industries.

Whereas up to the early 1950's the heavy industries, including
coal mining and shipbuilding, found it hard to meet demand,
diversification and vital new investment were retarded, and when
the boom finally collapsed after 1957 problems of overcapacity
and surplus labour emerged which are only gradually and with
immense difficulty being overcome.

The trend within Scotland is illustrated by the table, opposite,
which shows movements of individual components within the
Index of Production since 1963 (*N.B.* this Scottish index is based
on 1958 = 100 and so is not comparable with the Scotland/U.K.
comparison shown on the previous page.

It should be pointed out that the Index covers only about 50
per cent of the economic activity making up Gross Domestic
Product; some sectors such as trade, transport, finance and other
service industries are missed out altogether, and agriculture must
be separately assessed. The Index is thus far from being a
complete indicator of general economic performance.

TREND OF SCOTTISH INDEX OF INDUSTRIAL PRODUCTION, 1963/71 (1958 = 100)

	1963	1964	1965	1966	1967	1968	1969	1970	1971
TOTAL, ALL INDUSTRIES	115	124	129	131	129	133	136	136	135
Total Manufacturing Industries	113	123	129	130	126	129	132	133	131
Food, Drink & Tobacco	131	144	158	162	154	152	161	173	179
Food	102	104	104	107	108	109	106	111	110
Drink & Tobacco	160	185	212	219	201	196	217	237	249
Chemicals & Allied Industries	116	128	127	129	127	130	138	149	148
Metal Manufacture	96	117	123	112	103	112	119	126	122
Engineering & Allied Industries	110	119	125	131	128	129	129	127	122
Engineering & Electrical Goods	117	127	136	147	145	145	146	138	132
Shipbuilding & Marine Engineering	71	69	72	69	56	64	65	62	62
Vehicles	146	170	165	172	173	179	171	193	188
Metal Goods n.e.s.	107	117	118	113	102	106	111	114	104
Textiles, Leather, Clothing & Footwear	109	113	117	115	107	113	114	107	103
Bricks, Pottery, Glass, Cement etc.	111	125	128	127	121	127	127	112	107
Timber, Furniture etc.	99	108	114	108	106	117	116	115	115
Paper, Printing & Publishing	117	121	122	121	119	124	128	126	123
Other Manufacturing Industries	104	109	116	116	116	130	131	130	132
Mining & Quarrying	86	84	82	77	77	70	65	61	87
Construction	126	138	140	149	155	171	169	163	165
Gas, Electricity & Water	153	160	174	182	194	204	217	218	223

Source: *Scottish Abstract of Statistics.*

E

Manufacturing industries with growth better than average (Index: 1958 = 100)

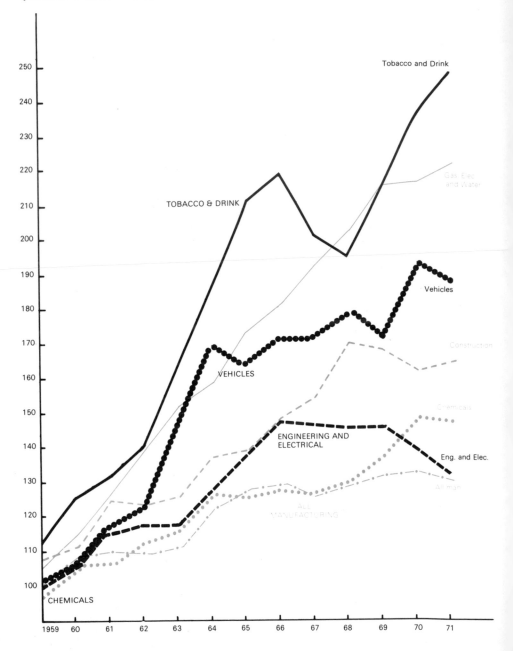

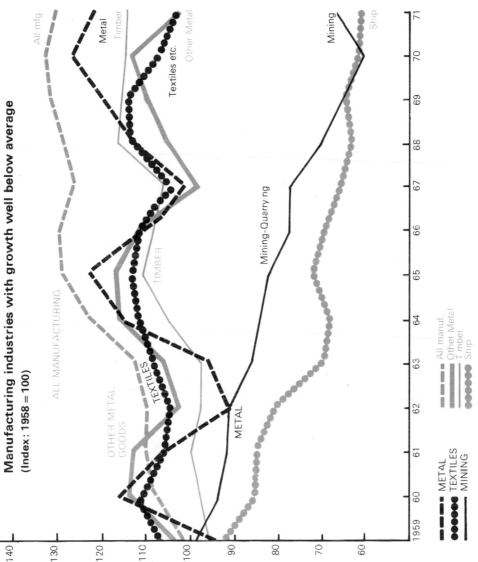

Manufacturing industries with growth well below average
(Index: 1958 = 100)

1971 saw a downturn in Scottish output after two years' standstill and, although the Industry Act 1972 will aid the recovery presently under way, the recession has been sufficient to arrest the growth of most industries, including some of Scotland's most buoyant sectors. Taking a longer view, it is not difficult to distinguish those industries which have had growth rates of either well above or well below the average for Scotland. The movement of the relevant indices is shown in chart form on pages 56 and 57. The contrast between the performance of the shipbuilding and mining industries, and that of drink and tobacco, vehicles or construction should be assessed with reference to the employment figures for the sectors in question to give a further measure of the agonies of an economy in transition.

The Transitional Industries

The fundamental changes in the economic position of the U.K. after her former overseas markets had reached maturity, and world competition in traditional fields mounted, created problems which struck at the roots of Scotland's economy. The main problem, though, has not been the decline in staple industries so much as the failure, in part, to develop alongside them the industries of the mid-twentieth century, especially the mass-production consumer goods industries. This adjustment, or rather conversion, of resources is an often under-rated process and in Scotland's case it has not been aided by the region's comparative remoteness from the mass markets of the Midlands and south of England.

Massive efforts have been made to reorganise and streamline the older, traditional industries, and if these have not always been fully successful, it is a reflection of the size of the task, with social and political factors often seemingly over-riding economic logic. A short profile of five of such industries is given on the following pages.

Coal Mining

The key factor in the early establishment of industry in Scotland was the presence of large quantities of accessible, good quality coal. Today, despite a continuing long-term contraction of the industry, there are 32 National Coal Board collieries in operation, and accessible reserves are estimated at around one thousand million tons, sufficient for another century at present rates of extraction.

In 1958, Scottish coal still employed 85,000 people; this figure has now shrunk to less than a third of that total, and Scottish-mined coal is now around 9 per cent of the national total. The trend of employment and output since 1963/64 (when a financial year was adopted in place of the calendar year) is shown below. The growth of productivity should especially be noted. (The 1971/72 results reflect the prolonged overtime ban in late 1971, and the ensuing seven week strike from January 9 1972.)

PRODUCTION AND EMPLOYMENT IN SCOTTISH COAL 1963/64–1971/72

Year	Production (million tons)	Employment (number)	Output per man-shift (cwt)
1963/4	16·5	50,800	28·1
1964/5	15·5	47,000	29·2
1965/6	14·9	44,900	30·9
1966/7	14·4	41,800	32·4
1967/8	14·0	35,900	34·4
1968/9	12·6	31,500	37·1
1969/70	11·1	30,100	36·8
1970/1	11·2	30,100	37·9
1971/2	10·4	28,400	38·1

Source: National Coal Board.

Scottish coal is the responsibility of two of the National Coal Board's 17 areas, designated Scottish South and Scottish North respectively, with the dividing line passing to the south of Glasgow, via Airdrie and Linlithgow to the Forth. Thus the South area comprises the Ayrshire and Midlothian fields, plus what remains of the southern part of the Central Coalfield, while the North area contains the three main coalfields in the east, in East Fife, Cowdenbeath, the Upper Forth, and the north-western flank of the Central Coalfield (Stirling and North Lanarkshire). From July 1973, NCB reorganisation will mean a single adminis-tration for all of Scotland's pits.

It is striking that—both in response to market factors and as deeper and more difficult seams must be tapped to maintain output—many of the mines in operation today have been established within the last twenty-odd years or are new sinkings. Several—including Seafield (Kirkcaldy), Monktonhall (Midlothian) and the Longannet complex north of the Forth, are capable of outputs in excess of one million tons a year.

Increasingly, the coal industry in Scotland as elsewhere has become dependent upon electricity generation for its market. Of the total Scottish coal output in 1971/72 of 11·9 million tons (the difference from the table above consisting of opencast production) 6·5 million tons went for electricity generation in Scotland, and well over one million tons to power stations elsewhere in Britain; 1·5 million tons of coking coal went to the steel industry, and the remainder to other markets including domestic and industrial coal.

This situation has produced integrally-planned coal/electricity complexes of which Monktonhall (supplying Cockenzie power station) and Longannet (linked to the South of Scotland Electricity Board's new 2,400 MW station of the same name) are the prime examples. Coal's dependence on electricity is unlikely to decrease, and Coal Board analysts in Scotland see demand from this source rising to 8 million tons annually, thus helping to stabilise the industry at something like its present size.

To a large extent the future of Scottish coal is a political issue. The electricity generating industry has campaigned (with some success) for a more flexible fuel policy, and does not foresee its use of Scottish coal rising above the present level. However, the Government's newly announced package of aid for the coal industry, which includes subsidies to offset the costs of burning more coal in SSEB power stations in the next few years, is likely to alter the Board's policies to some extent, and is warmly welcomed by the Scottish coal industry.

Shipbuilding

No industry has mirrored so precisely the fortunes of industrial Scotland over the last century and a half as shipbuilding. Scottish engineers, with their skill in steam-engine building and ironworking, were natural leaders in steamship development, and the Clyde became the greatest nineteenth-century shipbuilding centre in the world. Scottish prosperity was built on the Clyde, and the Clyde looms large in Scotland's present-day problems of adjustment.

Shipbuilding in Scotland, in fact, has been called the perfect example of an ailing staple industry, suffering from a combination of its own inefficient practices and unfavourable market forces. On the national canvas, Britain as a whole during the post-war period has steadily lost ground to foreign competitors such as Japan and West Germany. Even at the start of the 1960s, the U.K. was the world's second-largest shipbuilding nation; by the end of the decade she had fallen to fourth place.

Scottish yards have built a dwindling share of Britain's output, and a series of crushing blows to morale, calling into question the entire future of merchant shipbuilding on the Clyde, were until recently the main outcome of rationalisation attempts. The trend of output tells its own story:

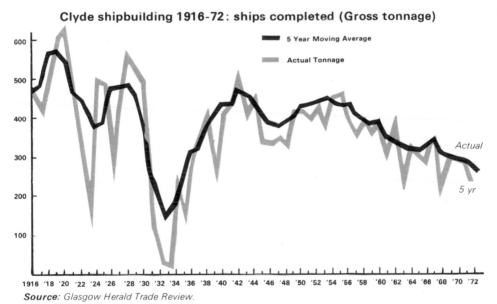

Clyde shipbuilding 1916-72: ships completed (Gross tonnage)

■ 5 Year Moving Average

■ Actual Tonnage

Source: Glasgow Herald Trade Review.

Similarly, the trend of employment has been downward, with the total directly involved in hull construction and finishing work falling from around 50,000 after the war to 20,000 today. (The number has been roughly steady at this figure since the mid-1960s.)

The Fairfields experiment (partnering private enterprise and Government), the Geddes report in 1966, the subsequent re-organisation of the main Clyde shipyards into two groups Scott Lithgow (lower reaches) and Upper Clyde Shipbuilders in 1967 and 1968 respectively, and the eventual collapse of UCS in mid-1971—all are events too well documented to need repetition here.* Nevertheless some reference must be made to the past in pointing to the future.

The formation of UCS took place in anything but auspicious circumstances, with a background of accumulated losses totalling £2·4 million. Additional losses from pre-merger contracts were later found to total £12 million, and to these further losses of almost £10 million were added from contracts entered into after the merger. The group moreover experienced both management and labour problems which precluded the realisation of any durable benefits from the merger. (Yarrow, the one profitable member of the group, withdrew in 1970 and continues independently.)

The new Govan Shipbuilders (comprising the former UCS yards at Govan, Linthouse and Scotstoun) set up by the Government in the wake of the UCS collapse, became fully operational in September 1972 and starts out with several advantages notably absent from the debut of its ill-fated predecessor. Apart from a 'clean sheet' position, launching aid totalled £35 million (of which no less than £17 million was to cover losses on existing contracts) and there is the prospect of a new era in labour relations. The fourth UCS yard, the former John Brown's on Clydebank, was of course rescued from closure by the Marathon Manufacturing Co. of Texas, after the famous 'work-in' lasting 17 months, and is undergoing conversion to make offshore drilling platforms and other equipment for the oil industry.

The Marathon takeover and launch of Govan Shipbuilders, coupled with the continuing success and stability of Scott Lithgow and the independent Yarrow, mean that overall employment in Clyde shipbuilding has barely suffered (the May 1972

---

* For an account covering events up to late summer 1971, the reader is referred to *Structure and Growth of the Scottish Economy*. Johnston, Buxton & Mair. Collins 1971.

total of 20,823 was in fact slightly higher than the previous year; however a later fall will automatically be recorded since the Marathon Clydebank employees will no longer be classified to shipbuilding). One important trend masked by the overall figures has however been under way—the gradual transfer of labour from the Upper to the Lower reaches:

Trend of Shipbuilding Employment on the Clyde 1968/72

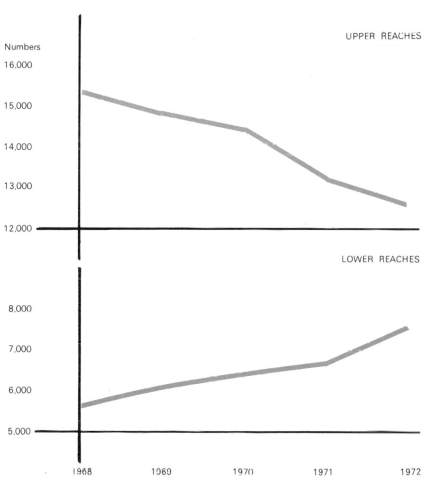

Source: Clyde Shipbuilding Association.

of the self-sufficiency of Scottish industry. The failure of that same industry to respond to the rise of new markets, and in particular to create consumer goods industries, however, delayed the establishment of continuous sheet production processes. It was only in 1962 that the continuous strip mill at Ravenscraig, near Motherwell, Lanarkshire, came into operation, and in its train a new motor industry for Scotland.

As recently as 1966 (in the report of the Benson Committee set up by the then British Iron & Steel Federation) Scotland was recognised as being a self-contained market in steel products. The spread of production is indicated below:

OUTPUT OF STEEL AND STEEL PRODUCTS IN SCOTLAND 1967/71 (000 tons)

	1967	1968	1969	1970	1971
Crude steel	2,600	3,072	3,296	3,330	2,939
Alloys	179	201	232	236	210
Finished steel:					
Plates	632	726	727	749	623
Rails & heavy rolled products	329	315	343	383	284
Light rolled products	262	243	299	338	222
Tubes etc.	185	188	183	220	198
Sheets	520	624	732	773	744
Others	54	52	60	61	49

Source: *Scottish Abstract of Statistics.*

During the same period as these figures span, though, Scotland has had to face the reality of planning on a national scale by the new British Steel Corporation, with its 'own' steel industry becoming a mere regional component, albeit an important one, in the whole. Since 1967, a number of closures affecting production of sections, angles, rods, barrel hoops and other finished products with local markets have taken place and also, inevitably, technical and planning services have been withdrawn and moved south—in most cases to regions with their own crop of economic problems.

In fact, a good deal of rationalisation had already taken place in Scottish steel prior to the state takeover, which also arrested far-reaching plans for expansion—including a plan by Colvilles for a major ore terminal at Hunterston on the Ayrshire coast, where deep water would permit access by the largest ore carriers then (or even now) envisaged. Such a terminal, allied to a new 'green field' steel complex, is in line with successfully applied thinking behind modern steelworks development in Japan and elsewhere, and Europe offers very few such natural sites.

Other possible development schemes for Hunterston which include steelworks have since been put forward by the Scottish Council (Development & Industry) and by private interests, and a major consultants' report has been prepared jointly for the Hunterston Development Company and the Scottish Office. Apart from the rare deep water/flat land combination, and the whole question of adequate steel supplies to Scottish industry, much of the significance of Hunterston is rooted in social questions (the area suffers from excessively high unemployment).

The five-year period of uncertainty since nationalisation is now ended with the December 1972 announcement of the Government's plans for the future of British steel, entailing a massive £3,000 million investment programme over 10 years. Scotland's share of this is to amount to £400 million, but the vision of a major green field steelworks at Hunterston is dead. The Steel Corporation is to spend £27 million on a new ore terminal at the site, and Hunterston may be used for a small direct reduction pellet plant (the site is now open to consideration for other purposes, of course).

Main investment in Scotland, however, is to centre on the doubling of capacity at the Ravenscraig strip mill to 3·2 million tons (metric) a year—in fact announced earlier—and the building of a new electric-arc steelworks producing up to one million tons (metric), probably at Hallside near Cambuslang. Scottish steel production will rise over 10 years by about 25 per cent to 4·5 million metric tons.

Scotland is more fortunate than some regions in that the programme entails no new redundancies beyond those already anticipated. Since nationalisation, Scotland has come off fairly well in terms of closures—despite an overall shedding of 30,000 workers by BSC since 1967. Redundancies in Scotland totalling 7,500 over the next five years will trim the Scottish labour force down to about 18,000 (the new schemes will generate up to 1,000 jobs). In the process, nearly all the old, labour-intensive open-hearth furnaces will be closed down. These at present supply over half of all crude steel output in Scotland, and the 34 such furnaces comprise over a third of the total surviving in Britain.

Although the future pattern of steelmaking is a natural disappointment to those Scots who had hoped for more, Scotland will undoubtedly remain a major regional component in the industry. Ravenscraig is one of five main 'heritage' sites to feature in BSC's long term plans, and on the basis of figures so far available, Scotland's share of British steel output will actually rise.

In conclusion, it should not go unrecorded that private enterprise survives in Scottish steel in the shape of William Beardmore, of Parkhead, Glasgow, now part of the Thos. Firth & John Brown Group, but once a company of world importance in steel, shipbuilding and engineering with over 20,000 employees. Trimmed to a single plant employing 1,400, Beardmore's now produce some 60,000 ingot tons of special steels annually, and a recently announced £1·1 million plant redevelopment scheme has dispelled fears of possible closure. With a modernised forge, and new or improved heavy and light machine shops, Beardmore's will be able to enter new product fields including those demanded by North Sea oil.

Alongside Beardmore's, a relative newcomer is Cameron Ironworks, an American company, established at Livingstone in 1964 and whose products include metal forgings and extrusions with emphasis on advanced alloys.

Textiles

This was another of Scotland's earliest industries and her first major exporter. It is frequently not realised that an important slice of economic activity in Scotland is still devoted to this sector, which employs about 80,000 with another 31,000 in clothing and related trades. The Scottish textile industry has in general attracted less attention and aid than the industries discussed in the foregoing. Yet Scottish textiles have in large measure shared the problems and experiences of these heavy industries and have been subject to changes no less profound.

The present pattern of employment is illustrated below:

EMPLOYMENT IN SCOTTISH TEXTILE AND CLOTHING INDUSTRIES, 1971 (000's)

Knitwear & Hosiery	19·2
Woollen & Worsted	14·1
Jute	9·9
Carpets	9·4
Spinning & Weaving	9·7
Textile finishing	6·2
Man-made fibres	1·3
Other Textile Processing	4·7
Made-up Clothing (other than Knitwear & Hosiery)	32·2
Total Employment	106·7

Source: *Scottish Abstract of Statistics*

Some 65 per cent of this labour force is female. The first four categories shown are the principal ones to consider in respect of the Scottish textile industry itself. Scotland displays a greater versatility in textile making than any other region. The wide geographical spread of the industry is also a feature. Spinning and weaving of tweeds (including the famous Harris) takes place in the Border country as well as in the western Islands and in Orkney and Shetland. Fully-fashioned knitwear is a speciality of the Border country, centred on Hawick, while the cut and sewn knitted outerwear industry is centred on Ayrshire. Jute is traditionally associated with Dundee and Tayside.

The tweed industry has made particularly successful use of its Scottish tradition allied to high quality, and since the war exports have never fallen below 40 per cent of output. The industry has been rationalised and has acquired up-to-date marketing skills. Thanks to a similar process in the cloth industry, no less than 42 per cent of all exports by members of the National Association of Scottish Woollen Manufacturers were sent to EEC member countries, even before Britain's own membership became effective. Recently, immediate prospects of the knitwear industry were damaged by a strike resulting in £1½ million lost output and the industry is in any case both subject to intense competition and rapid swings in fashion. However, Scottish knitwear is world-renowned for quality, and there are signs of a return to buoyancy in this sector.

The Scottish carpet industry—which includes such names as Templetons, BMK and Grays,—is now third largest after those of Worcester and Yorkshire in terms of numbers employed, and has steadily prospered in recent years, with both woven and tufted sectors in the process of expansion and modernisation. A close relationship has been achieved between carpet manufacture and the old jute industry of Dundee.

Although output of jute yarn and piece goods (and employment in the jute industry) continue to decline, an impressive degree of diversification has been reached in the industry within a relatively short period. Sacks and baling material now account for less than 10 per cent of output, and backings for tufted carpets are the most important product. Jute has however faced a major challenge from a new material, polypropylene, a petro-chemical by-product which yields a narrow tape suitable for weaving into an alternative material to jute cloth. This has now captured 60–70 per cent of the British market for tufted carpet backings.

A result has been the emergence of a broader-based textile industry on Tayside where, although redundancies directly attributable to the growth of polypropylene total some 3,000, the big jute companies have now entered the polyolefin textile business themselves. One of the earliest examples was a joint venture, Polytapes, set up between Sidlaw (the former Jute Industries) and Low & Bonar. Tayside now claims the largest concentration of polypropylene units in Europe, with specialist companies alongside the old jute concerns. An official Tayside study now foresees a large-scale potential growth for the region.

The biggest single factor in Scottish textiles is undoubtedly the Glasgow-based Coats Patons Group, with annual turnover (1971) of £303 million, including 68 per cent foreign sales and £27 million direct exports. Coats Patons are the largest thread-makers in Britain and in spite of recent contraction, the Group's mill at Ferguslie, Paisley, is the only cotton-spinning plant of any consequence in Scotland. Increasingly, though, the Group is diversifying into wool-based textile interests which offer greater profit potential. Big names in synthetic textiles with Scottish plants include ICI and Monsanto, and among prominent clothing manufacturers which have been attracted to Scotland recently are Lyle & Scott, Levi Strauss and Lee Cooper.

In sum, Scottish textiles are a classical case of adaptability in response to market forces and technical change. Many problems have been solved and, whilst many remain, the outlook is brighter than for some years.

Agriculture

Farming is an industry basic to Scotland and which remains one of its biggest. The value of output has increased year by year, and agricultural employment is still of the order of 55,000 (including 13,000 in forestry and fishing). The trend of output is shown below:

VALUE OF SCOTTISH AGRICULTURAL OUTPUT 1964/65 TO 1971/72

	1964/65	1966/67	1968/69	1970/71	1971/72
Value of Output at current prices (£m.)	198·4	206·5	223·6	263·5	281·4
Index of Value	100·0	104·1	112·7	132·8	141·8
Index of net output[1]	100	101	105	121	120

Source: *Scottish Abstract of Statistics.*

[1] Gross output at constant prices less the value of all goods and services purchased outside the agricultural sector.

Approximately three-quarters of the value of Scottish farming output is represented by livestock and livestock products. The chart overleaf shows the composition of output in value terms for the most recent year, 1971/72.

F

The structure of Scottish farms in size terms is broadly similar to that of the U.K. as a whole, although Scotland has higher than average proportions of both large and very small farms, the latter consisting mainly of Highland Crofts. Mixed farming predominates, but in line with the topography, a high proportion of

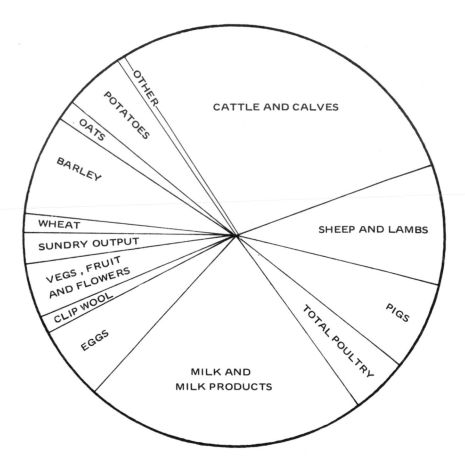

rough grazing and hill land is found (three-quarters of total agricultural land area compared with just over a third nationally).

Trends have been at work within both livestock and crop sectors. Sheepfarming, and the rearing of dairy cattle, have both declined, while the beef herd has assumed more importance. Scotland's success in beef breeding is without equal, and breeds such as Shorthorn and Aberdeen Angus are world renowned. Scotland's share of U.K cattle rose from 16·8 per cent in 1959 to 17·7 per cent in 1972, the increase being due to the expansion of beef herds. Scotland's importance as a pig farming centre has also increased.

Land suitable for crops is mainly limited to the east coast and central valley. Cereals are (as shown in the chart above) the most important crop in value terms, chiefly barley. The principal root crop is turnips and swedes, grown primarily as winter fodder for livestock, and Scotland produces some 60 per cent of the national total. Scotland furnishes, too, nearly a fifth of the nation's potatoes.

Equivalent gains in farming efficiency in Scotland have taken place as in England and Wales, and the recent trend to higher livestock prices augurs well for the future of Scottish hill farmers in the EEC (although the exact form of subsidy which they will receive has not yet been stated, and Scottish conditions are vastly different from those applying in 'equivalent' areas of Europe). On the other hand, Scotland's geographical position will place producers in crop and dairy sectors at some price dis-advantage unless special assistance is granted.

Forestry

Scotland's forests are an important natural asset, as well as a significant employer in upland areas, where alternative uses of land, even for farming, are limited. Much of the Forestry Commission's replanting programme since the 1950s has been concentrated in such areas, and almost 40 per cent of Scotland's present forest area has been planted since 1960—a measure of the pace of replanting.

Britain is the world's largest importer of timber, to the tune of 90 per cent of requirements. Only 8 per cent of land area is used for forestry, compared with an average of 30 per cent for Europe. Nearly half that area is in Scotland, consisting of some 1,850,000 acres (748,670 ha.), divided roughly equally between the Forestry Commission and private owners.

Scotland offers climatic conditions especially suitable for the growing of conifers and certain softwoods and—subject to overall

Government policies—there is the prospect of reafforesting up to a further three million acres (1·2 million ha.). During the latest year, to 31st March 1972, 91,000 out of the 128,000 acres planted on private and Commission land were in Scotland, most of it new planting.

This investment in Scottish forestry has attracted timber-using industries, of which the best-known example is the £15 million pulp and paper mill of Wiggins Teape at Fort William, Inverness-shire. After technical problems and a period of slack demand, as well as fierce competition from Scandinavian producers, the prospect at Fort William is now brighter, and the growth of the chipboard industry has led to the establishment of several new Scottish plants, notably an £11 million project by Scottish Timber Products at Cowie, near Stirling. Such developments go a long way to offset the difficulties of access to forest areas and distance from markets.

Fisheries

It is reliably estimated that about 20,000 people are dependent on the Scottish fishing industry for their livelihood, and the industry directly employs some 9,000. The old Scottish tradition was of strictly local inshore white fisheries, mainly for home consumption, either sold fresh or dried for winter use. Deep-sea trawling did not commence until about 1880. Aberdeen, main home of the Scottish trawler fleet, is now Britain's third most important fishing centre after Hull and Grimsby.

The value of Scottish landings has grown steadily and is now about £30 million annually. White fish is still the main catch, but Scotland is now the main source of herring for European markets in consequence of the overfishing of other areas, and sales of shellfish are booming, both these catches now earning some £4 million per year each. The industry has benefitted from the more realistic prices now being obtained for all types of fish, and an expansion of the fish processing industry as well as of direct exports is foreseen.

Scotland has also increased its importance as a fisheries centre relative to other regions. A 67 per cent increase in the volume of fish landed in Scotland from 1951 to 1971 compares with a decline of 30 per cent in England and Wales during the same period, with a consequent increase in Scotland's share in total landings from 25 per cent to 46 per cent. This status is consolidated by the presence in Aberdeen of the Torry Research Station, which is the main Government laboratory concerned with fish technology, and the Marine Laboratory of the Department of Agriculture and Fisheries for Scotland, as well as private research stations.

These steadily increasing quantities of fish are being caught by a contracting fleet—now totalling about 2,500 vessels compared with 3,000 a decade ago—due to gains in efficiency. However, despite progressive re-equipment, it is estimated that as many as 2,000 vessels need re-equipping or replacing. Uncertainty concerning the future has led, too, to a decline in new vessel orders, although under a Highlands & Islands Development Board scheme £4 million will be invested in 250 new boats, mainly in less developed areas such as Caithness and Orkney. Fleet owners continue to face huge rises in vessel and operating costs, and the radical changes in the laws governing inshore fisheries proposed in the 1971 Cameron report have caused widespread concern. Fishermen are fearful of losses through oil pollution and, despite the ten year transitional period secured for Scottish fisheries in the EEC entry terms, the industry's future outlook is punctuated by unknowns.

Other Industries

The scope of the older or traditional industries in Scotland is of course much wider than those discussed above, and successful transitions have taken place in, for example, the heavy engineering and electrical engineering industries. Scotland's food, drink and tobacco industries both form part of the traditional sector and are—as clearly shown on page 55—the fastest-growing present day sector in the Scottish economy. Canned foods, biscuits, soft drinks, beer and tobacco have all shared in this activity. Whisky and brewing, especially, have remained buoyant. The latter retains a distinctive Scottish character (without having wholly escaped the tide of rationalisation in the U.K. industry as a whole) and is a considerable exporter of beer.

Scotch whisky itself can claim to play a unique and distinct role in the Scottish economy. Employing directly 23,000 people, with thousands more in ancillary trades, it is a major employer in its own right. As an exporter, it is without peer in Scotland, accounting for one quarter of attributable foreign currency earnings. Since 1952, exports have grown at an annual rate of 9 per cent in volume and 11 per cent in value, to reach over 70 million proof gallons in 1971, valued at £227 million.

During the past four years, an estimated £100 million has been invested in expansion and new facilities. Although matters of concern face the industry—notably securing fair terms of trading in export markets and the harmonisation of EEC excise duty rates—there can be no doubt as to its long term prosperity as 'Scotch' increases in popularity the world over.

Unemployment and Migration

All the industries discussed in the foregoing have changed and adapted, with varying degrees of success, to modern conditions. The price of transition is still being paid, however. Consistently throughout the post-war era, Scotland has had a higher level of unemployment than Great Britain as a whole. During the 1960s the rate was in fact higher than in the previous decade—despite

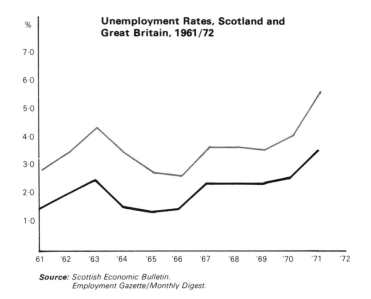

Unemployment Rates, Scotland and Great Britain, 1961/72

Source: Scottish Economic Bulletin.
Employment Gazette/Monthly Digest.

the new regional policies—due to the relative prosperity enjoyed by the traditional industries for most of the 1950s. Only later did a major under-utilisation of Scotland's labour resources become apparent:

The massive rise in unemployment since 1969 is attributable to a variety of causes including severe inflation, slack market conditions, and a low level of investment. In 1972, although a continuation of the upward trend is shown, a reduction in unemployment began in the early summer and continued during the remainder of the year. Confidence has to a substantial degree returned and the economy in general has also entered a more sustained growth phase. The cumulative effect of regional policies, more stability in the old industries and the employment potential of new fields of activity should in due course narrow the gap between Scotland and the national average.

Unemployment is in any case unevenly spread throughout Scotland, the Highlands and those areas most heavily dependent on the old industries suffering most. The following shows the position for the existing Planning Regions for the most recent five years:

UNEMPLOYMENT PERCENTAGES BY SCOTTISH PLANNING REGIONS 1967/71

	1967	1968	1969	1970	1971
Glasgow	4·6	4·5	4·3	4·9	7·0
Falkirk/Stirling	3·6	3·0	2·8	3·4	5·2
Edinburgh	2·8	3·1	3·1	4·0	5·3
Tayside	3·0	2·8	2·9	3·9	5·6
Borders	2·2	1·9	2·0	2·8	3·8
South West	6·1	6·2	6·4	5·9	6·6
North East	3·2	3·3	3·6	3·9	4·6
Highlands ·	8·1	7·8	7·9	8·0	8·6

Source: *Scottish Abstract of Statistics.*

The under-utilisation of Scottish manpower—and hence the potential spare capacity of the region—is thrown into sharper relief when the effects of emigration are taken into account. The overall pattern of emigration is shown in Chapter One (p. 6) but the phenomenon assumes even more significance in the context of employment, since net emigration to the rest of the U.K. especially bears a strong relationship to the 'push-pull' effects of respective economic conditions in Scotland and other regions. Historically, a close relationship has been shown between the trend of emigration from Scotland and the unemployment rate, with the former lagged 12 months behind. Ironically, the link has recently been less close as unemployment in other regions has risen, offering Scots less incentive to make a move.

During the 1960s Scotland lost virtually its entire natural population increase through emigration. Worse, the lost population tends to consist not of the unemployed or elderly, but of highly employable prime labour. Such emigration is not abnormal, but Scotland has suffered through failure to replace the outflow by an equivalent flow of immigrants. Only the creation of attractive opportunities within Scotland and an atmosphere of general confidence can restore the vital balance.

The New Industries

With the gap between average weekly earnings in Scotland and the U.K. as a whole all but closed (Scottish earnings in manufacturing industry now run at around 97 per cent of the national average) it is clearly these last two factors rather than inequality of reward which have caused the stagnation in Scotland's working population. It is important therefore to examine the extent of progress in building the Scotland of tomorrow and in creating the dynamism that is needed to shake off the 'depressed area' tag. Changes in the pattern of employment, and the relative growth of different industries, were discussed at the beginning of this chapter. There are many specific signs, though, of this new dynamism. Some are in fact already in the form of well-established industries. Two, especially, have created important new technologically-based elements in the Scottish economy. Each is discussed briefly below.

Vehicles

The motor industry is no newcomer to Scotland, but of earlier ventures all that survived into the post-war era was the Albion commercial vehicle plant at Scotstoun in Glasgow (now part of British Leyland's Bus & Truck Division). Scotland's 'new' motor industry is a direct result of Government regional policy. This led first of all to the opening by the then British Motor Corporation in 1960 of a truck and tractor factory at Bathgate alongside the main A8 Glasgow-Edinburgh road, with a planned capacity of 1,000 heavy trucks and 750 tractors per week. In 1963, the Linwood (near Paisley) plant of Rootes Motors was opened, expressly designed to produce a new car, the Hillman Imp, and representing an investment of £25 million. In addition there are Scottish plants of both General Motors (Euclid) and Caterpillar—both of these, incidentally, antedating the British investments.

Both Rootes and British Leyland plants and that of Albion Motors at Scotstoun have suffered more than their share of problems, with change of ownership (most significantly the acquisition by Chrysler of control of Rootes) taking place amidst erratic market conditions and problems of labour productivity which prevented either plant from achieving anything like full potential.

After these protracted initial difficulties, the Scottish segment of the British motor industry has reached a sounder base. Chrysler for instance has persevered with the earlier Rootes initiative, bringing total investment at Linwood to £50 million, and now the medium-sized range of Chrysler U.K. cars is produced alongside the Imp. Although a shortage of Scottish-made components still exists (illustrating the difficulties of achieving a balanced modern economy in a relatively short time) both Chrysler and British Leyland have decisively broadened the scope of their plants. Chrysler makes body panels and a high proportion of components such as gearboxes and back axles at Linwood, and Leyland has introduced a high degree of autonomy at both Bathgate and Scotstoun. All BL's tractor production is now concentrated at Bathgate, and Scotstoun not only exports 50 per cent of truck output but provides axles and gearboxes for other Leyland plants.

With developments such as these, a new note of both realism and long term confidence has been struck, and the Scottish motor plants—already substantial employers—are set to become significant contributors to the regional economy.

Electronics

The most spectacular incursion of a totally new industry—and fastest growing single industry in Scotland—has been electronics. Starting with the original wartime Ferranti plant at Edinburgh, with its associated training centre, there has developed an industry which has been called the catalyst of Scotland's industrial renaissance. The total number of firms is now over 70, and the 30,000 payroll makes electronics bigger in employment terms than shipbuilding, coal mining or iron and steel.

Nowhere has the transformation been more marked than in Fife where in 1951, with coal on the decline, engineering provided a mere 2,000 jobs. Electronics and other types of engineering now employ 14,000, or 12 per cent of total employment, and the New Town of Glenrothes is the acknowledged 'capital' of Scottish electronics.

The map overleaf shows the calibre of firms with an investment in Scotland, and the concentration of the industry in the central belt.

It is in electronics that the outstanding success in attracting overseas industry to Scotland has taken place. Among the main incentives has been the availability of Government aid (see Chapter 2); however the quality and availability of labour, easy communications, and the high quality of educational and training facilities have combined to form a powerful attraction. Glenrothes, for instance, is within 90 minutes' drive of no fewer than seven universities, and close links have been formed between universities and firms.

With a predominance of overseas-controlled firms, there was a natural tendency for the Scottish plants to concentrate initially on assembly work, but there has been a marked change, with the growth of distinct R & D operations within Scotland and export of know-how in some cases to parent companies. One Scottish firm, Nuclear Enterprises, has an American subsidiary, Nuclear Equipment Corporation in California, making Scottish-designed products under licence. In 1973, Scotland becomes the production centre for a new Honeywell computer range, and IBM, Univac and ICL are also represented in the computer field.

Perhaps inevitably, the emphasis on production of electronic equipment and systems has so far failed to create the balance

THE ELECTRONICS INDUSTRY IN SCOTLAND

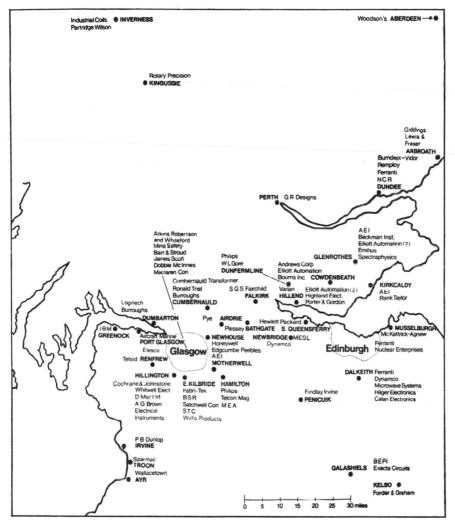

Industrial Coils ● INVERNESS
Partridge Wilson

Woodson's **ABERDEEN** → ●

Rotary Precision
● KINGUSSIE

Giddings.
Lewis &
Fraser
ARBROATH

Burndept – Vidor
Remploy
Ferranti
NCR
DUNDEE

PERTH G R Designs

Atkins. Robertson
and Whiteford
Mine Safety
Barr & Stroud
James Scott
Dobbie McInnes
Maclaren Con

Philips
W L Gore
DUNFERMLINE

Andrews Corp
Elliott Automation
Bourns Inc **COWDENBEATH**

AEI
Beckman Inst.
Elliott Automation (2)
Emihus
Spectraphysics

GLENROTHES

KIRKCALDY
AEI
Rank Taylor

Cumbernauld Transformer
Ronald Trist
Burroughs
CUMBERNAULD

S G S Fairchild
FALKIRK

Varan Elliott Automation (2)
HILLEND Highland Elect.
Porter & Gordon

Logitech
Burroughs

DUMBARTON

Pye **AIRDRIE**
Plessey **BATHGATE S. QUEENSFERRY**

Hewlett Packard

MUSSELBURGH
Mc Kettrick-Agnew

IBM
GREENOCK

Aircraft Marine
PORT GLASGOW

NEWHOUSE
Honeywell
Edgcumbe Peebles
AEI
MOTHERWELL

NEWBRIDGE ● MESL
Dynamco

Edinburgh

Ferranti
Nuclear Enterprises

Elesco
Telsid **RENFREW**

Glasgow

HILLINGTON
Cochrane & Johnstone
Whitwell Elect
D Mac Ltd
A G Brown
Electrical
Instruments

E.KILBRIDE HAMILTON
Fabri-Tek Philips
B S R Telcon Mag
Satchwell Con M E A
S T C
Wilfo Products

Findlay Irvine
● **PENICUIK**

DALKEITH Ferranti
Dynamco
Microwave Systems
Hilger Electronics
Calan Electronics

P B Dunlop
IRVINE

Sparmac
TROON
Wallacetown
AYR

GALASHIELS

BEPI
Exacta Circuits

KELSO ●
Forder & Graham

0 5 10 15 20 25 30 miles

Source: 'Scotland' Magazine.

necessary for the complete integration of the industry into the Scottish economy; reliance on suppliers outside Scotland for components and the absence of strong local markets mean that the industry is relatively vulnerable to conditions elsewhere. In 1971 the industry felt the chill wind of recession, with the downturn in capital goods industries and world overproduction of microcircuits. Several closures have taken place and a few U.S.- and British-owned firms have moved operations south of the border.

Latest reports, though, are of a cautious return to optimism, and with no question mark over the long term growth of electronic systems, the Scottish industry has now reached a size and momentum which will assure its future. Slowly, too, 'spin-off' is beginning, into new Scottish firms and as a result of industry/university partnerships, and these and other multiplier effects are healthy long term auguries. The industry is a major hope in stemming the Scottish 'brain drain'.

Motors and electronics are naturally far from being Scotland's only two new industries. Office machinery, electrical appliances, petro-chemicals—a host of diverse undertakings have come to join the traditional Scottish industries in their modernised or transitional state.

The part played by the New Towns in this second Industrial Revolution is central. The attraction of new industries, within the context of prevailing regional policies, is the necessary con-comitant of rehousing urban populations and of creating vital modern communities. The focal point of Glenrothes in the electronics industry is referred to above, and Glenrothes has two million sq. ft. (186,000 sq.m.) of new industrial space in use, Irvine 2·3 million (214,000 sq.m.), Livingstone so far 1·5 million (140,000 sq.m.), Cumbernauld 3 million (281,000 sq.m.) and East Kilbride 5·5 million (515,000 sq.m.), making a total of 14·3 million sq. ft. (1,335,000 sq.m.) in these five designated areas alone. This compares with, a total of 46 million sq. ft. (4·3 million sq.m.) completed over the whole of Scotland between 1961 and 1970. (N.B. the latter figure relates to projects over 10,000 sq. ft. only.)

The New Towns are optimally sited close to main roads or motorways, airports and seaports; all have ready access to nearby

universities or higher education centres, and Development Corporations ready to encourage and assist incoming industry in all
possible ways.

Changes in the structure of Scottish industry are not confined
to the nature of output. Foreign capital now has a very considerable stake in the region. Up to date information is scarce,
but in 1966 it was stated in evidence to the Select Committee on
Scottish Affairs that foreign-controlled firms were responsible for
16·5 per cent of total Scottish turnover, and for almost 14 per
cent of total employment.

North America is the dominant non-British element, and by
1968 American-controlled firms accounted for over 10 per cent of
total employment in Scottish manufacturing, 12 per cent of total
output, and an estimated 27 per cent of manufactured exports.
At the beginning of 1969, according to a Scottish Council survey,
there were 89 U.S.-controlled companies manufacturing in
Scotland, with a combined turnover of £365·7 million and
employing 73,300 people.

The significance for employment is more clearly pointed by the
results of a study by the Department of Social & Economic
Research of Glasgow University, which shows the following
pattern within the Central Clydeside Conurbation as at December
31st 1968.

Ownership of Firm	Employment (No.)	Per cent
Scottish	134,542	42·5
Rest of U.K.	133,889	42·3
North American	40,424	12·7
E.E.C.	4,826	1·5
Other European	2,517	0·8
Others	10	—

The field covered by American investment is wide. In 1968,
automotive machinery and accessories accounted for 27 per cent
of sales by U.S.-controlled firms, and there is also a heavy investment in instruments, electronics and office machinery. Other
products include food, drink, watches, clocks, construction

equipment, textiles, clothing and sewing machinery. The former Rootes plant at Linwood is now, of course, also American-owned.

This transatlantic influence has brought undoubted benefits, and has largely compensated for the lack of investment in new industry from native sources. U.S.-controlled firms have been found to employ higher proportions of men than the average, and output per worker has increased much faster than in the rest of Scottish industry. The American firms have been heavy exporters.

Although fears of American 'domination' of Scottish industry are groundless, it is significant that greater efforts are now being devoted to promote the advantages of Scotland as a manufacturing location in Europe, and EEC membership will no doubt stimulate this further, especially given the declared Community objectives as regards regional policy.

While some feel that Scotland will inevitably become less Scottish, others look for a re-establishing of the old direct links between Scotland and Europe. Essentially, the creation of a better-balanced economy, full employment and a resurgence of confidence are the main objectives shared by all.

4 Oil from the sea

The Background to Offshore Exploration

The discovery of oil and gas in commercially exploitable quantities beneath the North Sea constitutes potentially the biggest single stimulus to Scotland's economy in history and is already forming the basis of the recovery of confidence looked for at the end of the last chapter. The scale of the offshore operations and the potential gains to Scotland even on the most conservative of forecasts and derived from services and supplies only (i.e. assuming no direct participation in exploration or revenues) are immense.

Few realise that the world's first commercial oil industry began in Scotland, close to the site of what is now Livingston New Town. It had been known for centuries that oils, tars, bitumens etc. could be obtained from underground sources, yet it was here in the Lothians, in 1850, that a young Glaswegian James Young (later to be known as 'Paraffin' Young) first began retorting crude oil from locally mined shale and refining it into marketable products—coining the term 'cracking' still used today. This was nine years before the world's first productive oil well was drilled at Titusville, Pennsylvania.

Although the costs of producing shale oil ultimately became prohibitive, the one remaining refinery at Pumpherston (adjoining Livingston) was still in operation till about 1960, producing 19 million gallons of oil a year and providing direct employment for some 3,000 people. For this reason if no other, Scots are entitled to take a close interest in the new, infinitely larger surge of activity off the coast well over 100 years later.

The earliest example of offshore petroleum production is that of the Summerland oil field in Santa Barbara, California in 1894, but the first really important developments took place at Lake Maracaibo, Venezuela, in the 1920s. Drilling in open and unprotected waters, though, did not commence until 1938, in the Gulf of Mexico. By the early '60s, offshore oil production

85

amounting to about four million barrels a day was taking place off the coasts of twenty countries. Today about 10 per cent of the world's oil and 5 per cent of its natural gas production come from the Continental Shelf adjacent to these countries.

Interest in the North Sea as a possible hydrocarbon producing area began indirectly with the discovery in 1959 of the Slochteren gas field on the Dutch mainland. A massive geophysical programme then commenced, with the realisation that similar gas-producing structures could exist beneath the southern part of the North Sea. The 1958 Geneva Convention of the Law of the Sea gave countries the right to explore and exploit the resources of the Continental Shelf area. Enabling legislation in Britain in 1964, and agreement with other interested countries on a straight line median basis for dividing the North Sea area, paved the way for the initial award of Petroleum Licences and drilling commenced.

The first commercial gas dicovery was made in October 1965, and five major gas fields are now in production in the British sector. The first oil discovery was the Ekofisk field in the Norwegian sector, made by the Phillips Petroleum Company in 1969. Since then, the great concentration of effort has been on the search for oil, with the field of activity shifting to the northern sector off the Scottish coast.

Underlying the near-desperate need prompting these new searches for oil in savage weather conditions and inhospitable waters is the fundamental statistic that during the present decade the non-communist world will consume as much oil as in the entire 19th century and twice as much again in the 1980s. With nearly two-thirds of the world's known resources in the Middle East (some 340 billion barrels) there is no doubt of continuing dependence on sources in that area, but sharp rises in the cost of crude oil from OPEC (Organisation of Petroleum Exporting Countries) nations have stimulated the search for supplies from more politically stable backgrounds preferably under the control of petroleum *consuming* nations. Further ahead, a major world energy crisis is foreseen if new discoveries are not made.

Results and Prospects

To date, over 500 wells for exploration, appraisal or production

purposes have been drilled in the North Sea since 1964, 380-odd
in the British sector, and those in the deeper waters in the north
costing on average one million pounds each. One in eight drilled
in Scottish waters has found oil—a remarkable average and a
tribute to the geological skills of the oil companies.

The search has attracted the world's leading oil companies,
singly or in partnership, along with Britain's public sector energy
interests and financial and industrial groups. The oil discoveries
in the British sector so far are set out in the table on page 88.
In addition, an important gas find—the Frigg field—has been
made in Block 25 on the median line between Britain and Norway,
west of the Shetlands (to be shared between the two countries).

The location of these discoveries is shown in the map on page
89. So far all the finds have been close to the international
dividing line and some distance from the mainland. It will also be
noted that successive finds have in general been progressively
further north. In particular, since the Brent discovery, the deep
water round the Shetlands has been the focus of activity in the
British sector. It was the famous Block 211/26—now the
Cormorant field—for which Shell/Esso paid £21 million in
auction. The latest round of licence allocations has introduced a
new area to the north west of the Orkney and Shetland islands,
and also off the Welsh coast, indicating a gradual anti-clockwise
pattern of exploration.

What is the implication of these discoveries, first, in oil production terms? *Official* estimates are that by the mid-1970s
sufficient reserves will be proved in the British sector to sustain
a daily production rate of one million barrels, and that actual
production of around $1\frac{1}{2}$ million barrels daily could be coming
ashore (with a major share from Scottish waters) by the early
1980s. This would be equivalent to some 75 million tons a year—
little short of the present total offshore production of the United
States, and establishing Britain among the world's major offshore
producers. (It would still equate the entire North Sea reserves,
however, with one moderate-sized Middle East field, and the
investment required will be approximately ten times the level of a
typical Middle East field per daily barrel output.)

It is important to compare these estimates with forecasts of oil
consumption:

G

OIL DISCOVERIES IN THE NORTH SEA (BRITISH SECTOR)

Company/Consortium	Block No.	Name of Field	Date of Discovery (or announcement)	Estimated Potential Output (Barrels per day)
Phillips/Petrofina	30/13	Josephine	Sept. 1970	100,000
BP	21/10	Forties	Oct. 1970	400,000
Shell/Esso	30/16	Auk	Jan. 1971	50,000
Gas Council/Amoco	22/18	Montrose	Nov. 1971	50,000
Hamilton Bros.	30/24	Argyll	Nov. 1971	200,000
Hamilton/Burmah	30/2	—	June 1972	Gas/Condensate
Shell/Esso	16/8	—	July 1972	?
Shell/Esso	211/29	Brent	Aug. 1972	300,000
Shell/Esso	211/26	Cormorant	Sept. 1972	Unproven but possibly comparable to Brent
Mobil/Gas Council/Amoco	9/13	Beryl	Sept. 1972	?
Signal	211/18	—	Sept. 1972	?
Occidental	15/17	Piper	Jan. 1973	200,000

Source: Compiled from various sources. Estimates of potential output subject to change.

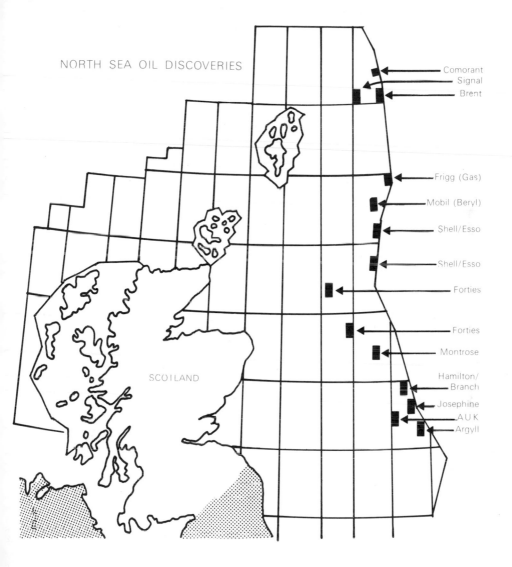

NORTH SEA OIL DISCOVERIES

Comorant
Signal
Brent

Frigg (Gas)

Mobil (Beryl)

Shell/Esso

Shell/Esso

Forties

Forties

Montrose

Hamilton/
Branch

Josephine

AUK

Argyll

SCOTLAND

FORECAST OF U.K. DEMAND FOR OIL
(Million metric tons equivalent)

1971	1974	1977	1980
103·0	124·9	138·9	153·3

Source: BP

Thus in theory by about 1980 Britain could be self-sufficient for half her total oil needs—a dramatic change from being 100 per cent dependent on imports. However, oil company estimates put early 1980's production from the North Sea as a whole closer to 150 million tons a year (three million barrels a day) with two-thirds of this coming from the U.K. sector. The report prepared by IMEG* for the Government published in January 1973 goes further, suggesting a possible U.K. output of 2·1 to 2·6 million barrels a day by 1980, rising to around 3 million barrels by 1985. These figures hold out the possibility of self-sufficiency in oil for Britain, or even a new status as an oil exporter. The IMEG report puts the forecasts in perspective:

FREE WORLD: FORECASTS OF OIL AND CONDENSATE PRODUCTION OFFSHORE (Million Barrels Daily)

	U.K.	Other NW Europe	Rest of world	Rounded Total
1972	—	0·06	10·2	10
Increase 1972–75	0·3	0·47	5·7	6–7
1975	0·3	0·53	15·8	16–17
Increase 1975–80	1·8–2·3	0·27–0·49	5·5	8
1980	2·1–2·6	0·80–1·02	21·3	24–25
Increase 1980–85	0·6–1·0	0·20–0·31	6·5	7–8
1985	2·7–3·6	1·00–1·33	27·8	31–33

Source: IMEG.

* *'Study of Potential Benefits to British Industry from Offshore Oil and Gas Developments'.* International Management & Engineering Group (HMSO).

Even if these forecasts are met, *trade* in oil will remain, and indeed grow. North Sea oil, while of good quality and low in sulphur content, is 'light' in specification and hence does not fully match U.K. domestic requirements, with their emphasis on heavy industrial fuel oils. A proportion of British oil will therefore be exported for refining abroad, while heavier crudes will be imported to give the right blends for U.K. refineries.

Technology and Equipment

Although offshore oil exploration and production are, as shown in the foregoing, well-established practices, the demands of the North Sea are well in advance of previous technology. Apart from geological complications, offshore work involving weather conditions and water depths such as the North Sea offers—particularly in northern latitudes—has never previously been attempted.

The North Sea has an average depth of no more than 308 ft. (94m.) and its deepest point is little more than 600 ft. (183m.); however, its funnel-like shape, wide open in the north and narrowing down to a mere 20 miles (32 km.) at the Dover Strait, can lead to violent storm surges lasting for days on end, wind gusts of over 100 miles per hour (160 kph) being commonplace. In the most northerly locations, drilling has so far only been possible for a maximum of four months during the summer. Winter wave heights are over 15 ft. (5m.) for 20 per cent of the time and 65 ft. (20m.) is typical in severe storms, while water temperature falls to 4°C.

Such conditions demand hardware to match. Initially, drilling units had to be brought in from other parts of the world, including ship-type mobile rigs such as those of the 'Glomar' type developed for U.S. offshore operations in shallower and more hospitable waters. Although these rigs are still in use, custom-built drilling platforms have now been developed, capable of operating in the most exposed waters all year round. There are two types, jack-up units (which stand on the sea bed) and semi-submersibles such as Shell's £3½ million 'Staflo'—the rig which was used to discover the Auk and Brent fields—which are mobile floating platforms with partly submerged frameworks. The latest generation of semi-submersible rigs will be floating structures of some 20,000 tons displacement, able to move under their own power between locations and drill wells up to 25,000 ft. (7,500m.) in water depths of over 600 ft. (183m.). More advanced jack-up platforms able to work in depths up to 300 ft. (91m.) are also becoming available.

The cost of these unusual craft is of the order of £10 million each. These costs—and the size of the structures—are dwarfed by the scale of the permanent, fixed production platforms required to bring the oil ashore. Those for the BP Forties field, for instance, will have a main sub-structure or jacket with base dimensions 250 ft. × 200 ft. (76m. × 61m.) and weighing 18,000 tons—the same quantity of steel as in a 150,000 d.w. ton tanker.

The first are already being built on land. They will be launched, towed horizontally to the site, then tilted to the vertical in an operation of extreme delicacy. Piles and conductor tubes for the wells (up to 27 are to be drilled on each platform) will weigh a further 9,500 tons, and decks and equipment 3,000 tons on top. Each platform when fully equipped and installed will cost £40 million, and its electrical power requirements will equal those of a town of 50,000 people.

Similar structures will be developed for the northerly Brent and other fields; each will be 700 ft. high (212m.), with piles extending a further 200 ft. (61m.) into the seabed. When installed, they will withstand winds of 120 miles an hour (193 kph). Some impression of their size is conveyed in the comparison below. It is expected that building of production platforms of all types in

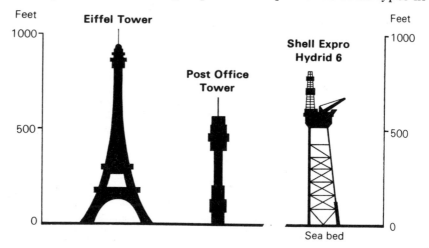

Scotland will reach about ten a year, and at present nine are under construction.

Although development has so far been primarily in terms of steel structures the potential for concrete platforms and combinations of steel and concrete has also been under study, and planning permission has been granted for a construction yard for concrete platforms at Artdyne Point, Kyles of Bute. McAlpines are the contractors and the platforms will be built to a French design. Underwater systems embodying seabed well-heads in pressure chambers have also been developed by Lockheed in the U.S.—a spin-off from space technology—and are being evaluated for the North Sea.

Bringing the oil ashore presents a further challenge to existing technologies. With a choice between tankers and pipelines, both methods have been adopted, and considerable experience in laying submarine pipelines has been gained in the southern, gas-bearing sector of the North Sea. In the case of the Forties field, a pipeline is to bring the oil ashore at the nearest land point, Cruden Bay near Peterhead (a distance of 115 miles (184 km.)) and thence onward to BP's Grangemouth refinery. Oil and gas separation will take place at Grangemouth and there will be a new crude oil loading terminal in the Firth of Forth. Cost of the undersea pipeline will be equivalent to a four-lane motorway— a 32-inch (80cm.) diameter pipe, steel-reinforced and coated with $2\frac{1}{2}$ in. of concrete. For most of its distance, the pipe will be between 330 and 420 ft. (100m. to 127m.) beneath the surface.

Shell, on the other hand, are to deliver oil from the Auk field by tanker (probably to Teesside), while for the Brent field a system combining tankers with a floating well-head storage system is under consideration, as is also a pipeline to Shetland.

Finance and Timescale

From the figures already quoted, it is evident that colossal sums of money are involved in the quest for oil in the North Sea; even larger sums are entailed in producing and landing the oil. For the development of the Forties field, BP has raised the largest-ever private bank loan—£360 million. Shell has given a breakdown of the costs of developing a field with a daily flow of 250,000 barrels which has received wide currency.

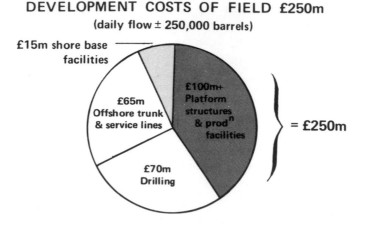

DEVELOPMENT COSTS OF FIELD £250m
(daily flow ± 250,000 barrels)

£15m shore base facilities

£65m Offshore trunk & service lines

£100m+ Platform structures & prod^n facilities

£70m Drilling

} = £250m

(Shell further suggests that rates of return on investment where exploration has been successful will average 15 per cent—respectable rather than bonanza proportions.)

To produce the *minimum* estimate of 75 million tons of oil a year by 1980, six such fields would be needed, suggesting a total development expenditure of £1,500 million. However, on the basis of IMEG and other forecasts, the total could easily be twice this or £3,000 million over 10 years. Figures as high as £5,000 million have been quoted in responsible quarters. The IMEG report in fact suggests an expenditure of some £300 million on offshore equipment and services yearly in the U.K. until 1985 (to this must be added a further £150 million yearly in the rest of Europe and £880 million elsewhere in the world—a £1,330 million market annually).

Suggested breakdown of the British share by 1980 is as follows:

	£ million
Survey work	4
Drilling	55
Platform construction	80
Platform modules	3
Drilling equipment	3
Production equipment	16
Deck·plant equipment	1
Power plant	7
Drilling services	25
Pipelines	80

Source: IMEG.

All these estimates refer to the development phase of the existing sector of the North Sea oil fields. Development may in fact last much longer than this if new discoveries are made. The pace of activity is still growing. In 1972 13 rigs were at work in Scottish waters in the peak season; a total of 25 is foreseen for 1973, and 35 the following year. Overall, the life cycle of an offshore field may be over 30 years. Shell give the following estimates:

Exploration	2–6 years
Construction	5–6 years
Production	
Build-up	3–5 years
Plateau	5 years
Decline	8–10 years

From this it is obvious that whatever the future success rate in discoveries, the oil industry is here to stay in Scotland—until well into the 21st century. This presents both challenge and opportunity on a daunting scale.

The Gains for Industry

The opportunities for industry lie in the field of engineering and equipment, and on-shore services and supplies. At a Scottish conference in early 1972 (before the Brent and Cormorant strikes were announced) the Chairman of Shell Transport & Trading declared a belief that two-thirds to three-quarters of the investment in Scottish waters could come to Scotland if the opportunities were grasped and fulfilled. BP suggest that the proportion of both capital and operating costs for the Forties field spent in Scotland will be 'substantial'.

If it is conservatively assumed that one-third of capital investment comes to Scotland (including non-Scottish firms) and one-half of operating expenditures, the former could total £1,000 million over ten years and the latter £500 million—altogether £150 million yearly. The capital expenditure alone is the equivalent of 1·4 per cent of Scotland's 1970 Gross Domestic Product. However, the multiplier effect (as chain reactions spread through the economy) and the direct effect of income from operations, could result in an increase in Scottish GDP of between two and five times the initial demand injection, or up to £750 million annually.

On this basis, a rate of growth of between four and seven per cent can be forecast for Scotland during the 1970's.

The implications of this for Scotland are immense, especially in view of the 'turnround' situation it represents compared with the position described in Chapter 3. This topic will be returned to. But in the narrower field of industrial activity, the ultimate objective for Scotland is of a Scottish-based industry founded on the experience of the North Sea which would be an exporter of offshore equipment and technology worldwide. (One American estimate is that 265,000 oil and gas wells will be drilled over the next decade alone.) It is recognised that such an industry must be able to compete effectively outside its home market. To further this end, an Institute of Offshore Engineering has been established at Edinburgh's Heriot-Watt University. The Institute is expected to establish a leading British role in stimulating research into new methods of exploring very deep sea waters and extracting oil and gas from them. An M.Sc. course in Petroleum Technology has also been established at Aberdeen University. Other universities and technical colleges too are offering courses in this new science.

So far, though, the offshore contracting scene has been dominated by American experience and technical backing. This alone is bound to influence the placing of contracts for equipment and services. Scottish and other British companies have been slow to become involved in offshore installation work or pipelaying. In December 1972 it could be said that of the 12 contract drilling companies based in the U.K. only one was British; of 17 rigs under construction for northern waters not one was being built in Britain (although a number of smaller rigs had previously been built in British—including Scottish—yards); of 26 fixed platforms installed to date, none had been made in this country.

It has been pointed out that rig and platform building is not the same thing as shipbuilding, and the necessary underwater technology just was not available from British sources in the early stages. British firms have from the start been well placed to supply pumps, valves, prime movers, communications equipment etc., but competition is fierce, and knowledge of the opportunities and their implications has been limited. However, official sources take the view that heavy steel fabricators, the construction equipment industry and process plant manufacturers could also develop equipment and processes for the oil industry.

Partnerships between British and foreign companies have been proposed as one way of speeding up British involvement, and a variety of methods of Government initiative and support have been suggested. Now, the Government has set up an Offshore Procurement Office within the Department of Trade & Industry to promote and encourage British participation, with a Scottish Oil Office located in Glasgow.

As a measure of the ground to be made up, the IMEG report of January 1973 estimated that only about 25 to 30 per cent of the money spent in Britain so far has gone to wholly British companies. IMEG forecast that by the late 1970s this share could reach 35–40 per cent of the annual total (or £100 million to £120 million at 1972 prices). However, the share *could* be as high as 70 per cent if the right forms of stimulus are applied (IMEG recommended that the 'shopping lists' of offshore operators should be scrutinised and their British content taken into account in the award of future licences). It is forecasts of this kind, allied to Shell's belief that up to three-quarters of this investment might come to Scotland, which make the implications for Scotland so vast as almost to defy comprehension.

The Initial Effects

The involvement of local industry is increasing under its own momentum. Production platforms for both Auk and Forties fields are being built in Scotland, and Marathon's arrival on Clydebank will bring purpose-built platforms from the site of the old John Brown slipways. A Scottish-American partnership is to re-open an Ardrossan (Ayrshire) yard after 42 years' closure to build supply vessels, platforms and rigs. The same group is to tender for offshore drilling work. British companies involved with building production platforms (not necessarily in Scotland) include:

> Redpath Dorman Long (British Steel Corp.)
> Wimpey (with the U.S. Brown & Root)
> Cleveland Bridge (with Mid-Continent Supply)
> Laing (with the French EPTM).

Over 20 companies are now prepared to construct deck modules. A growing crowd of local entrepreneurs has taken advantage of the many opportunities in the service field.

The case for American co-operation with Scottish firms has been most forcefully put by the North East Scotland Development Authority, which mounted a major mission to Houston, Texas in the autumn of 1972 and is a focal point in oil developments in the region. Already, though, the Moray and Cromarty Firths have become the main centre for production of platforms, and it is in North East Scotland, along with the eastern Highlands, that the impact of oil has been most sharply felt. This impact is by no means confined to the mainland, with Orkney and Shetland already becoming principal service bases for rigs (in summer 1972, seven rigs were serviced by helicopter out of Sumburgh airport in the Shetlands) and envisaged as pipeline reception centres.

Most of all, the oil boom is crystallised in the City and surroundings of Aberdeen. This northernmost of Scottish cities with its prosperous farming hinterland merging into the 'golden rectangle' of Speyside distilleries has been transformed almost literally overnight into a fledgling Houston of the north. Aberdeen's long seafaring traditions, active fishing industry and ancient connections with Europe have stood the city in good stead in adapting to and assimilating the new polyglot oil community.

Already, 130 companies directly connected with the offshore industry are established in and around the city, while several hundred others are directly or indirectly connected in a service capacity. Nearly 2,000 new jobs have already been created— mostly for local people—and the total is forecast to rise to 5,000 by 1975, with a further 5,000 in spin-off jobs. Aberdeen is in fact displaying all the classic signs of boom, with sharp rises in property values and pressures on hotel accommodation, communications and other services. Unemployment in the area is lowest in Britain outside south-east England. Busiest of all is Aberdeen harbour, where quayside space is at a premium and supply ships servicing the rigs come and go round the clock. A £1·5 million scheme to convert the existing closed docks into a tidal harbour is under way, and £10 million expenditure on new docks is envisaged.

From the oil men's point of view Aberdeen offers not merely the nearest developed harbour and communications point to the present exploration and production areas, but an historic city with a rich cultural and educational tradition, bidding fair to become a world centre for underwater technology. Never before has offshore oil been discovered next to such a community.

Although Aberdeen undoubtedly merits its new title of Britain's offshore capital, the effects of the oil boom are felt throughout north-east Scotland. The impact on neighbouring Peterhead, 30 miles to the north, is proportionately even greater. Here, £2½ million improvements to the enclosed Harbour of Refuge will provide another major service base for rigs. A £2½ million service base is being built at Montrose, further south; Dundee too is envisaged as a support base, and the effects are felt as far south as Leith.

To the north, though, the potential effects are even more far-reaching, and the visible results of the oil finds most evident. At Nigg Bay on the Cromarty Firth the biggest dry dock in the world is under construction by Highland Fabricators (the Wimpey/Brown & Root consortium). This is being used initially to build one of the two production platforms for the Forties field (the other is being built on Teeside). The facility represents an investment of £12 million. A Bill establishing a Port Authority for the Cromarty Firth—till recently more used to ferries and pleasure steamers—is due to become law in 1973.

The Highlands & Islands Development Board—which has for years campaigned to attract industry and stem emigration—estimates that the next three years will see up to 7,000 new jobs created along the Moray Firth between Nairn and Tain—the land of Macbeth—giving an overall population growth of 20,000 in the same period. The Board's Operation Counterdrift, set up to bring back emigré Highlanders, has on its list 10,000 names of Scots who will return home in response to the right opportunities.

As the oil industry moves north and west, northernmost Scotland and the Islands are becoming candidates for development. Wick and Thurso on the Caithness coast (present populations 7,000 and 8,000 respectively) are considered promising sites for onshore developments, and the American Chicago Bridge company has plans to establish itself at Dunnet Bay, just five miles from John O'Groats. The Highlands & Islands Development Board has commissioned a new study of the potential of ports in the region as oil servicing bases. Shetland has plans to produce a comprehensive development scheme, designed to ensure long term benefits for the islands from the present spate of construction activity. In Shetland's Sullom Voe area this could cover 20,000 acres if plans by the Nordport company are allowed to go ahead. The proposed complex includes rig and platform fabrication yards, tank farms, tanker terminals, gas liquefication plants and possibly refineries.

It is impossible here to do more than cite examples of both the type of development involved and the interests responsible. All major oil companies involved in the search have supply and service bases onshore. P & O have established a new service company, Sea Oil Services in Aberdeen, with further expansion due in Montrose and possibly Shetland. A proposal by Total Oil Marine for a £5 million gas terminal at Crimond on the Aberdeenshire coast is under consideration, to land the output from the Anglo/Norwegian Frigg field. 1,500 ft. of quayside to be built at Peterhead is to be leased to Aberdeen Service Co. (North Sea) Ltd., a subsidiary of Sidlaw Industries. South East Drilling Services (SEDCO) have set up a training school in Aberdeen for workers on the fleet of new rigs expected over the next two years, and others are proposed.

Particularly significant is the decision by two major American manufacturers of oilfield equipment to set up in the north east. VETCO Offshore and Baker Oil Tools will both occupy factories on Aberdeen County Council's Bridge of Don Industrial Estate. For Baker, it is the company's first factory outside the U.S., and is to supply demand from Eastern Europe and the Middle East as well as the North Sea.

The overriding importance of all these developments, though—irrespective of actual Scottish participation in the companies concerned—is that they comprise *volunteered private investment* on a scale without parallel in living memory, in an area where previously the full weight of regional policies has been unable to stem the tide of depopulation. Although infrastructure developments are discussed elsewhere, the movement of the entire British

European Airways helicopter service base from London-Gatwick to Aberdeen's Dyce airport (alongside the private enterprise Bristow Helicopters) and the start by BOAC of feeder services between Aberdeen and Prestwick, connecting with flights to and from New York and on to Houston, bear witness both to the sudden concentration and long range growth potential of activity in north-east Scotland.

The Implications for Scotland

In the shorter term, benefits to the Scottish economy can be seen in terms of employment, the creation of business opportunities of all scales, the revitalisation of remote and declining communities, and a general and substantial inflow of money. Already, though, widespread concern has been expressed at possible dangers such as the permanent despoliation of areas of natural beauty by a rash of unco-ordinated developments, the effects of offshore activity on the fishing industry, and above all the transitory nature of the oil boom.

There is evidence to show that fishing may actually be stimulated, but in relation to the last of these fears, it should be clear from the analysis of offshore oilfield life-cycles already given (p. 95) as well as from the sheer scale of investment, that oil will be no passing ripple in Scottish history. With drilling perhaps two years away from its peak, a cycle of at least forty or fifty years can confidently be predicted.

This prospect in fact raises severe problems for the overall future development of Scotland. A growth rate of 7 per cent or more during the 1970s is foreseen, and oil could easily result in the creation of 120,000 new jobs overall. The effects of offshore oil discoveries on local economies are well documented—many oil producing countries including Venezuela, Iran and Saudi-Arabia have achieved growth rates well above European averages and, although the effects for Scotland will be less marked in that North Sea oil is a British rather than a Scottish asset (see below) Scotland's population is small in comparison to the size of the likely discoveries.

Oil is therefore a central factor in the planning of Scotland's future which is taking place simultaneously within Government and private agencies as described in Chapter 2. Apart from the impossibility of predicting the success rate of future exploration, offshore oil has—as already noted—never before been found alongside a fully developed local economy, so that precedents are in short supply. The danger that oil will cause environmental damage and may create temporary employment peaks (e.g. during the exploration phase) is recognised in St. Andrew's House and at Westminster, and without putting too heavy a brake on progress, planning is being held to the rate where local authority views and development plans can be taken into account in drawing up the overall scheme.

A special committee within the Scottish Economic Planning Board has been established to co-ordinate the entire North Sea situation, and this will work in close co-operation with the new branch of the Petroleum Division of the Department of Trade & Industry in Glasgow. The DTI is to publish an annual report on the offshore industry, of which the first has already appeared (January 1973). Official reports have been commissioned by the Secretary of State from the Countryside Commission and Nature Conservancy to identify 'untouchable' coastal sites, and a study of the social and economic consequences of oil (with particular emphasis on employment) is to be undertaken by the Department of Political Economy of Aberdeen University. To strengthen the planning mechanism in response to oil, a Minister of State with special responsibility for oil has been appointed, and the Scottish Oil Development Council has been formed, with 27 members appointed by the Secretary of State and drawn from industry and Local Government, along with Development and Conservation interests.

The Scottish Council's Growth Stategy Study will also emphasize the social consequences of oil, and is itself being undertaken with the collaboration of both Government and oil industry representatives. The objective is to put forward guide-lines for infrastructure development which correspond to the optimum (not necessarily the fastest) rate of growth. The same concerns are naturally present in the West Central Scotland Plan.

Ahead of publication of such plans road improvements (such as the widening of the slow and narrow A9 Stirling-Inverness route) have been put in hand, and harbours in the north-east extended for their new role. Airports such as Aberdeen, Inverness and Sumburgh (Shetland) are to be improved to take the bigger aircraft and more frequent services their swelling traffic demands.

The entire long range planning function in Scotland is in fact influenced by oil, not least because a completely new shape is foreseen for the Central Belt, with a new axis reaching from the north-east down to Ayrshire.

So far, West Scotland has shared only to a minor extent in the oil boom. Production platforms must be built on flat land near deep water at the nearest practicable point to their eventual site, hence the green field developments in the north-east and north; service and supply installations too are bound to be located at the nearest point. The potential resources of the north-east are limited, though, in terms of manpower, and with half Scotland's population located in what is to be the new Strathclyde region there is danger both of imbalance and underutilisation of Scotland's collective resources.

Rig building is getting under way on Clydeside and in Ayrshire, and opportunities for heavy and general engineering firms are enormous in view of the absence of such industries in the east. Disseminating the knowledge and creating the confidence to enable Scottish firms to go for this business is a major concern of Government and planners. The creation of improved environmental conditions to enable Glasgow to keep its place as Scotland's principal commercial centre is an urgent priority.

It is in this context that the question of Hunterston and the Ayrshire coast has been crucial. With the prospect gone of seeing Hunterston as a deep water port serving a big new complex for the nationalised steel industry, attention has turned to other possible developments in which oil figures largely, notably the use of the deep water potential for the import of crude oil, export of refined petroleum products, and shipment of the heavy engineering products which Scottish industry will hope to produce in the future for world offshore markets. Oil indeed could be the catalyst for the 'Oceanspan' concept.

There are plans too (by the Italian ORSI Group and by Chevron) for an oil refinery at Hunterston, and clearly the extent of refining capacity to be built in Scotland as a whole will have

H

a significant effect on Hunterston's future. With Scotland itself remaining a relatively small market for petroleum products, and nearly all existing U.K. refineries in the south and underutilised, the question of further processing capacity being located in Scotland still has to be resolved. Refineries are open to opposition on environmental grounds, and in any case once completed have only modest labour requirements (2–300), so limited net social advantages.

Revenues and their Allocation

The most contentious aspect of oil and Scotland's future concerns the revenues which may be derived from the oil itself. While the discoveries and their implications have been tinder to the old nationalist fires, North Sea oil is of course *not* 'Scotland's oil' and to the oil companies themselves it is not even British oil but an international resource. This has been no damper to appeals for Scots to have a larger share of the proceeds and a bigger say in their disposal. Scotland's case is based on the benefits which will accrue to the nation as a whole, and the much greater revenues which might be extracted if the Government adopted a tougher policy towards the oil companies.

During the early phases of exploration the Government's policy was to encourage rapid and thorough exploration, and for this reason blocks were awarded by Ministerial discretion to applicants thought likely to satisfy certain basic conditions (the auction system was introduced later) and comparatively modest licence payments exacted, starting at £25 per sq. km. annually and rising eventually to £350. These are coupled with a simple $12\frac{1}{2}$ per cent royalty on production. From these sources it is estimated that by 1980 the Government will be receiving £100 million a year. In addition, of course, the oil companies pay Corporation Tax on profits.

These are not the only benefits to the nation. Every ton of home-produced oil will save Britain at least £6 (at present rates) in foreign exchange. With forecasts of production up to 150 million tons a year, the implications for the Balance of Payments are enormous, and a saving of around £500 to £800 million a year could be derived.

However, pressures have been exerted from some Scottish sources—including Members of Parliament—for the Government to renegotiate existing licences on more stringent terms and to write into current and future licences conditions for the purchase of Scottish and other British equipment. Unfavourable comparisons are made with the policy of the Norwegian Government regarding its own sector of the North Sea, which has set a more leisurely pace for exploration and insisted on direct State participation once oil is found coupled with the use of Norwegian goods and services wherever possible. The granting of further concessions off the West Coast has been suspended until a new policy emerges.

In Britain the public sector is represented in the exploration programme by the National Coal Board and the Gas Council, plus of course the Government's half share in BP and—in the industrial sector—its ownership of the British Steel Corporation. Direct Government participation through a special State agency can be ruled out (except possibly following a change of Administration).

However, the terms for licence allocations have already started to become tougher. A tightening up of control and of tax regulations is foreseen, and the Government has already taken steps to impose U.K. taxation on profits from exploration of the British Sector of the Continental Shelf. The prospect, though, of revenue being directly returned to the region where—or off whose shores—it originates is scant, without precedent, and to many people full of dangers.

Rather, the direction of Government thinking is likely to go further towards encouraging and facilitating Scottish participation in exploration activities and shore-based services within the framework of the forthcoming generation of long-range plans and infrastructural developments. This chapter has made it abundantly clear that the nettle—or rather, thistle—is there to be grasped, and that the results for the Scottish economy are likely to be dramatic and sustained.

5 Infrastructure Two: Services

The Scottish Clearing Banks

The Commercial Banks in Scotland have had a long-standing intimate involvement with the growth and development of the Scottish economy. Despite the changes described below and elsewhere in this chapter, the business of the Scottish banks remains firmly linked to its own 'market' and the banks retain their original character to a large degree. The Bank of Scotland was founded in the year 1695 expressly for the promotion of trade, and later the Scottish banks led the world in the development of branch banking. Their contribution to the economic development of 19th century Scotland was enormous.

After the Bank of England Charter Act in 1844 the Scottish banks retained their separate right to issue their own notes and Scottish notes continue to account for some four to five per cent of bank notes in circulation in Scotland.

During the present century, rationalisation has been at work on a massive scale amongst both English and Scottish banks. A series of mergers has reduced the total number of Scottish banks to three of which two remain substantially Scottish owned, while the third is wholly owned by the Midland Bank Limited. Most recently the Royal Bank of Scotland merged in 1968 with the National Commercial Bank of Scotland to form the National and Commercial Banking Group, followed in 1969 by the merger of the British Linen Bank and the Bank of Scotland. The structure of the three Scottish Banking Groups is set out in the Table overleaf (page 108).

There are several important distinguishing features in the asset structure of the Scottish banks. Historically (pre-1914) the Scottish Banks enjoyed a much higher ratio of investments to deposits than the English banks. This position became even more heightened during the 1930s and the 1939–45 war when pressure on advances was at a low level. In 1938 the Scottish banks' invest-

STRUCTURE OF SCOTTISH BANKING GROUPS 1972

Present Name	Constituent Banks	Founded	Capital & Reserves £ million	Deposits £ million	Advances £ million	Branches	Affiliation
Bank of Scotland	Bank of Scotland Union Bank of Scotland British Linen Bank	1695 1830 1746	43·2	529·9	312·2	472	Barclays Bank 35%
The Royal Bank of Scotland Ltd	The Royal Bank of Scotland	1727	69·7	730·6	481·6	595[1]	National & Commercial Banking Group (Lloyds Bank 16%)
	Commercial Bank of Scotland Ltd.	1810					
	National Bank of Scotland Ltd.	1825					
Clydesdale Bank Ltd.	Clydesdale Bank Ltd.	1825	29·5	308·8	149·1	361	Midland Bank Ltd. (100%)
	North of Scotland Bank Ltd.	1836					

Source: *Institute of Bankers in Scotland.*
[1] *Includes 87 sub-offices.*

ments represented 57 per cent of deposits as compared with 28 per cent with the London Clearing Banks. In the post-war era the Scottish banks have been able to finance the tremendous expansion in advances by the sale of securities, whilst still preserving reasonable ratios. The investments: deposits proportion has fallen but at around 24 per cent is still approximately double the average level for the London banks.

Scotland has no Central Bank and the control over the money supply exercised by the Bank of England over the Scottish banks is lower than for the London Clearing Banks due to the Scottish note issue. For every £1 of their own notes issued the Scottish banks are required to hold £1 cover in Bank of England notes. The result is an increase in assets for the Scottish Banks which cannot be smaller than the value of their own notes in circulation. Effectively, though, the Scottish banks are subject to the same constraints as their English counterparts and these differences do not materially increase their credit creating powers. There is, though, a tradition of longer term lending among the Scottish banks than in England—a trend now being followed by the whole banking system.

In addition, of course, the Scottish banks are now governed by the new credit control measures introduced by the Bank of England in 1971, replacing the former quantitative directives with more flexible rules, allowing the banks to buy in from money markets additional deposits to finance profitable lending.

Outline statistics for the Scottish Clearing Banks over the 1967–1971 period are shown in tabular form on page 110.

Merchant Banks and North Sea Finance

The existence of this distinctively Scottish banking sector implies to some extent a separate money market from the City of London; however, other institutions and foreign banks have till recently been slow to establish separate bases in Scotland. The position is now changing fast, providing competition for Scottish banks not only for traditional banking business but for the whole range of financial services required in a modern growth economy.

The Bank of America—the world's largest bank—has established itself in Edinburgh. The Bank of Nova Scotia has

SCOTTISH CLEARING BANK STATISTICS 1967–1971

		1967	1968	1969	1970	1971
Deposits[1]	£ Million	1,025	1,106	1,142	1,069	1,151
Current Accounts	£ Million	411	446	461	444	479
Deposit Accounts	£ Million	454	488	503	521	557
Other Accounts	£ Million	159	172	178	105	115
(Total Deposits as percent of London Clearing Banks)		10·5	10·6	10·8	10·5	10·2)
Scottish banknotes outstanding	£ Million	136	142	148	155	164
(Scottish banknotes as percent of Bank of England notes)		4·5	4·5	4·5	4·5	4·4)
Main Assets						
Liquid Assets	£ Million	368	393	392	415	444
Special Deposits	£ Million	10	11	11	13	13
Investments	£ Million	234	272	285	270	280
Advances and other Accounts	£ Million	503	520	548	586	634
(Investments as percent of deposits)		22·8	24·6	25·0	25·3	24·3)

Source: *Monthly Digest of Statistics*
Scottish Economic Bulletin.

[1]Changes in accounting procedures in January 1970 are estimated to have reduced gross deposits by over £60 million. Similar changes took place within the London clearing banks.

branches in both Glasgow and Edinburgh and Standard & Chartered is in Glasgow where Credit Lyonnais has also established itself. The arrival of other banks from North America and elsewhere is confidently expected as the renaissance of Scotland's involvement in direct trading and investment activities grows. The traffic is not all one way since the Bank of Scotland has an interest in the Banque Worms et Cie of Paris and the Royal Bank of Scotland has an interest in the Australian Associated Securities Group. However, for the present the Scottish banks are more concerned with the opportunities present on their own doorstep.

It is in the realm of the highly specific financial services, mostly described under the heading of 'merchant banking', that the Scottish scene is changing fastest. The arrival of a whole new financial community—an admixture of Scottish enterprise and the expansion into Scotland of English and foreign institutions—has been seen. At the start of the 1960s, Scotland had only two merchant banks. The number has now grown to at least eight depending on precise definitions.

The Glasgow-based British Bank of Commerce founded in 1935 was reformed and enlarged in 1960 and a substantial minority interest is held by Samuel Montagu. Scottish Industrial Finance, the second of the two 'original' native institutions, started life in 1946 as an issuing house set up by a number of Scottish Investment Trusts and since 1964 has been owned by ICFC (Industrial and Commercial Finance Corporation).

Edward Bates & Sons (described in more detail below) set up a Scottish office in 1963, specialising in portfolio management work. In 1965 National Commercial & Schroders was formed as a joint venture to handle acceptance business, short term investment and new issues. The Schroder interests were subsequently bought out by the then National & Commercial Banking Group and the name is now National Commercial & Glyns Limited. Also in 1965 came Scottish Financial Trust, originally a subsidiary of Birmingham Industrial Trust and now part of First National Finance Corporation, which provides equity and loan capital for companies not yet ready to go public.

A Glasgow branch of London-based Singer & Friedlander was set up in 1969 with the main function of promoting acquisitions and mergers among Scottish businesses. The same year saw the formation of Noble Grossart as an aid to Scottish Industrial Development (extending eventually to portfolio management and related services) by four Scottish Investment Trusts: Ailsa Investment Trust, American Trust Company, Scottish Investment Company and Scottish Northern Investment Trust. The latest arrival, in 1971, is Dalscot in which a major shareholder is Dalton Barton, now merged with Keyser Ullmann.

The new institutions retain their basic concern with the usual range of Merchant Banking services, such as the provision of long term finance for industry, portfolio management, advice on business growth and mergers and so forth. They bring to Scotland a new range of financial skills and provide services more directly geared to local requirements than is generally possible from a London base as well as promoting the retention of interest-bearing deposits within Scotland.

Even in the already encouraging climate resulting from regional policies during the 1960s, though, these functions have been overshadowed by the opportunities offered by North Sea Oil. In this essential area of financing the enormous capital expenditures in exploration and development of the oil fields, institutions with at least a Scottish flavour have been very much to the fore.

Many of the ventures in question have common or related origins. Edward Bates & Sons, an old established Liverpool banking concern once associated with Cunard and which, as noted above, established a Scottish office in 1963, was acquired in 1970 by Atlantic Assets Trust. This is among six investment trusts managed by Edinburgh investment managers Ivory & Sime, and has been described as the root of the tree from which most of the North Sea development and support companies have sprouted. Funds under management by Ivory & Sime have risen to some £500 million from £15 million in 1949; they also include two property investment companies of which one, Mount St. Bernard Trust of Preston is 50 per cent owned by Atlantic Assets. This is the parent company of Onshore Investments, one of whose subsidiaries is the Nordport Company, which is concerned with major development proposals in the Shetlands. Other subsidiaries plan developments in the Cromarty Firth and Peterhead areas with the aim of providing fully serviced land and financial and construction service 'packages' for the oil and gas industries.

As the chief organising vehicle for the oil activities of Atlantic Assets, Edward Bates have been concerned with the launching of a number of new enterprises. They include two companies, Caledonian Offshore and Viking Oil, set up to invest directly in oil exploration and the Viking Resources Trust and Viking Resources International NV. The KCA Drilling Group Limited provides drilling services for oil and gas exploration, while North Sea Assets Limited is a £20 million unquoted public company specialising in support services for North Sea development and backed in all by 135 institutions and companies.

A successful flotation of Edward Bates took place in 1972, involving the retention of 32 per cent ownership by Atlantic Assets and the purchase of a 25 per cent stake by London Merchant Securities. The new capital raised will enable Bates to attract deposits of at least £200 million and places it among Britain's major merchant banks.

North Sea Assets was set up jointly by Edward Bates and Noble Grossart, one of the livelier new Scottish institutions. Noble Grossart has, in addition, formed two exploration companies, Pict Petroleum and Caber Oil. Noble Grossart are also participants in a new property development company, International Caledonian Assets, in association with the House of Fraser, which will develop properties in England and on the Continent as well as in Scotland.

The joint stock banks have not been left out of this activity. The Royal Bank of Scotland and the Bank of Scotland have invested a combined total of at least £30 million in North Sea ventures of which perhaps one half went towards British Petroleum's mammoth £360 million loan for the Forties Field. In addition the Royal Bank of Scotland has a share in Caledonian Offshore (Edward Bates) and the Bank of Scotland in Pict Petroleum (Noble Grossart). The Clydesdale Bank—despite its many existing branches in North East Scotland—has set up a special sub-branch at Nigg Bay to cater for the needs of the Cromarty Firth construction activity and this is expected to be the forerunner of others. Direct bank lending to supplier firms and to local authorities has also been stepped up. The Bank of Scotland is taking steps to increase its capital by one quarter so as better to serve the oil related needs of its customers and to make funds available for direct participation.

Other Financial Institutions

There is no doubting the level of interest and enthusiasm for oil-related investment among the Scottish financial community. It would be invidious to draw comparisons with industry, but Scottish banks' investment managers and the new merchant banking groups have, by their far-sightedness and resources, paved the way for Scottish industry to take fullest advantages of the opportunities discussed in the previous chapter.

Assistance to industry is by no means confined to the names already mentioned. A range of other institutions exist including official and statutory bodies administering the *ad hoc* supply of funds in addition to the various government incentives described in Chapter 2, hire-purchase companies, leasing companies, factoring organisations and the like. Some Investment Trusts will entertain direct proposals from industrial and commercial firms.

The latter are one of the types of financial institution traditionally associated with Scotland. Scottish Investment Trusts control about one-third of total British funds invested in such trusts. Based chiefly in Edinburgh and Dundee they have a substantial reputation for their skills in foreign portfolio management—especially American—and until the recent growth in the merchant banking sector were a cornerstone of Scotland's claim to support a financial community of international status. Scottish Investment Trusts have combined assets of close on £2,000 million.

The life insurance companies are another important force on the financial scene. Edinburgh is the home of some of the oldest and most respected of Britain's life insurance companies and after London is the most important centre in the country of the control and deployment of life assurance funds. The Scottish Widows' Fund and Life Insurance Society was founded in Edinburgh in 1815 and the formation of the Associated Scottish Life Offices dates from 1841. By the end of the 19th century twelve independent Scottish insurance companies with headquarters in Edinburgh were firmly established, six of these transacting life business only while the rest accepted other classes of risk. Today there are nine major life insurance companies in Scotland, of which six are in Edinburgh and three in Glasgow and one major general insurance company—General Accident—whose head office is at Perth. The

Scottish life companies control about one-eighth of total British life funds.

Other financial institutions have their principal emphasis as consumer savings media and savings form a topic discussed separately in Chapter 8. Under this heading fall Unit Trusts, Building Societies, the Trustee Savings Banks and the various facilities available within the National Savings movement. In terms of their overall place alongside the institutions already discussed it can be noted here that both the Trustee Savings Banks and Unit Trusts have a special place in Scotland. In particular the banking services forming part of the National Savings movement—e.g. the Trustee Savings Banks and Post Office Savings Bank—are more popular savings media in Scotland than elsewhere with Scottish TSB deposits amounting to about 20 per cent of the U.K. total.

It is more difficult to isolate the Scottish content within the Unit Trust movement, although this has been simplified by recent changes in the organisation of leading Trust managers. A number of Trusts under Scottish management are directed towards the Scottish investor or centre on Scottish securities.

The dominant Unit Trust group in Scotland is Scotbits Securities Limited, a subsidiary of the Save and Prosper Group. Apart from Scotbits itself, the best known of the Scottish Unit Trusts, Scotbits also offer Scotgrowth, Scotincome, Scotshares and trusts tailored for specialised investors such as 'Scot Exempt Growth' and 'Scotlaps'—the last being geared to the needs of Local Authority Pensions Funds. Scotbits Securities (until 1970, Scottish Save and Prosper Group Limited,) also includes two trusts from the Scottish subsidiary of Ebor Securities Limited, now also within the Save and Prosper Group. Ivory & Sime are also advisers to one of the Ebor Funds. Major shareholders in the Save and Prosper Group include Atlantic Assets and the Bank of Scotland along with other merchant banking and insurance interests.

Other Scottish based Unit Trusts include Crescent Funds (Edinburgh Securities), Jascot Securities, Target, Pistol & Eagle Funds (Target Trust Managers (Scotland) Limited), Scots Units (National Group of Unit Trusts) and Clyde General High Income and Conversion Funds (M & G (Scotland) Limited) Barclays

Unicorn has a share distributor in Edinburgh. Funds controlled by Scottish based Unit Trusts are estimated to account for around 10 per cent of the national total and the Scottish banks occupy an important position as trustees.

Finally, Building Societies with their specialised but important place in capital markets are a less significant force in Scotland than elsewhere. The largest English Building Societies such as the Halifax or Abbey National each have larger operations in Scotland than all 28 Societies registered in Scotland. In part this is due to the preference for other forms of savings media but it is also true that a Scottish Building Society movement failed to develop on the same scale as in England.

Historically low rents and the greater part played by Local Authorities, with proportionally lower incidence of home ownership, are the main reasons. The result is that Scottish Building Societies handle only one-tenth of home loan business in Scotland and account for only half of one per cent of Building Society lending in Britain.

The Stock Exchange

As with other financial institutions the Scottish Stock Exchange has a number of distinguishing features and its activities have, during the last decade, been subject to a process of far reaching changes which will have been completed by the time this book appears in print. In the final move the Scottish Stock Exchange as a separate entity is in fact due to disappear.

The Council of Associated Stock Exchanges (CASE) formed in 1966 brought about a reduction in the number of provincial Stock Exchanges from 21 to 6. In the following year the Federation of Stock Exchanges formalised arrangements between provincial Exchanges and led to more inter-exchange business. Prior to these events, though, at the beginning of 1964, the four main Scottish Stock Exchanges, in Glasgow, Edinburgh, Dundee and Aberdeen were merged into one, with trading floors in Glasgow and Edinburgh.

Since 1971 a single trading floor—a new floor reopened by Prince Philip after reconstruction has been in operation.

Since March, 1973 the Scottish Stock Exchange, along with the remaining provincial Stock Exchanges have formed part of one single Stock Exchange system throughout Britain known as the United Stock Exchange. The implications of this reorganisation are discussed below. However, it will imply no dramatic change in the number of Scottish Stockbroking firms or the volume of business traded in Scotland. Membership of the Scottish Stock Exchange currently consists of 192 individuals in 32 firms. These are located as follows:

Aberdeen	2
Dundee	2
Edinburgh	8
Glasgow	19
Stirling	1

Naturally, since Glasgow has become the sole trading floor the tendency has been for broking firms to concentrate in that city, but several of the best known firms are located in Edinburgh and the larger firms tend to have branches in other centres, including towns such as Inverness, Perth, Dumfries and Falkirk. Rationalisation and a recent increase in membership have stepped up average membership from four in 1968 to six at the end of 1972, although Scottish firms are still small in comparison with their London equivalents (average around 13 members).

The Table on page 118 shows the trend in the volume of business on the Scottish Stock Exchange. Dealings in ordinary shares account for a dominant—and growing—proportion of business, a major difference from London which is primarily a market in gilt-edged securities (in fact gilt-edged business is almost entirely confined to London). Thus turnover on the Scottish Stock Exchange represents only a little over one percent of the London total, but this rises to around five per cent for ordinary shares alone.

The average size of transactions is naturally smaller than in London—between 20 and 30 per cent of the London average—but the comparison is only partly valid since London stockbrokers count the transfer of a security from one client to another as two transactions, whereas the figures for the Scottish Stock Exchange count a transaction between two Scottish Brokers as a single deal. Hence an unknown element of duplication exists between the two sets of figures.

TREND OF BUSINESS ON THE SCOTTISH STOCK EXCHANGE 1967–1972

	1967	1968	1969	1970	1971	1972
Total turnover £ Million	359·1	421·6	430·5	454·0	644·5	748·6
(Ordinary Shares only £ Million	244·3	328·1	300·8	350·1	492·2	626·5)
Total turnover as percent of London S.E. Total	1·0	1·3	1·4	1·2	1·0	1·3
Ordinary Shares	4·2	3·6	3·5	4·0	3·7	3·1
Transactions (000)	268·9	320·1	274·1	277·2	328·0	355·7
(Ordinary Shares only (000)	213·4	258·6	214·3	217·1	264·0	300·2
Average size of transaction (£)	1,335	1,318	1,572	1,638	1,965	2,105
Average size of transaction as percent of London[1] Total	18·6	26·9	29·9	22·4	20·3	29·8
Ordinary Shares	76·7	74·0	73·1	75·0	73·3	69·9

Source: *Financial Statistics.*
Council of the Scottish Stock Exchange.
Council of the London Stock Exchange.

[1]*Comparison not fully valid due to different procedures in recording transactions. See text.*

Although business will outwardly continue much as usual the March 1973 change to a single Stock Exchange will provoke some considerable reorganisation. At present, although cases where Scottish dealings in nationally quoted shares are heavy enough to exert a dominant influence on price are rare, slightly different terms are usually available from local jobbers, often giving distinct dealing advantages. Where stocks to be traded are not quoted in Scotland (as for instance with some gilt-edged) the business is usually put through a London broker and the commission split. A few Scottish brokers known as 'shunters' also specialise in dealing on the London Exchange on behalf of other brokers in blocks of shares too large or 'wrong' for the Scottish market.

The new system gives Scottish brokers direct access to London jobbers so that 'shunting' will come to an end, and Scottish broking firms will be able to set up direct facilities on the floor of the London Stock Exchange, either by having their own 'box' or by means of mergers or associations with London brokers.

Although this might seem to presage the end of the need for a Scottish trading floor Scottish brokers will, of course, continue to do business with each other locally and their skills and knowledge will be in no less demand. The local Exchange is also a hedge against major failures in communication systems. Scottish quoted companies of national importance will continue to rely upon the presence of trusted local advisers in this, as in other aspects of financial life, and as shown earlier in this chapter there is a strong inward movement of financial institutions to Scotland.

The tradition of service to the small private investor survives more easily in the provincial exchanges than in London, and Scottish brokers with their smaller size and greater emphasis on equity dealing are particularly well placed in this regard. Scottish brokers find that private business—much of it carried on with families from one generation to another—is steadier than that offered by institutional clients, which can suffer spasms when the institutions simply stay away from the market. Scottish brokers place great store by the advice that they can offer private investors, often extending this to Bonds, Unit Trusts or other investments for which a stockbroker's services are not strictly necessary. Increased mechanisation of the actual dealing processes (the Scottish Stock Exchange was the first to install a computer) and

I

the processing of paperwork will in fact, in the view of some, enable more time to be devoted to giving proper service to private clients.

Services for Business and Research

In general the widest cross-section of industry and commerce is formed of those whose interests are represented by Chambers of Commerce. In Scotland the 'focal' Chambers of Commerce are those of the four cities, Glasgow, Edinburgh, Dundee and Aberdeen. Each of these has an affiliated 'family' of local chambers. In addition at regional level there is the Scottish Chamber of Commerce in Glasgow, formerly the Scottish Council of Chambers of Commerce. The formation of a single Chamber to represent Scottish interests reflects both an attempt at coordination for the sake of harmony and some broadening of the traditional objectives.

The Glasgow Chamber of Commerce dates from 1783 and has the distinction of being the oldest in Britain. Its formation followed the collapse of the tobacco trade after the American War of Independence and helped to rebuild Glasgow's fortunes on cotton and other industries. The Edinburgh Chamber is younger than that of Glasgow by a full two years.

The services provided by the Chambers of Commerce cover a vast range from handling export documentation to providing translation services or simply arranging introductions. Representing a broad mixture of local interests, the Scottish Chambers are an admirable forum through which incoming businesses can obtain contacts and ensure a hearing for their own viewpoint. In the period leading up to Britain's entry to EEC the four main Scottish Chambers have, like their counterparts in English cities, been fulfilling a vital educational role in preparing industry for entry with advice and seminars on topics such as VAT, European Company Law and specific legislative provisions such as the new requirements for information on company letterheads.

One aspect of EEC entry affecting the Chambers of Commerce themselves is the Public Law Status which implies an eventual change from being purely voluntary organisations, to becoming statutory representative bodies to which all commercial and industrial undertakings are obliged by law to belong. Although the full implications (which would inevitably involve some rationalisation and change of character) are still being assessed, the Scottish Chambers are participating fully in discussions initiated by the Association of British Chambers of Commerce and in keeping their members fully informed.

The contribution of Scottish Universities and other higher educational establishments to the industrial and commercial life of the region is a large and impressive one. There are now eight universities in Scotland; these are listed below with their dates of foundation:

University of St. Andrews	1411
University of Glasgow	1451
University of Aberdeen	1494
University of Edinburgh	1583
University of Strathclyde	1964
Heriot-Watt University	1966
University of Dundee	1967
University of Stirling	1967

Thus there are now four entirely modern institutions alongside the ancient and respected University foundations of Scotland. Two of these—Strathclyde in Glasgow and Heriot-Watt in Edinburgh—are technological universities in especially close liaison with industry. At Strathclyde a centre for industrial innovation puts research undertaken in the university to work in promoting industrial development. At Heriot-Watt, 'Unilink' provides industry with consultants, special training programmes and access to university research equipment and services, together with facilities for carrying out advanced R & D work alongside university teams working in related fields. Degree courses in business studies are run at both universities. Dundee University can provide advice and practical services to industry in a wide variety of fields and is in the process of establishing a centre for industrial research and consultancy, while Stirling runs an Industrial Projects Service and both short and degree-length courses in Technological Economics.

Such activity is by no means confined to the new universities. Glasgow University's tradition of cooperation with industry dates back to at least the middle of the 18th century when one James Watt was instrument maker to the University, and the Departments of Town and Regional Planning, Social and Economic Research and Managerial and Administrative Studies are closely involved in the swiftly changing economic and business scene of Scotland today. Edinburgh's particular speciality is in the field of nucleonics, although a wider-ranging consultancy and liaison centre has now been established. Both St. Andrews and Aberdeen Universities have technical and consultative links with industry and Government departments. The latter, through its Department of Political Economy, is presently engaged in a Government study of the implications of the oil discoveries for the region.

In addition to these service activities a wide range of courses in Management Studies is offered by the universities. A Scottish Business School (with divisions at Glasgow, Edinburgh and Strathclyde Universities) has also been established. Short postgraduate courses are to be a feature of its work. The Regional Computing Centre, at Edinburgh, links Glasgow, Edinburgh and Strathclyde Universities as well as Government departments and industry.

Outside the universities the Dundee School of Economics (now operating within Dundee College of Technology) has a particularly strong tradition in management education and a four-year sandwich course in Business Economics is offered by Robert Gordon's Institute of Technology in Aberdeen. The new (1972) Glasgow College of Technology has established an Industrial Safety Management Centre and at Paisley a B.Sc. degree in Engineering with Marketing has been developed alongside the many science based courses already available.

It is not surprising to find that many of the leading Management Consultancy firms have opened offices in Scotland. Scotland's industrial revival is generating a growing local demand for their services as a complement to the resources of the academic foundations, and the growth of student interest in management studies should ensure both an adequate flow of native recruits into service organisations and a new generation of fully professional Scottish managers.

Scotland is, in addition, the home of a number of governmental laboratories and research establishments. These include the Torry Research Station of the Ministry of Agriculture, Fisheries and Food at Aberdeen (concerned with the investigation of all aspects of fish technology) and the National Engineering Laboratory (Department of Trade and Industry) situated at East Kilbride. A number of research units of the Medical Research Council are in Scotland.

Tourism and Hotels

In spite of its legendary scenic beauty and the drawing power of its history and culture for overseas visitors especially, it is only recently that the full tourist potential of Scotland has been appreciated and efforts to develop a modern tourist industry made.

The main change has been with the setting up of the Scottish Tourist Board, along with similar boards for England and Wales, under the Development of Tourism Act of 1969. The new statutory board replaced its voluntary predecessor with an organisation fully competent in functions such as marketing, public relations and research and with fully defined responsibilities and an annual Grant-in-Aid which for 1971/72 was in the region of £400,000. Biggest single item of expenditure for the Board is publicity—£181,000 in 1971/72. The Board has, however, initiated a comprehensive series of research studies.

Included in the Board's responsibilities has been the development of regional Tourist Associations. Tourism already falls within the scope of the Highlands & Islands Development Board, but other associations largely founded by Local Authorities have been set up covering the North East, East Central, West (Clyde), South West, and Edinburgh and the Lothians. A Scottish Tourism Consultative Council has also been formed under the Chairmanship of the former Lord Provost of Glasgow and representing the interests of a large number of bodies concerned with different aspects of Tourism.

Tourism in Scotland has two natural markets—visitors from elsewhere in Britain, and abroad. As regards British holidaymakers, distance is seen as a barrier for the further regions and strategy so far has been to promote Scotland to those regions within comfortable motoring reach, so as to enlarge the car holidays market. Promotions during the last two years have centred on Yorkshire, the Manchester area and Bristol (the latter being considered a promising new market due to the completion of motorway links). In 1971 Scotland received 3·91 million holiday-makers from the U.K. whose average expenditure was £28·8 each.* For those staying four nights or more, three-quarters came by car—illustrating the accuracy of the STB's promotional strategy. The following shows the regions visited:

	Holidays 4 nights or over %	All holidays %
Highlands and Islands	32	26
North East	10	10
East Central	16	10
West	19	25
Edinburgh and Lothians	7	13
Borders	5	5
South West	11	8

Source: BHTS 1971.

Although the present pattern is largely one of touring holidays, the real scope is seen to lie in 'activity' holidays, especially for families with children, and Scotland is abundant in facilities for water, mountain and other recreational pursuits—including winter sports. Extension of the tourist season, especially by second holidays taken in the spring or autumn, is an important objective.

Outside London, Scotland holds a special place for overseas visitors. A conservative estimate is that some 12 per cent of visitors to the U.K. visit Scotland and the proportion is much higher for North Americans. The Edinburgh Festival is a particular attraction. A survey by the Scottish Tourist Board in August and September 1971 among visitors to Edinburgh Castle and Holyrood Palace—two prime tourist attractions in the capital—found that over half those interviewed came from overseas and one-fifth were from the U.S.A. Expenditure by foreign tourists in Scotland totals some £50 million annually.

A major activity during the early years of the STB has been administering the Hotel Development Incentives Scheme in the

* British Home Tourism Survey carried out by N.O.P. Market Research Limited for British Tourist Authority.

region. As at 31st March, 1972 the Board had approved no fewer than 440 applications under the scheme (introduced under Part II of the 1969 Development of Tourism Act) and had paid out £1,476,000 in grants for 108 projects. The indications are that a total of about 5,500 bedrooms will be added to Scotland's hotel accommodation as a result of the scheme. However, the greatest improvement is in bathroom accommodation with over 90 per cent of rooms built under the scheme having private bathrooms or showers compared with a previous average of only 11 per cent for all hotel accommodation in Scotland.

Many of these projects have been on a modest scale (average grant less than £14,000) but some notable new additions to Scotland's hotels have resulted. The Excelsior at Glasgow Airport (Scotland's largest hotel) and its near neighbour the Normandy were both opened in 1971/72, as was the Post House at the Aviemore resort centre in the Highlands. 1973 has already seen an important new addition to city centre accommodation in Glasgow with the opening of the 252-bedroom Albany—with colour TV in all rooms, and several important new projects have been undertaken in Edinburgh, notably, the King James Hotel.

Establishments with less than 10 bedrooms are beyond the scope of the HDI Scheme, but have been able to benefit as Tourist Development Projects (also using Government funds (£300,000 in 1971/72)) channelled through the Scottish Tourist Board. These small hotels and guest houses—generally family run—have been called the backbone of the Scottish tourist industry. The table on page 126 shows why.

The picture is confused by the large numbers of establishments in all categories whose size is unknown. No official registration or classification scheme for hotels is in force in the U.K., although a voluntary scheme covering most categories of accommodation has now been agreed by both English and Scottish Tourist Boards. A recent NEDO Report* credits Scotland with a total of 5,076 hotels giving 60,381 bedrooms. The distribution is as shown on page 127.

Obviously a large proportion of these hotels fall within the STB definition of guest houses. The majority are unlicensed: 2,670 compared with 2,406 licensed hotels.

* 'Hotel prospects to 1980': Hotels and Catering Economic Development Council, October 1972.

HOTELS, GUEST-HOUSES AND FARM-HOUSES IN SCOTLAND, 1972

	Number of Rooms							
	1–3	4–9	10–25	26–50	51–100	Over 100	No details	Total
Hotels	61	950	1,132	248	102	28	769	3,290
Guest-Houses	3,254	1,543	121	5	1	1	737	5,662
Farm-Houses	270	133	4	1	—	—	46	454
Total Establishments	3,585	2,626	1,257	254	103	29	1,552	9,406

Source: *Scottish Tourist Board.*

HOTELS AND BEDROOMS IN SCOTLAND (Jan. 1970)

	Coastal	Rural	Urban Under 100,000	Urban Over 100,000	Total
No. of Hotels	1,882	1,241	1,365	588	5,076
No. of Bedrooms	22,735	12,540	16,100	9,006	60,381
Average Bedrooms per Hotel	12	10	12	15	12

Source: *Hotels & Catering EDC (Op. Cit.)*

From both these sets of figures it is clear that the average size of tourist accommodation units is very small; and yet Scotland possesses a range of establishments at the other end of the scale— the mushrooming field of conference facilities—which is unique in variety and atmosphere.

Most of the larger (and especially newer) hotels can handle conference business—Glasgow's new Albany hotel can accommodate up to 700 delegates for instance and has closed-circuit television, multi-lingual translation facilities and other advanced aids—but efficient conferences can be held in locations ranging from coastal resorts such as Oban, Rothesay or Aberdeen to picturesque small towns like Strathpeffer in the Highlands or Peebles in the Borders. Two locations specially worthy of mention are Gleneagles, world renowned for its golf courses and the Aviemore centre in the Highlands, which though primarily a winter sports centre has become a major venue for large-scale conference and seminar activity.

A service to conference organisers is provided by the Scottish Convention Bureau which is affiliated to the Scottish Tourist Board.

Broadcasting and Entertainment

As in the rest of the country, television services are provided in Scotland by both Independent Television and the BBC. Both services transmit on both VHF and UHF frequencies, on 405 and 625 line standards respectively. 405 line transmissions will eventually be terminated and both black and white and colour services are provided on 625 line UHF, the majority of both ITV and BBC programmes now originating in colour.

The National UHF system is planned so that services for any particular area come from a single transmitting mast, shared by both BBC and the Independent Broadcasting Authority. This means that viewers require only a single receiving aerial for all programmes. Bringing UHF service to Scotland, especially in the North East and Highlands, requires a relatively large number of transmitters and the areas reached are considerably smaller than those covered by the old VHF 405 line stations. Additional main and relay stations will be built until coverage is comparable with the VHF system.

The main transmitting centre for Central Scotland is at Black Hill near Airdrie which reaches Clydeside and a large part of Central Scotland. Other transmitters are at Craigkelly a few miles north of Edinburgh, and Darvel near Kilmarnock which opened in late 1972. A local relay station opened at Lethanhill in March 1973. In the North East the first main UHF station opened in 1971 at Durris to the South West of Aberdeen. Stations at Angus and Perth were added during 1972, and during 1973 a further main station at Rosemarkie, and Rumster Forest is scheduled for early 1974, plus a further two local relays of the Durris transmitter. Later another main station will be added to the network at Knock More.

Maps of the areas covered by each of the transmitters already in use and showing relay stations due for opening during 1973 are on pages 130, 131 and 132.

Independent television programmes in Central Scotland are provided by Scottish Television Limited and in the North East by Grampian Television Limited. A common sales organisation, Scottish Television and Grampian Sales Limited (STAGS) handles sales, promotional and advertising business for both stations and provides certain additional services to advertisers. (See Chapter 9). Advertising does not apply to BBC services.

Scottish Television provides more than 100 programmes a year specifically for Scottish audiences, apart from making a growing contribution to the National Network, whose output occupies the bulk of programme time. Average output of locally produced programmes is over 10 hours a week. The old Gateway Theatre in Edinburgh was reopened by STV as Scotland's first colour television theatre. Various local feature and entertainment programmes are also produced by Grampian Television in addition to news broadcasts and the station has taken a keen interest in North Sea Oil developments.

Local BBC television programming in Scotland continues to expand—especially in drama. The BBC maintains a national Broadcasting Council for Scotland which, like its counterpart for Wales, assists in controlling the policy and content of programmes produced mainly for reception in the region.

So far the only sound radio services available to Scottish listeners are those of the BBC (although commercial programmes from Radio Luxembourg are widely listened to—see Chapter 9).

North~East Scotland

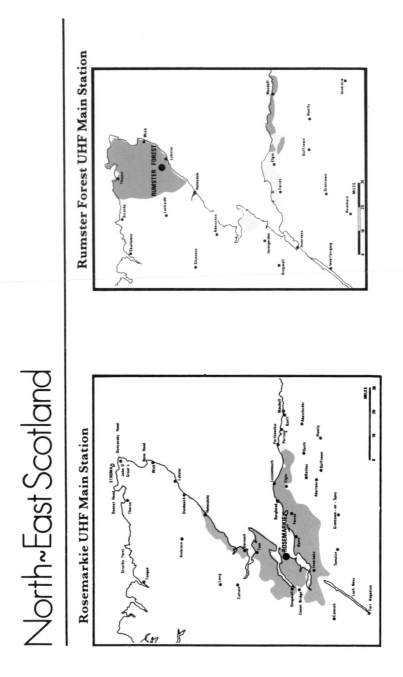

Rosemarkie UHF Main Station

Rumster Forest UHF Main Station

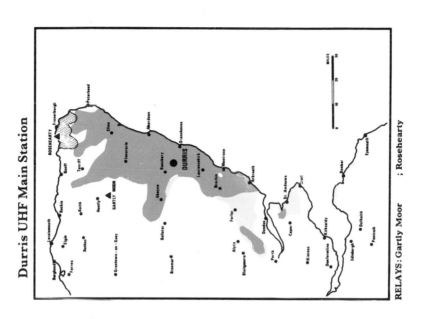

Durris UHF Main Station

RELAYS: Gartly Moor   ; Rosehearty

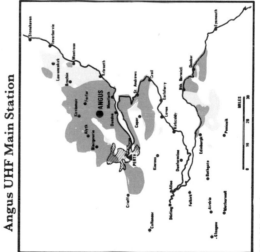

Angus UHF Main Station

RELAY: Perth

Central Scotland

Black Hill UHF Main Station

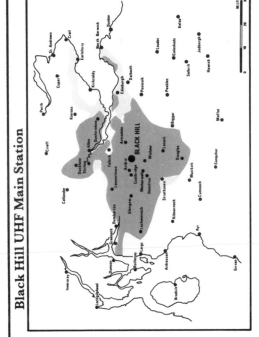

Darvel UHF Main Station

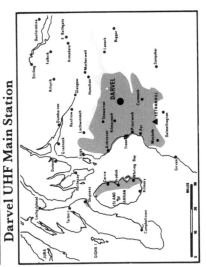

RELAY: Lethanhill

Craigkelly UHF Main Station

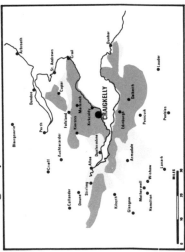

Colour UHF 625-line transmitters
now in operation or due by the end of 1973

● **MAIN STATION**

Principal Service Area
Signal expected to be stronger than that from any overlapping station.

Supplementary Service Area
Signal expected to be satisfactory, but may be weaker than alternatives.

▲ **RELAY STATION** ▨ Relay Coverage

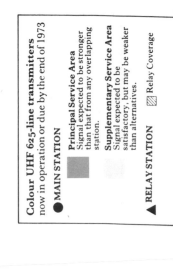

Scotland is well served by VHF radio transmitters, which carry BBC Radios 2, 3 and 4. (Radio 1 is broadcast on medium wave only and medium wave duplicates the VHF transmission of the other 3 channels).

None of the BBC's 20 local radio stations is located in Scotland; however, Glasgow is among the first group of major cities which will have local commercial radio stations and Edinburgh is one of the second group. The first commercial stations are expected to be on the air by the end of 1973. The contract for the Glasgow station has been awarded to Radio Clyde among whose backers are The Glasgow Evening Citizen (Beaverbrook Newspapers,) George Outram, publishers of the Glasgow Herald and Evening Times, Scottish Television, The Clydesdale Bank and Stenhouse Holdings.

An older medium, the cinema, offers both entertainment and advertising services. Scots—especially in Central Scotland—continue to be more frequent cinema-goers than the average, and the proportion going to the cinema at least once a year is second only to London. However, the pace of cinema closures in Scotland has been faster than elsewhere, and this has continued during the last few years, with numbers falling in the 1969–71 period by 11·8 percent compared to 6·3 percent for Great Britain as a whole.

The most recent figure for the total number of cinemas in Scotland is 154, providing a total of 165,685 seats. This total is broken down to show the two Independent Television areas within Scotland as follows:

	Scotland Total	Central Scotland	N.E. Scotland
Cinemas	154	120	56
Total Seats	165,685	135,691	54,135
Average Seats/Cinema	1,076	1,131	984

Important changes have been taking place, though, in the size structure of cinemas, the trend being noticeably towards smaller auditoria. The table overleaf shows the present structure alongside the changes which have taken place during the past few years.

SCOTTISH CINEMAS—SEATING CAPACITY

Seats	No. of Cinemas	Seating No.	Capacity Per cent	Percentage change in No. of Cinemas 1969–1971	Percentage change in No. of Cinemas 1970–1971
0– 500	21	7,912	4·8	–11·4	+11·4
501–1,000	56	42,249	25·5	–11·4	–12·4
1,001–1,500	47	57,659	34·8	–5·6	–1·9
1,501–2,000	21	35,615	21·5	–21·5	–24·0
Over 2,000	9	22,250	13·4	—	—
Total	154	165,685	100	–11·8	–6·7

Source: *Screen Advertising Association.*

Openings of new smaller cinemas in Scotland are, as the table shows, only a recent trend, and cinema managements have been slower than elsewhere to put in hand the necessary construction or conversion work. The slower overall rate of closures for the whole nation is partly a result, in fact, of an earlier start in other regions to building multi-screen complexes incorporating two or more separate auditoria. Scotland now has three 'twins', and two 'triples', as follows:

TWINS:

> Glasgow (Sauchiehall St.) ABC 1 & 2
> Edinburgh Dominion 1 & 2
> Wishaw Classic 1 & 2

TRIPLES:

> Glasgow (Renfield St.) Odeon 1, 2 & 3
> Edinburgh ABC 1, 2 & 3

As the above indicates, the major national cinema chains extend to Scotland, with the ABC/EMI and Rank chains accounting between them for 43 of Scotland's 154 cinemas.

	Number
ABC/EMI	26
Caledonian Associated Cinemas	24
Rank	17
J. B. Milne	12
Sir A. B. King	6
Classic	5

For an analysis of cinemagoing and 'media' aspects of the cinema, see Chapter 9.

K

6 Physical communication

EVEN TODAY, AT THE threshold of the supersonic era, the inescapable fact of Scotland's physical distance from the principal centres of population and industry in southern England and from the Continent is a pre-occupation of Scottish planners and leaders of the business and social community alike. High speed travel by surface and air has brought Scotland 'nearer' to these centres and future developments will minimise the effects of distance still further. Much of the pre-occupation, however, relates to the improvement of facilities and services provided within the framework of current transportation technology.

A specific region in Scotland's position has more to gain than others from 'hybrid' services in which two or more traditional forms of transport combine to provide a single service. Roll-on/roll-off container services are one example. Scotland, as indeed the whole country, is a long way from an integrated transport policy, let alone possessing an integrated system, but would be a major beneficiary among regions of the U.K. from such a policy. On a regional scale within Scotland, such a policy is being developed in the west, where one outcome of the Greater Glasgow Transportation Study has been the formation of a Regional Passenger Transport Authority to co-ordinate road, rail and underground systems in consequence of the massive redevelopments taking place in and around the city.

The need for an integrated policy is heightened by the strain on existing transport systems imposed by the North Sea oil developments, and indeed transport considerations are an important part of the present wave of long range planning activity in Scotland. The need for further upgrading and extension of existing plans for infrastructure improvements is widely recognised if communications bottlenecks in exploiting the North Sea resources are to be minimised and Scotland is to play its fullest part within the E.E.C.

Priorities now extend to new links to remote and previously

137

declining areas as well as to improving trunk routes within Scotland and facilitating communications with the rest of the country and abroad. Present and anticipated developments are reviewed in the following pages, together with an outline of the main structure of transport services both within each category and in the mixed or hybrid class.

ROADS AND ROAD TRANSPORT

Road-building
Present dual-carriageway mileage in Scotland consists of 230 miles of trunk road, including 76 miles of motorway. By 1975 the figure will have increased to some 310 miles of which 135 will be motorway. These figures give Scotland 8·3 percent of dual-carriageway road in Great Britain and 7·5 percent of motorway mileage, showing that Scotland has certainly had no more than its fair share of modern road building—in fact, rather less.

Since the Scottish Development Department took over responsibility for Scottish roads from the old Ministry of Transport in 1956 the main aims have been to provide Scotland with a modern road network linking the industrial areas of central Scotland to each other and to the English road system to the south. The Government White Paper published in 1969 (Cmnd 3953) 'Scottish Roads in the 1970s' set forward a new official strategy envisaging an expenditure of £580 million during the decade. In 1972, in response to North Sea and other developments, additional new trunk road projects costing £66 million were authorised. These figures contrast with an annual expenditure level in the early 1960s of around £15 million.

The map on page 139 illustrates the existing trunk road pattern and shows improvements completed or planned for the first half of the 'Seventies. The M8 motorway link between Glasgow and Edinburgh was completed in 1970, giving 36 miles (57·6km.) of continuous dual highway between the two cities. Extensions to the city boundaries at either end are now planned, and to the west of Glasgow the M8 already extends 7 miles towards Greenock, with work on the remaining 4 miles due to start in summer 1973.

The M8 connects at Newbridge with the M9 Edinburgh-

Proposed Road Programme for 1970's

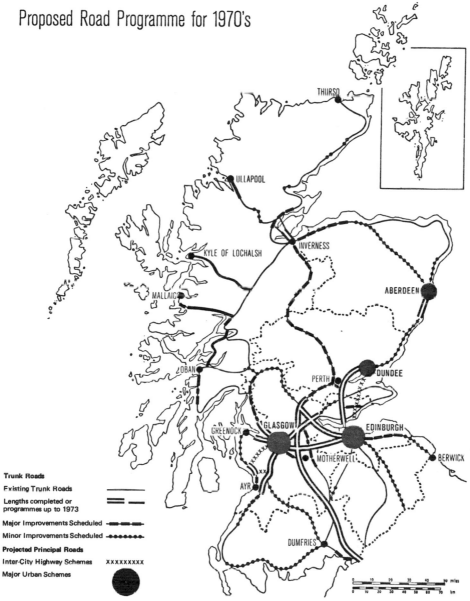

Trunk Roads

Existing Trunk Roads

Lengths completed or
programmes up to 1973

Major Improvements Scheduled

Minor Improvements Scheduled

Projected Principal Roads

Inter-City Highway Schemes   XXXXXXXXX

Major Urban Schemes

Stirling motorway, of which two sectors totalling 20 miles (32km.) are open, while the remaining stages of the Stirling by-pass to connect with the M80 to Glasgow at Pirnhall should be completed by the end of 1973. The M73 connects the Glasgow-Stirling route with the M74/A74 Glasgow-Carlisle road, Scotland's main artery to the south, to meet the M6 at Carlisle. The M73 provides the main by-pass to Glasgow on the East of the city connecting at Baillieston with the A8/M8 to Edinburgh. The A74 itself is estimated to carry upwards of three quarters of all commercial road traffic between central Scotland and the Border, and upgrading to motorway standards has long been needed; traffic now has the benefit of motorway conditions until well clear of the Glasgow area and the work will progressively extend south.

Meanwhile the M90 Forth-Perth motorway has run into legal obstacles over the route of the final 16 miles north to Perth, which will delay this section, due to start in summer 1973, together with the M85 Perth by-pass.

Inevitably—due to geography as well as to the location of industry—motorway building in Scotland has been concentrated into the central belt. Now priorities are altering with the need for better routes to the rapidly developing oil centres of the north and north east. The new batch of schemes gives priority to modernising the A9 Perth-Invergordon route—in terms of a major re-alignment rather than motorway building, but taking a new route across the Black Isle north of Inverness with a high-level bridge over the Beauly Firth and a bridge and causeway over the Cromarty Firth.

The A85 road between Perth and Dundee is also to be improved, and in response to increased traffic between Dundee and Aberdeen the A929/94 route via Forfar is to undergo major upgrading, with by-passes to Laurencekirk, Brechin and Stonehaven. In consequence, the A92 coast road is to be 'de-trunked'. The road between Aberdeen and Peterhead and other routes in the west highlands and north of Dingwall (including that up to Wick in Caithness) are also to benefit.

Planned modernisation of the A82 Glasgow-Inverness route now extends as far as the Loch Lomond-site road. In the west, major schemes are in hand for the A75 from Dumfries to Stranraer and the A76 and A77 routes to Ayrshire. And a Glasgow-Ayrshire motorway will be started in 1974.

The emphasis of all these schemes is on rapid, free-flowing transit between centres; however, urban road building has been a particular, even spectacular feature of Glasgow's redevelopment. The new road system is based on an inner-ring motorway four and a half miles in length and embracing the commercial centre of the city, with four radial arteries leading to Renfrew, Monkland, Maryhill and Hamilton. Total envisaged cost at 1965 prices was £200 million. The north and west flanks are already open, including the dual five-lane Kingston Bridge over the Clyde, and—allowing for controversy and some re-routing on environmental grounds, the remainder is due for completion by about 1980. Thus a continuous motorway route will be provided across the city from the Renfrew by-pass to the Edinburgh road and the Hamilton by-pass. A traffic-loading of some 75,000 vehicles per day on the north and west flanks is then foreseen. Other by-pass routes are already provided by the Clyde Tunnel and, further to the west, the Erskine Bridge, linking the industrial areas of the west with central Scotland, and Dunbartonshire with the south, while avoiding Glasgow altogether.

Comparable schemes for Edinburgh have been slower in implementation, due in part to the rejection in 1967 (after an enquiry by the Secretary of State) of original plans for an inner-ring road. Ensuing controversy has added to delays and only in November 1972 was a new £104 million 'Blue Print for the 1990s' unveiled. Environmental questions centring on preserving Edinburgh's historic centre have weighed heavily in these radical new plans, involving the creating of new pedestrian areas, private car restrictions and special bus routes, as well as ring and relief routes and new eastern and western approach roads. The new proposals remain subject to enquiry while the problems mount in urgency.

The pace of development of oil-related activities means that previous assumptions as to the growth and pattern of road traffic are still open to question. Many Scottish interests would like to see still further improvements and an acceleration in the existing programme. Upgrading of the Perth-Inverness road to full dual carriageway status is urged along with an acceleration of building the M74 southwards and improvement of the A1 and other routes south from Edinburgh—especially to Northumberland and

Teesside. The allocation of central funds may well increase in response to these representations following receipt by the government of reports and assessments of the need for infrastructural developments recently completed or now under way (see chapter 4).

Road Freight

Approximately 120,000 goods vehicles are licensed in Scotland of which nearly half are of 30cwt. (1,524kg.) capacity or over. 'A' licences—vehicles available for general haulage work—amount to some 12,000.

Road haulage services are the province of both State and private interests. In the private sector about 85 percent of licensed hauliers are represented by the Road Haulage Association, with about 1,000 Scottish members. Scotland is one of 15 areas within the RHA organisation, and within Scotland there are eight sub-offices at Wick, Inverness, Dundee, Aberdeen, Dumfries, Edinburgh, Glasgow and Ayr. Scottish RHA members are represented in each of the various RHA functional groupings—such as livestock, bulk liquids and tipping.

Members own an average of five vehicles each and the relatively few large organisations concealed within this average dominate the road freight market—especially in sectors such as whisky and machinery and mechanical engineering.

The main public sector haulage companies forming part of the National Freight Corporation are also members of the RHA (an exception being Tartan Arrow, on account of a technicality), and normal commercial relationships operate between the two sectors.

The National Freight Corporation is said to be the largest transport system in the non-communist world; yet it holds a mere 7 to 8 percent of the freight distribution and warehousing business in the U.K., and only 4 to 5 percent in Scotland. Of its various subsidiaries, the former Scottish Division of British Road Services became known on 1st January 1973, as Scottish Road Services, one of seven autonomous operating companies within BRS. The business of Scottish Road Services is in general haulage, with the bulk of shipments being over the border between

England and Scotland, in roughly equal flows. Scottish Road Services has 18 depots and 5 sub-depots in Scotland, and those at Glasgow, Edinburgh and Dundee provide the principle scheduled services to England for traffic emanating from the Clyde/Forth valley.

A new distribution depot has recently been opened in Glasgow, to break bulk shipments from the south for distribution to customers' outlets in Scotland. Scottish Road Services maintains close connections with the New Towns and the various Development Authorities and stresses the reliability of its overnight services to cities as far south as Birmingham. Main growth area of business is long term hire of vehicles in customers' own liveries—'leased' without drivers, or on 'contract hire' including driver and maintenance.

Scottish Road Services is now running direct continental services, carrying complete sealed vehicle loads, using 12-metre 'tilt' trailers built to TIR specifications, and with full CMR (Convention Merchandises Routiers) insurance cover. These services were till mid-1972 left to other concerns within the National Freight Corporation such as Containerway & Roadferry and Pickfords. Following a re-grouping of international services within the Corporation the latter now operates, in association with Tartan Arrow, a direct continental air freight service currently engaged in setting up operating depots in major European cities to compete with local operators.

Nationally, the haulage services of Scottish Road Services— similarly to the other former BRS regions—dovetail into the Freightliner services run by British Rail, and through road services between Scotland and the south have been virtually withdrawn in view of the more rapid transit service available by rail. Containers are delivered to and collected from railheads by local BRS vehicles.

The road/rail relationship is even closer in the case of small loads and parcels of up to one ton. These are the province of BRS Parcels, run as an entirely separate business within the National Freight Corporation but with normal commercial relationships with its sister companies. BRS Parcels has six Scottish depots and three sub-depots. Only in the case of Argyll —with a special traffic pattern and no rail services—do parcels and general haulage companies operate on a common basis. BRS Parcels, in turn, parallels closely the services of National Carriers Ltd., formerly part of the Sundries Division of British Rail. NCL, too offers a nationwide parcels service, but with more emphasis on collection and delivery to and from a large number of points than BRS parcels' more centralised and strategically-located activities, run more closely in association with local private sector haulage concerns.

Road Passenger Transport

Unlike goods haulage, passenger transport by road in Scotland is almost entirely the province of the public sector, with all services operated by the Scottish Transport Group with the exception of bus services in the four cities. These are run by the City Corporations, although the cities are naturally terminal points for inter-city and long haul services run by Scottish Transport Group Companies.

The Scottish Transport Group came into being as a result of the 1968 Transport Act, although somewhat earlier the Road Traffic Act of 1930 brought into existence the embryo Scottish Bus Group whose passenger transport interests were subsequently taken over by the British Transport Commission in 1947. Over the years independent operating companies were progressively absorbed, and the road passenger operating subsidiaries of the Scottish Transport Group are now as follows:

Scottish Bus Group Ltd.
W. Alexander & Sons (Fife) Ltd.
W. Alexander & Sons (Midland) Ltd.
W. Alexander & Sons (Northern) Ltd.
Central S.M.T.* Co. Ltd.
Highland Omnibuses Ltd.
Scottish Omnibuses Ltd.
Western S.M.T.* Co. Ltd.

In addition to road transport the ferry services to the Western Isles are also operated by the group through two companies, David MacBrayne Ltd. and Caledonian Steam Packet Co. Ltd., the former owned as to 51 per cent by the Secretary of State

* Originally Scottish Motor Transport.

and 49 per cent by the Scottish Transport Group and the latter now wholly owned, purchased from British Rail.

The group comprises certain other interests including two travel agency businesses and two hotels. It also publishes the monthly *Scotland's Magazine* in association with the Scottish Tourist Board. The pattern of operating revenue for the Scottish Transport Group since its formation is shown below.

SCOTTISH TRANSPORT GROUP: GROSS REVENUE FOR YEARS 1969-71

		1969	*1970*	*1971*
Road passenger services	£m	29·00	28·82	37·12
	%	87·5	87·6	88·7
Shipping	£m	3·43	3.49	3·90
	%	10·4	10·6	9·3
Travel and tourism	£m	0·24	0·25	0·30
	%	0·7	0·8	0·7
Insurance	£m	0·46	0·34	0·52
	%	1·4	1·0	1·3
Total revenue		33·13	32·90	41·84

Source: *Scottish Transport Group*

The dip in revenue in 1970 was due to an unprecedented series of industrial stoppages; however, despite the growth of receipts the passenger transport operations have shown a gradual decline as illustrated by the following figures:

	1969	*1970*	*1971*
Vehicle miles (millions)	168·2	148·1	152·2
Passengers carried (millions)	555·7	463·8	454·3
Traffic vehicles (end of year)	4,721	4,712	4,580

It is expected that the rate of passenger loss will slow in the future. An important growth area, however, is express services—both between Glasgow and Edinburgh and between both cities and the south.

Motorways have brought Glasgow-London down to 9 hours including stops, and fastest scheduled Edinburgh-London timing is 10 hours, while fares are less than half the rail equivalent.

Within Scotland, one particular role of the bus services is to fill gaps left by the closure of railway lines. Such services are often by their nature uneconomic (rail closures themselves resulting from lack of traffic) and in such cases are maintained on social grounds by arrangement with local authorities and the Traffic Commissioners, with subsidies up to 75 percent of operating costs obtainable. Even so a large element of cost-subsidisation is necessary to balance the economics of other services.

Ferry Services

Of the two shipping companies, services in the Firth of Clyde area are run by the Caledonian Steam Packet Company whilst MacBrayne's operates the principal ferry services to the Western Isles. The Stranraer-Larne service to Northern Ireland is run by British Rail.

The total number of vessels operated by MacBrayne's is 13 with a combined gross tonnage of 10,118 whilst the Caledonian Steam Packet Company has 19 vessels with a combined tonnage of 8,629 and one hovercraft. Total passengers carried by the two companies in 1971 were 4·2 million of which four-fifths were carried by Caledonian Steam Packet. The MacBrayne's services, in which there is a strong social as well as tourist element (including the carriage of mail and considerable quantities of freight) are subsidised by the Secretary of State.

Policy of the Scottish Transport Group is to transfer traffic as rapidly as possible to modern roll-on/roll-off vessels and already drive-on car ferries operate on the great majority of routes. As well as these comparatively large vessels, however, a fleet of 12 small ferries, each carrying about 6 cars, is also being introduced. These provide greater flexibility to meet the needs of the highly seasonal tourist traffic (a vessel such as the *M.V. Clansman* may carry 500 passengers in summer and as few as 20 in winter, while full ocean-going safety standards must be observed at all times).

Route policy is to secure the shortest possible sea crossings and for instance a new Stornoway-Ullapool service is to operate from April 1973. Changes of this type, however, involve the co-operation of the Scottish Development Department in road improvements and of harbour authorities in the construction of pier facilities. These may be sophisticated structures costing £250,000 when drive-on ferries must operate in conditions where the tidal rise and fall may be up to 30 feet and weather conditions highly variable.

Tourist cruising remains an important, if highly seasonal, aspect of Scottish water transport and picturesque vessels such as the *Maid of the Loch* continue to operate on Loch Lomond and other lochs whilst the Group operates Europe's last sea-going paddle steamer, the *Waverley* on the Firth of Clyde.

RAIL

Summary of Traffic

The Scottish rail services form an integral part of the British Rail network covering the whole country. During the so-called 'Beeching era' of the early 1960s, hundreds of small stations were closed as were subsidiary, sparsely used routes and branches. Facilities were rationalised and a general reorganisation took place, leaving a streamlined rail system able to serve the main priorities of large scale passenger and freight transport. At the same time the 1968 Transport Act introduced grant-aid to cover those loss making services retained for social reasons.

As the result of these changes, the Scottish rail network today totals just under 2,000 miles, compared with nearly 3,400 miles in 1960.

The table on page 148 shows the trend of operations, and a map of the passenger service network appears on page 152.

It is thus clear that closing some 40 per cent of total track length has had no lasting effect on passenger traffic; in fact the underlying long term trend continues to be upward. Freight traffic has fallen but at around 20 million tons a year remains very substantial, and traffic outside the traditional heavy sectors (coal and steel etc.) is rising steadily. The only further closure contemplated is the Dingwall-Kyle of Lochalsh line which British Rail

SUMMARY OF BRITISH RAIL (SCOTTISH) OPERATING
STATISTICS 1960-1971

	1960	1968	1969	1970	1971
Lines open for traffic (miles)	3,369	2,091	1,999	1,955	1,948
Passenger journeys (millions)	64·9	67·0	68·4	70·7	66·5
Freight traffic (in tons)					
Total	29·8	20·9	21·1	20·8	20·0
Coal and coke	17·2	12·0	11·5	10·6	9·8
Iron and steel	12·6	5·5	6·1	5·9	5·1
Other		3·3	3·5	4·3	5·1
Receipts total (£m)	43·8	34·3	35·8	38·0	40·5
Coach trains (£m)	18·1	17·8	18·5	20·7	22·9
Freight trains (£m)	25·7	16·5	17·3	17·3	17·6

Source: Scottish Abstract of Statistics.

plan to close at the end of 1973 subject to Department of the Environment permission and substitution of adequate road transport services. A road link with Inverness from the new ferry terminal at Ullapool will replace the existing Kyle line.

Inter-City Services
Faster timings stemming from investment in modern equipment have played the major role in increasing the attractiveness of rail transport. Edinburgh-London timings for instance were reduced from 7 to 6 hours in 1962 and are down to 5½ hours for 1973. More frequent trains with air-conditioned coaches have been introduced, along with connecting trains to serve points north of Edinburgh. The summer 1973 timetable includes two day-time through services—with timings much faster than previously —between Aberdeen and London (Kings Cross) together with three overnight trains, two of them catering for sleeping car passengers. The same route links Aberdeen, Dundee and Fife with Teesside and Tyneside.

Within Scotland, Inter-City services between Glasgow and Edinburgh run on the half hour with a best city centre to city centre time of 43 minutes, bringing steady increases in passengers carried despite competition from the now completed motorway link. 1973 timings between Glasgow and Aberdeen have been reduced (now under 3 hours) and new rolling stock introduced.

The Highland line to Inverness poses special problems in that the route is single track, with passing places, climbs over several summits (including the highest point on British Rail) and has extensive curvature due to the nature of the terrain. Nevertheless the journey between Glasgow and Inverness, which once took 6 hours with steam, was reduced to 5 hours with diesel in 1962 and is now down to 4 hours. A change planned for 1974 is a new direct service between Inverness and London (Euston) by day for the first time, supplementing the overnight 'Royal Highlander'. Resort developments at Aviemore and industralisation—including oil—further north have swollen traffic on this picturesque line.

Speeds and acceleration are now almost at the limit achievable with conventional diesel locomotives and the limitations of existing track and signalling. The Advanced Passenger Train (APT) under development by British Rail will ultimately bring Scotland-London timings down to 4 hours or so. Before this, though, there are plans for a High Speed Train (HST) based on APT principles but using diesel power at 125 m.p.h. (200 k.p.h.) and with braking distances comparable to existing 100 m.p.h. (160 k.p.h.) trains. HST will bring Edinburgh-London down to 5 hours. In the meantime, however, the biggest single advance in rail communications between Scotland and the south is the electrification of the Glasgow-London line.

Electrification as far north as Liverpool and Manchester was completed in 1967 and the first five years' operations brought a 100 percent increase in passengers carried on the services concerned. In 1970 the government go-ahead was given to extend this highly successful electrically powered service to Glasgow. At an investment of £55 million, this will bring average journey times between Glasgow and London down to little more than 5 hours from May 1974, with air-conditioned luxury coaches adding to the attraction of the route for businessmen and tourists alike. Services to other points south will benefit and the electrified line will

connect with diesel services to Edinburgh through Carstairs
Junction using through coaches.

Glasgow Improvements

As an extension of the main line electrification project the suburban
Hamilton Circle line is being electrified in a £1·5 million scheme
which will bring the well known 'Blue Trains' to a further area
of Lanarkshire with increases in the number of trains resulting
from electric power and reduced running costs. This service carries
a heavy commuter traffic as well as thousands of shopping
housewives.

The Hamilton electrification was one of the recommendations
in 'Planning for Action', part of the Greater Glasgow Transportation Study. Another recommendation was the reopening of
part of the former Glasgow Central Low Level Line between
Rutherglen and Kelvinhaugh. This line was closed in 1964 and at
the time was the last steam underground railway in the world.
Most of its former services duplicated those on newly electrified
surface routes, but although the old track was lifted, the track
formation and tunnels were retained by British Rail against the
possibility of a future reopening, and the new plan is to open the
Central Section between the new Hamilton service at Rutherglen
and the existing Airdrie/Helensburgh suburban electric network
near Partickhill Station, which would be rebuilt to co-ordinate
with Glasgow Corporation's underground line at Merkland Street
and local bus services.

Feasibility studies are not yet complete, but reopening the
Central Line would offer Glasgow the rare distinction of a new
fast cross-city rail service without the need for surface construction
or new tunnelling work.

Rail and Industry

More than three-quarters of the 21 million tons of rail freight
carried in Scotland each year is between private sidings belonging
to customers' undertakings. Every large industry is served by
company trains, whether traditional sectors such as whisky, coal
and steel or modern ones such as vehicle building, aluminium,

cement and oil. British Rail's carryings of oil from Grangemouth have reached an annual total in excess of three million tons and BR has responded actively to the demands of the new oil industry in the north east by co-operating in the speedy bulk transport of cement, steel and other items. Several thousand tons of steelwork were moved by train to a point north of Invergordon for the rig construction yard at Nigg Bay, and BR built a new quarter-mile siding for a pipe-coating plant at Invergordon within 3 weeks.

The Freightliner container services are, since the 1968 Transport Act, controlled by the National Freight Corporation, although British Rail retains a 49 percent interest and of course runs the trains. Scottish container services are growing rapidly, with terminals at Aberdeen, Edinburgh, Glasgow and Coatbridge. The Greenock Containerport also provides a feeder service into the national freightliner network, and Coatbridge is the terminal for the Euro-Scot international service as well as acting as a general clearing house for maritime containers. Services from Coatbridge link with the ports of Felixstowe, Harwich, Tilbury and Southampton.

British Rail can claim close operating relationships with many industries. The railway carries supplies to the Wiggins Teape Paper Mill at Fort William, and delivers pulp paper to the south. British Rail handles more than 120,000 new cars each year in Scotland, notably those built at Chrysler's Linwood Plant. Three million tons a year of iron ore are conveyed by train from the Glasgow quayside to Lanarkshire steel works and 'merry-go-round' trains of huge hopper waggons provide conveyor belt delivery of coal from mine to power station.

British Rail is co-operating actively in studies of various possible developments for Hunterston on the Ayrshire coast.

L

British Rail Scottish passenger network

AIRPORTS AND AIR SERVICES

Scottish Air Traffic

It is the jet plane which has done most to reduce Scotland's effective distance from the south and from Europe, bringing Glasgow and Edinburgh within an hour's flying time of London. Glasgow Abbotsinch, opened in 1965, is Scotland's largest airport, but the greatest passenger traffic growth has been shown by the two principal airports of the north east.

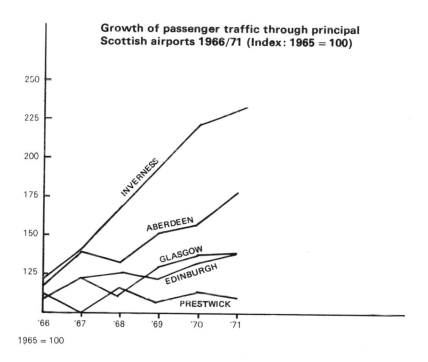

Growth of passenger traffic through principal Scottish airports 1966/71 (Index: 1965 = 100)

1965 = 100

A full summary of air traffic operation is shown on page 154.

Scottish air services encompass an astonishingly wide range, with the busy short to medium haul U.K. and European services flanked on the one hand by intercontinental services to and from Prestwick, Scotland's main International airport on the Ayrshire coast, and on the other hand, by the local services to the Islands where the airstrip may, as at Barra, simply be the beach and the plane a lifeline.

CIVIL AVIATION MOVEMENTS AT SCOTTISH AIRPORTS
1967-1971

	1967	1968	1969	1970	1971
			thousands		
Movements	121·3	140·2	176·0	188·2	215·9
Scheduled[1]	69.2	68·2	69·0	69·0	72·8
Chartered[2]	4·3	6·3	8·1	10·3	10·8
Other	47·8	65·7	98·9	108·9	132·2
Passengers	3,046·2	2,967·6	3,202·0	3,411·1	3,501·6
Terminal	2,762·9	2,689·1	2,905·6	3,102·7	3,198·7
Scheduled	2,592·0	2,478·5	2,608·5	2,729·4	2,750·1
Chartered	170·9	210·6	297·1	373·3	448·6
Transit	283·3	278·5	296·4	308·4	302·9
Scheduled	263·3	243·1	247·5	251·5	249·5
Chartered	20·0	35·4	48·9	56·8	53·4
Total passengers by airport:					
Aberdeen (Dyce)	120·2	114·0	130·0	135·5	153·6
Benbecula	30·4	29·3	30·4	33·2	35·8
Edinburgh (Turnhouse)	613·7	628·6	614·4	662·5	690·0
Glasgow (Abbotsinch)	1,548·1	1,409·3	1,630·7	1,724·4	1,764·3
Inverness (Dalcross)	65·1	64·5	89·5	103·6	108·4
Islay (Port Ellen)	17·9	15·7	16·2	14·8	14·6
Orkney (Kirkwall)	66·2	62·3	74·7	72·0	73·3
Prestwick	452·6	521·9	480·2	515·7	500·5
Stornoway	36·7	34·0	41·2	45·0	45·8
Shetland (Sumburgh)	25·0	23·5	26·0	32·2	43·5
Tiree	6·6	5·4	5·2	5·2	5·2
Wick	63·9	59·0	63·4	66·9	66·6
			Metric tons		
Freight	24,941	31,100	39,859	36,390	31,868
Scheduled	24,262	29,308	37,472	34,595	30,776
Chartered	679	1,792	2,387	1,795	1,092
Mail	4,113	3,976	3,797	4,003	3,585

Source: *Department of Trade and Industry.*
[1] All movements.
[2] Loaded movements only.

The largest carrier in Scotland is British European Airways, now under the control of the British Airways Board and headed for eventual merger with British Overseas Airways Corporation in the new British Airways. In the meantime, aircraft on BEA's Scottish services bear the name Scottish Airways—result of a recommendation in the Report of the Edwards Committee in 1969 that Scotland should have its own regional airline. BEA flies the main trunk routes connecting Scotland with other U.K. centres and also a network of internal Scottish routes, serving the tiny island airports to the north and west of Scotland (a typical route in this category being Glasgow-Inverness-Wick-Orkney-Shetland).

Turbo-prop Viscount aircraft, capable of flying in most weathers (though requiring more extensive ground facilities than its predecessors) have progressively been introduced on these Highlands and Islands routes, but on the Glasgow-Tiree-Barra route to the Western Isles, the 14-seater DeHavilland Herons previously in use will shortly be replaced by 19-seater turbo-prop Short 'Skyliners', which will also do duty as emergency air ambulances. Other services to the Islands are flown by Loganair, a subsidiary of the Royal Bank of Scotland, using aircraft of the 'Islander' type, and charter services are also available to any destination.

BEA competes on the Glasgow and Edinburgh trunk routes with British Caledonian Airways. BCAL is the 'second force' private sector airline advocated by the 1969 Edwards Committee report, and came into being in November 1970 as the result of a merger between the former British United Airways and Caledonian Airways (for a short period the name Caledonian/BUA was used).

British United had already established itself since 1965 as a scheduled carrier on the Scottish routes (using London-Gatwick as its terminal in the south) while Caledonian—which previously functioned solely as a charter airline—was originally built up from a group of Scottish shareholdings, operating from 1961 as Scotland's unofficial national flag carrier. British Caledonian can thus claim close connections with Scotland apart from its name— even though for operational reasons the airline is based at Gatwick in Surrey.

As well as domestic routes, a network of international services has been built up, covering a large number of destinations in Europe, Africa and South America. The then British United Airways took up the routes voluntarily relinquished by BOAC in 1964, and the entire British West African route network, together with the London-Paris (Le Bourget) run, formed part of the 'package' of routes transferred to British Caledonian by the Government on its formation.

In 1972, in fulfilment of one of its original ambitions, British Caledonian was granted a licence for transatlantic services. Scheduled services from London-Gatwick to New York and Los Angeles began on 1st April 1973—in competition with BOAC but bidding to increase the total British share of transatlantic traffic. In June 1973, direct services started from Glasgow-Prestwick and from Manchester to New York, again alongside the existing BOAC services. BCAL's 'Golden Lion' services will have a 1973 peak summer frequency of 42 flights a week on these four routes. The airline's Scottish links are strongly emphasised in the promotion of the American services—20 million Americans are of Scottish descent—and in the tartan uniforms worn by cabin and ground hostesses. All aircraft in the fleet bear Scottish place names, and the Lion Rampant of Scotland on the tail.

Further ahead, British Caledonian propose to include Boston, Houston, Dallas, Forth Worth and Atlanta among their trans-atlantic destinations. A recent (1972) innovation on the airline's domestic flights is 'Moonjet', Britain's first walk-on walk-off service, late night services between Glasgow or Edinburgh and London at a fare below the basic rail fare.

As indicated by the table on page 154, a substantial and growing volume of air freight travels to and from Scotland—much of it bound for export markets and almost all on scheduled services. BEA runs through container services from Scotland to Europe, with a purpose-built cargo terminal at Abbotsinch. Considerable quantities pass through Prestwick, where a new terminal is also under construction, and frequent scheduled BOAC services by jet freighter are run to North American and a variety of other destinations including Australia and the Far East. British Caledonian too carries large quantities of cargo on its scheduled services, and plans to extend its freight activities to the North Atlantic run.

Direct Continental Services

Growth and development of Scottish air services is inescapably bound up with important infrastructural improvements, and as such forms part of the wide-ranging analysis of the Scottish economy under way at the present time. A working party has been set up by the Civil Aviation Authority to study future air service requirements in Scotland, and the Regional Development Department is deeply involved in the question. The Highlands and Islands services of BEA inevitably lose money, despite the re-organisation to create a closer Scottish identity, and require cross-subsidisation from profitable routes. Various possibilities are under consideration including direct flexible subsidies, in which part of each passenger's fare would be paid to the airline by the government. Some form of rationalisation involving the indepen-dent Loganair is also a possibility.

An especially contentious question is that of direct air services between Scotland and the Continent. A long-standing cry in business circles is that these are wholly inadequate. At present the only direct year-round scheduled continental services are to Amsterdam and Copenhagen—although from Glasgow, Frankfurt and Dusseldorf can be reached via Manchester, Paris via Birmingham, and Amsterdam via Newcastle and Copenhagen as well as direct. Edinburgh's only European link is to Copenhagen via Newcastle—a newly started BCAL run.

The airlines maintain that the potential traffic volumes are in-sufficient to justify regular direct services, and some—such as Loganair's Aberdeen-Stavanger—have been tried unsuccessfully. BEA's view is that Continental flights must be shared between two provincial points (Glasgow and Birmingham for instance) and it is widely accepted that many business travellers prefer, in any case to go via London. The need to call at London head-offices is one factor, but a 1971 survey by the Scottish Council found the most important reason to be the frequency of connections from London-Heathrow especially—to continental destinations, where-as any direct service from Scotland would inevitably offer a lower frequency and hence be less convenient for many travellers. Thus a 'chicken and egg' situation prevails.

Furthermore, whereas first class interline connections are available from Amsterdam and Copenhagen, justifying the direct

Scottish flights to these cities, it was found to be predominantly to France and to Germany that the London connection was used—evidence that London is regarded as the 'normal' place to start a journey to Europe.

Britain's E.E.C. membership is expected to accelerate the growth of direct air services. Holiday tour and other charter business is already expanding fast—chiefly from Glasgow, but package tours to Majorca will be run from Aberdeen in summer 1973. In the long term the position is bound to be influenced by the location of major new U.K. airport developments (discussed below). In the meantime the emphasis is on meeting the current and anticipated needs of traffic generated by North Sea exploration activity.

The growth of services has already been impressive. BEA flights from Aberdeen to Sumburgh (Shetland) were formerly operated for six days a week in summer only. During winter 1971/72, three flights a week were kept going and frequency rose to nine flights a week in the summer. Frequency in winter 1972/73 was held at six a week and summer 1973 will see twelve flights a week. Aberdeen-London services were, till recently, maintained at a frequency of 18 flights weekly in summer and 12 in winter. Booming traffic caused the 1972 summer programme to be maintained through the following winter and summer 1973 services have been fixed at about 24 flights weekly, including one jet service on weekdays. Daily Inverness-London direct flights began in 1969, and although growth of traffic has been slower than anticipated, frequencies have been doubled for 1973.

One of the most telling innovations has been in the BOAC feeder service operated between Prestwick and Edinburgh and now extended to Aberdeen, to give North Sea Texans the facility of through services. This feeder is operated by Viscount aircraft.

Airport Improvements

The lack of adequate airport facilities is at present a serious brake on further improvements. The terminal facilities at Aberdeen for instance are badly in need of improvement and runway rebuilding is required before jet frequencies can be stepped up.

Dalcross airport at Inverness—the subject of a current study by the Highlands and Islands Development Board—needs radical runway improvements before the heavier jets can be accepted, although BEA hopes to bring jets to Inverness by 1975. Sumburgh in the Shetlands is becoming a key airport in oil developments, but poses special problems on account of high ground at each end of the runway causing even Viscounts to operate with a weight penalty. As the oil prospecting programme moves westwards around the Scottish coast, problems are foreseen in Orkneys and then Lewis and Harris.

All these airports are under local or regional authority control and the funds for the sweeping improvements required are not available from normal sources. There are strong pressures for responsibility to be taken over by the Scottish Development Department and indeed the need for incorporation of airport development in overall infrastructure planning is evident.

Of Scotland's major airports, Prestwick and Turnhouse (Edinburgh) are run by the British Airports Authority, while Glasgow's Abbotsinch is still run by Glasgow Corporation. The restructuring of local government will provide an opportunity for the BAA to take over Glasgow too, if agreement can be reached on terms. A £9 million project to provide a new runway and terminal building at Turnhouse has now been approved, deferring at least for the present the long mooted question of a Central Scotland Airport, which could replace Turnhouse, Abbotsinch and possibly Prestwick (although the latter, despite being under-utilised, has a special value through being almost entirely fog-free).

Such an airport—located on one of several possible sites between Glasgow and Edinburgh—has been the subject of official enquiries (including a working party under DTI chairmanship and including representatives from the Scottish Office, the Civil Aviation Authority, British Airports Authority and Glasgow Corporation) and is undoubtedly feasible technically—albeit at a cost of some £60 million. Protagonists of the concept see it as an opportunity to replace two—if not three—airports with one, with consequent environmental benefits and release of valuable land; and also as a means of putting Scotland at the hub of a vastly more extensive air communications system, as an air complement to Oceanspan. The decision to go ahead with building Maplin airport must be

Direct Passenger Services

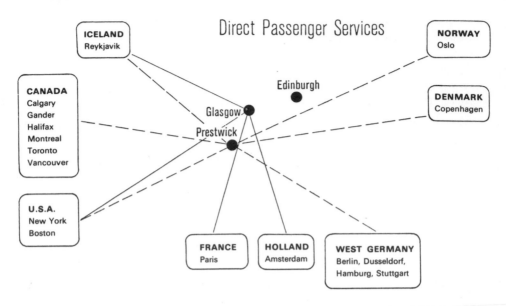

Direct Cargo Flights

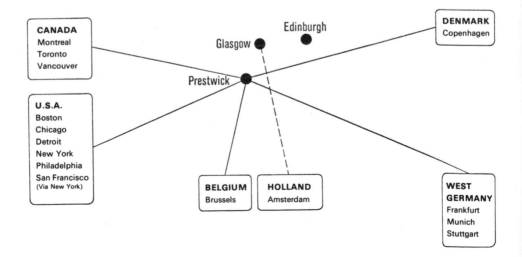

seen as a further blow to the concept of a new Scottish 'green field' airport—at least for the present, though the idea is unlikely to be abandoned.

Sea Traffic and Port Facilities

The sea has been Scotland's traditional highway for communication with the outside world, and even in the jet age Scotland retains its enduring confidence in the sea to give it independent access to any point in the world.

Recently, recognition of the strategic value of the deep water available on both sides of Central Scotland, and more especially in the west, has led to detailed studies (see Chapter 2) of the potential in a world context of major new port construction allied to a hinterland of associated industrial development and a 'land bridge' across the central belt, facilitating transhipment or inward and outward movement of goods in either direction.

Scotland offers all the key necessities for port growth—deep water (the Clyde gives over 100 feet (30·5m.) of natural deep water at all tides), land, labour, power, a developed hinterland and a potential for investment. Le Havre and Marseilles are the only two sites in Western Europe offering comparable scope for development.

Such a concept can only be approached in a strategic context and with due regard to international considerations. It is too early to say whether a major new port complex will emerge from the present round of Scottish development plans, and the implications of oil discoveries are still only partly known. Scotland already possesses advanced port facilities in both East and West, which are now starting to benefit from recent reorganisation as well as from investment stemming directly from oil.

The Clyde Port Authority was Britain's first estuarial port authority to be formed in the wake of the report of the Rochdale Committee in 1962. Established in 1966, it is Scotland's biggest port complex, extending to 450 square miles of water (1,166sq.km.) and including the ports of Glasgow, Greenock and Ardrossan. Clydeport provides the most modern and comprehensive facilities for importing raw materials (such as grain, iron ore, and oil) and exporting finished goods. The Clyde Estuary is already used by tankers of over 300,000 tons dwt, and the potential exists on the Ayrshire Coast to provide berthage for vessels of up to 1 million tons dwt—twice the size of any ship presently in existence.

The Forth Ports Authority was born of more diverse parentage. Created in early 1968, it consists of Grangemouth, Leith (Edinburgh) and the smaller facilities of Burntisland, Kirkcaldy, Methil and Granton, the last two of which have close connections with the coal and fishing industries respectively. Grangemouth and Leith are the two principal ports of the Scottish East Coast. The combined share of the Forth and Clyde ports of Scottish seaborne traffic is four-fifths, and that of Clydeport alone is half.

It is through the ports of the Forth and Clyde—respectively the two halves of the Oceanspan concept—that the principle ocean going services are operated. The Clydeport Container Terminal at Greenock, opened in 1969, handles the major part of the rapidly growing international container traffic to and from Scotland. The terminal has a minimum depth of 42 feet alongside, permitting round the clock working regardless of tide, and simultaneous docking facilities for two second-generation container ships. A rail freightliner terminal forms an integral part of the complex, which is also linked to the national motorway network. Scheduled container services operate from Greenock to the U.S.A., and other Atlantic destinations.

Additional container services are provided at the port of Glasgow, and groupage for these and for the Greenock facilities is provided by Clyde Container Services Ltd., a consortium of the operating interests. Meadowside Granary in Glasgow is one of the largest grain stores in the U.K., and an important transhipment centre. At Ardrossan, the largest single commodity handled is oil and refined petroleum products in connection with the neighbouring Shell installation, but Ardrossan is also a focal point for roll-on/roll-off and passenger services to Arran, the Isle of Man and Ireland.

Both Leith and Grangemouth have modern container terminals, and roll-on/roll-off facilities at Leith provide a direct link with Sweden. Regular cargo services by conventional or container ship are operated to the U.S.A. and destinations throughout Northern Europe. Leith can now handle vessels drawing up to 37 feet (11·2m.) or about 30,000 tons dwt, and industrial development within the dock area has been actively pursued. Leith, with spare dockside capacity, has proved to be an attractive centre for both transhipment and supply in relation to North Sea oil developments, and engineering and fabrication plants as well as warehousing facilities have been established. Alongside this, Leith remains a powerful draw for cruise liners, being only some two miles from the heart of Edinburgh.

Grangemouth has several intrinsic advantages which have consolidated its position as Scotland's second port. Although inland, Grangemouth is a deep water port capable with a new lock scheme of taking ships of up to 24,000 tons; by virtue of its position it is also adjacent to the motorway network. Grangemouth has especially benefitted however, from its connection with the adjoining petro-chemical complex. As well as oil traffic, container and conventional cargo services are operated between Grange-mouth and a variety of ports in North America, the Far East, Middle East and Europe.

Some mention has already been made (Chapter 4) of developments at other ports on the east coast of Scotland stemming from North Sea oil activity. For Aberdeen, especially, oil has created problems of capacity. This, Britain's third largest fishing port, and with strong trading connections with Scandinavia and the Baltic countries, has become the most important base for vessels servicing and supplying the oil rigs, and a harbour for the mobile rigs themselves. Other cargoes handled by Aberdeen consist predominantly of chemicals plus timber and materials related to the paper industry. Aberdeen can accommodate ships of up to 525 feet (162m.) in length and drawing $30\frac{1}{2}$ feet of water. Conversion of the existing closed docks into a tidal harbour and investment of £10 million in new docks will relieve the acute pressures caused by oil-related activity.

Other ports are in any case coming to take an increasing share of the load. As well as Leith, these include Dundee and the harbours of Montrose and Peterhead, both of which are undergoing radical improvements. Dundee is Scotland's fourth port after Aberdeen and the Forth and Clyde complexes, and can accommodate merchant vessels of up to 12,000 tons and oil tankers of up to 20,000 tons displacement, with a maximum draught of 28 feet. There are three riverside wharves and two impounded docks.

Several important improvements to the port of Dundee are envisaged or underway, including deepening the approach channel, extending the overall port area by land reclamation, and provision or roll-on/roll-off facilities. The port has the advantages of direct access to the national rail system and to trunk roads. A variety of cargoes are handled and there are regular sailings to Northern European ports and Central America. Dundee is increasingly coming into the orbit of oil developments. Already the supply base for BP's Forties field, the port is bidding to attract a larger share of oil business by establishing a supply base for off-shore rigs to be operated by Ocean Inchcape and shipbuilders Robb Caledon.

The summary of traffic through Scottish ports which appears overleaf does not, of course, reflect the growth of oil related traffic during 1972. The figures include coastwise as well as foreign traffic, and represent the sum of inward and outward movements.

In the years 1965 to 1971, a total of £30·2 million was spent on Scottish port projects, about 11 percent of the national total. Two-thirds of this Scottish expenditure went to East Coast ports, and in the absence of any radical new developments on the Ayrshire coast these proportions are unlikely to be reversed, as the East Coast ports are modernised and extended in response to the opportunities offered by Europe and by oil.

Apart from these factors, the trend towards containerisation for general cargoes and to very large vessels for oil and other bulk cargoes is tending to increase the advantages of ports with an open sea frontage at the expense of smaller ports generally and up-river docks especially.

Dock facilities on the upper reaches of the Clyde are likely to be the main casualties in Scotland, and the emerging counter-trend towards multi-barge carriers of the LASH type is seen as one way of reversing the decline of such facilities, and incidentally of reducing road congestion. The barges—nearly 100 of which can be carried on the mother vessel—are of a size to exploit the full potential of inland waterways as well as river estuaries, and the possibility of reopening the Forth and Clyde Canal to provide a new artery across Scotland has been publicly raised. A barge carrier service of the 'Seabee' type run by a U.S. shipping company has already been inaugurated between Leith and North American ports.

CARGO TRAFFIC THROUGH SCOTTISH PORTS 1967-1971

	1967	1968	1969	1970	1971
			thousand tons		
All Scottish Ports					
Dry cargo	10,616	13,271	13,447	13,008	13,603
Petroleum	11,900	12,646	13,169	15,431	18,079
Clyde Port Authority					
Dry cargo	4,852	5,316	5,542	5,717	5,756
Petroleum	6,358	6,936	7,368	8,533	10,653
Forth Ports Authority					
Dry cargo	3,808	4,464	4,569	3,979	4,287
Petroleum	3,163	3,270	3,332	4,169	4,905
Aberdeen					
Dry cargo	783	796	773	751	706
Petroleum	448	476	515	554	612
Dundee					
Dry cargo	242	257	199	218	178
Petroleum	484	393	457	691	670

Source: Scottish Abstract of Statistics.

7 Distribution

DISTRIBUTION

Structure and Trends

A periodic Census of Distribution is taken in Great Britain under the Statistics of Trade Act 1947. The third full census under the Act was taken in 1971, previous full censuses having related to 1950 and 1961. Sample censuses were taken in 1957 and 1966.

So far a minimum of regional information from the 1971 census has been published, and this in the form of provisional estimates only. Indeed the first part of the final results to be published by Her Majesty's Stationery Office as the 'Report on the Census of Distribution and Other Services 1971' is not expected to be published until towards the end of 1973, to be followed at intervals thereafter by a series of regional volumes.

For the present, therefore, a general analysis of retail distribution in Scotland must be based on the 1966 Sample Census, with trend information drawn from a comparison from that census and the previous (full) 1961 census. Trends in the case of Great Britain as a whole can be taken forward to 1971 in substantial detail— although still on a provisional basis—and an outline of the 1971 census results is shown in the following, together with such provisional data for Scotland as have been released.

A basic analysis of retail distribution in Scotland for 1966 is shown in the Table on page 168. In due course, it will be possible to compare these data directly with those for 1971. A note on definitions of the retail trade categories used is given in Appendix 3 —but it should be noted here that a multiple retail organisation is defined as one possessing ten or more branches, whilst an 'independent' has fewer than ten branches. Co-operative outlets are individual retail establishments belonging to co-operative societies.

RETAIL DISTRIBUTION IN SCOTLAND 1966

	All retail establishments		Cooperative Societies		Multiples		Independents	
	Establish-ments (No.)	Turn-over (£000)	Establish-ments (No.)	Turn-over (£000)	Establish-ments (No.)	Turn-over (£000)	Establish-ments (No.)	Turn-over (£000)
Total retail trade	48,464	1,066,229	4,930	158,270	6,546	304,393	36,988	603,567
Grocers and provisions dealers	11,933	297,413	2,336	85,757	1,333	72,863	8,264	138,792
Other food retailers	10,454	191,606	1,452	30,752	1,282	29,505	7,720	131,349
Confectioners, tobacconists, newsagents	7,667	113,410	18	623	705	15,365	6,944	97,422
Clothing and footwear shops	8,105	174,134	643	17,289	1,794	84,827	5,668	72,018
Household goods shops	5,352	112,835	230	7,858	846	30,569	4,276	74,408
Other non-food shops	4,633	76,937	171	3,177	390	18,821	4,072	54,939
General stores	320	99,895	80	12,814	196	52,442	44	34,639
Electricity showrooms	151	8,008	—	—	—	—	—	—
Gas showrooms	132	7,032	—	—	—	—	—	—

Source: *Census of Distribution 1966*

It is important to realise that the description of outlet categories relates to outlets categorised by the Census according to the main types of goods handled. It does not reflect the numbers of establishments selling particular commodities (for example, the number of outlets selling confectionery and tobacco is considerably greater than the number classified to this trade). The widening of the range of goods sold through non-traditional outlets is, of course, one of the features of retail trade during the past decade.

The principal trend within the sixties was the expansion of supermarket and self-service type trading, mainly—though by no means exclusively—operated by the multiple grocery chains. The result was the closure of thousands of independent grocery shops, and the conversion of many multiple and cooperative counter service stores to modern forms of trading. Other trades—such as the confectionery/newsagent/tobacconist type of outlet have been affected not only by the progressive encroachment of supermarkets into their traditional spheres of business, but by problems of remaining competitive—even given the advantage of convenience often enjoyed by small neighbourhood shops—after the abolition of resale price maintenance.

These trends have, of course, been reflected throughout Britain, and were already apparent during the first half of the decade. We give overleaf a comparison of trading through the main forms of retail organisation for 1961 and 1966 for all types of business.

Independent outlets were formerly slightly *less* important in Scotland than for the country as a whole (though the difference has narrowed), but the multiples, though still less important than in other regions, became proportionately more important and the cooperatives, though still much more important than for the whole country, became progressively much less important than they had formerly been in Scotland.

With a rising volume of trade carried on through fewer outlets, the average volume per outlet has clearly been rising even faster; however, important variations are present within the overall pattern.

The increase in business by the multiples has been very substantially in excess of their numerical increase, while the generally high levels of turnover—through higher prices, of course, as well as higher 'real' volumes of trade—have ensured an increase of the

RETAIL TRADE (by Value) BY FORM OF ORGANISATION (percentage)

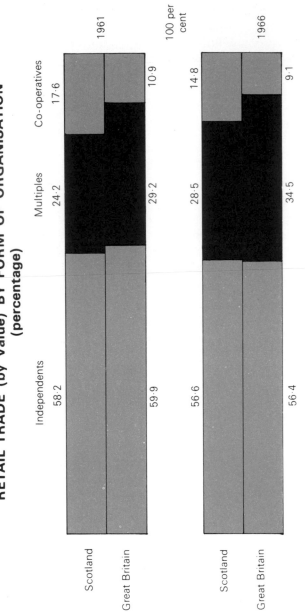

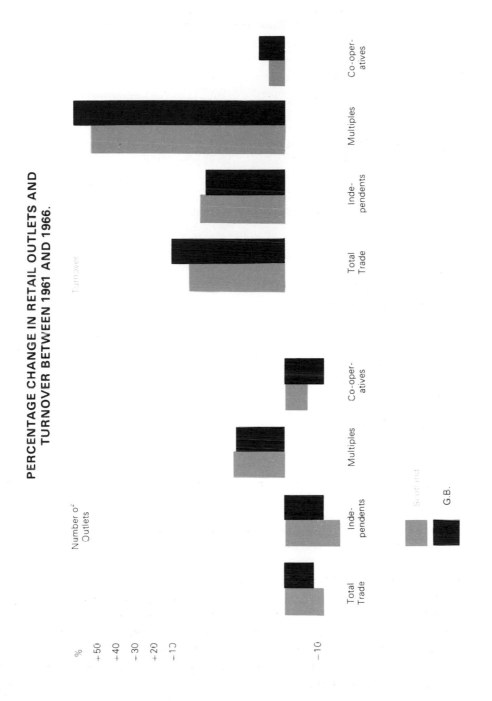

PERCENTAGE CHANGE IN RETAIL OUTLETS AND
TURNOVER BETWEEN 1961 AND 1966.

order of 20 per cent for the independents despite a numerical fall in strength of roughly the same proportions in Scotland within this five year period.

Scotland's importance in retail trade in Great Britain (the census does not cover Northern Ireland, where a separate census

SCOTTISH RETAIL TRADE AS A PERCENTAGE OF GREAT BRITAIN, 1961 & 1966

	1961		1966	
	Establish-ments	*Turn-over*	*Establish-ments*	*Turn-over*
Total retail trade	9·8	9·9	9·6	9·6
Grocers and provisions dealers	9·7	10·7	9·7	10·2
Other food retailers	10·6	9·5	10·0	9·2
Confectioners, tobac-conists, newsagents	12·3	11·2	12·1	10·8
Clothing and footwear shops	9·5	10·4	9·8[1]	10·1
Household goods shops	7·9	8·6	8·1[1]	8·7
Other non-food shops	8·3	8·3	7·5	7·5
General stores	10·5	8·9	10·6[1]	9·4
Electricity and Gas showrooms	12·0	7·9[2]	9·4	8·1

Source: *Census of Distribution, 1961 & 1966*

[1] Figures differ from those published in reports on the 1966 Census of Distribution due to reclassification of some credit traders calling on customers from clothing and footwear and household goods shops to general stores.

[2] Excludes charges for installation, repair and maintenance of appliances, which were included in 1966.

is taken) is almost precisely commensurate with the population base—9·6 per cent of national turnover and 9·9 per cent of retail outlets, compared with 9·8 per cent of Britain's population in 1966. However, the pattern by type of business varies considerably, with corresponding implications for retail sales per capita and per outlet. The above table shows the positions, with changes between 1961 and 1966.

COMPARISON OF TURNOVER PER OUTLET, SCOTLAND AND GREAT BRITAIN, 1961 & 1966

	1961		1966		Growth of Scottish t/o per Outlet 1961–1966 %
	Turnover per Outlet (£000)	As % of G.B.	Turnover per Outlet (£000)	As % of G.B.	
Total retail trade	16·3	100·0	22·0	99·5	35·0
Grocers and provisions dealers	17·8	111·3	24·9	105·5	+39·9
Other food retailers	13·5	89·4	18·3	92·0	+35·6
Confectioners, tobacconists, newsagents	9·3	81·7	14·8	89·7	+59·1
Clothing and footwear shops	17·2	108·9	21·5	103·9[1]	+25·0[1]
Household goods shops	17·1	108·9	21·1	107·7[1]	+23·4[1]
Other non-food shops	11·7	99·2	16·6	100·0	+41·9
General stores	209·0	84·3	312·2	88·1[1]	+49·4[1]
Electricity and Gas showrooms	24·6[2]	65·9	53·1[2]	86·1	+115·9

Source: *Census of Distribution 1961 & 1966.*

[1] Figures differ from those published in reports on the 1966 Census of Distribution due to reclassification of some credit traders calling on customers from clothing and footwear and household goods shops to general stores.

[2] Excludes charges for installation, repair and maintenance of appliances, which were included in 1966.

This position—and the changes illustrated—are examined in terms of turnover per outlet, with an index showing Scotland's position relative to Great Britain, in the table on page 173.

Turnover per outlet for 1961 was exactly the average for the whole country; by 1966 it had fallen to half of one per cent below the average. However, in 1966 Scottish grocers, clothing and footwear, and household goods shops all continued to do above average levels of business, and several categories (notably confectioners, tobacconists etc. and 'other food retailers'—dairy-men, butchers, greengrocers and so forth) increased their turnover by more than the national average.

The 1961 Census included other data which can usefully be recorded, despite the time interval since. The Central Clydeside Conurbation of Glasgow and its environs encompassed a total of 13,987 retail outlets with a combined turnover of £282·8 million, these figures accounting respectively for 26·2 per cent and 32·5 per cent of the Scottish total, while the Conurbation accounted in 1961 for 34·8 per cent of Scotland's population. The Census gave data for certain service trades, as follows:

	No.	Turnover (£000)
Hairdressers	2,868	6,822
Boot & Shoe Repairers	942	2,554

RETAIL OUTLETS IN SCOTLAND 1971, COMPARED WITH 1961 AND EQUIVALENT CHANGES FOR GREAT BRITAIN

	Scotland 1971	Scotland 1961	Scotland % change	U.K. % change
Total retail shops	44,561	53,386	−16·5	−11·4
Grocers and provisions dealers	10,869	14,063	−22·7	−26·4
Other food shops	9,261	12,291	−24·7	−18·0
Confectioners, tobac-conists, newsagents	4,902	8,649	−43·3	−25·9
Other retailers	19,529	18,383	+6·2	+7·5

Source: *Business Statistics Office*
Census of Distribution 1961

Turning to the new 1971 Census, preliminary figures enable the broad trends in retail distribution to be assessed as between Scotland and Great Britain over the 1961–1971 decade. The regional figures take the form of a count of registered traders and as such are not strictly comparable with earlier censuses (nor with the eventual results of the 1971 census itself). However they offer a fair guide to the changes which have taken place.

Thus the trend for proportionately larger numbers of shops to close down in Scotland than for the whole country has been maintained, and the toll has been especially heavy among the predominantly independent confectionery/tobacconist/newsagents shops. Rate of closure of grocery outlets has been slower in Scotland, though, than the national average and it must be presumed that an above average turnover per outlet is maintained within this group. The numbers of retail shops for each of the present counties in Scotland for 1971, with a breakdown showing grocery and certain other retail categories, are given in Appendix 2.

Appendix 2 shows a breakdown of the 1971 Census results for Great Britain nationally, indicating numbers of outlets and turnover by form of organisation and type of business in greater detail than has been discussed above. The overall number of outlets fell by a further 4 per cent between 1966 (year of the previous Sample Census) and 1971. This compares with a 7 per cent fall between 1961 and 1966, and the fall was due almost entirely to reductions in the numbers of food shops and confectioner/tobacconist/newsagents.

Retail turnover grew by 37 per cent between 1966 and 1971, but a 28 per cent average price rise over the period limits the increase in 'real' sales volume to around 7 per cent.

Numbers of clothing and footwear shops fell by 2·4 per cent, but turnover increased by 30·7 per cent. Despite the fall in the number of food shops, grocery turnover increased by 37·3 per cent and business in other food shops by 25·2 per cent, suggesting further increases in supermarket-type trading. Small stores of the confectioner etc. type contracted by 14·7 per cent, but increased business by 24·1 per cent—suggesting a further degree of concentration in this sector also. The trends within the principal sectors with respect to both 1966 and 1961 censuses are illustrated on page 176.

TRENDS IN RETAIL TRADE IN GREAT BRITAIN 1971, SHOWING PERCENTAGE CHANGES SINCE 1966 & 1961

	Since 1966		Since 1961	
	Establish-ments	*Turn-over*	*Establish-ments*	*Turn-over*
Total retail trade	−3·8	+36·7	−10·5	+72·4
Grocers and provision dealers	−12·8	+37·3	−26·7	+69·9
Other food retailers	−9·7	+25·2	−17·8	+50·8
Confectioners, tobacconists, newsagents	−14·7	+24·1	−22·9	+62·6
Clothing and footwear shops	−2·4	+30·7	−6·3	+64·5
Household goods shops	+11·9	+50·1	+22·1	+104·5
Other non-food retailers	+14·6	+54·3	+17·1	+122·5
General stores	+43·0	+46·5	+14·8	+68·0
Market stalls and mobile shops	n.a.	n.a.	−30·5	+7·8
Electricity and Gas Board showrooms	−21·7	+52·5	−15·5	+171·9
Mail order businesses	+36·6	+44·3	+21·6	+173·0
Automatic vending machine operators	+7·1	+0·1	+130·8	+167·5
Boot and shoe repair shops	−28·1	−2·7	−43·5	−0·3
Hairdressers	−1·1	+21·7	+17·3	+69·9
Laundries, launderettes and dry cleaners	+43·0	+16·1	+75·8	+77·8
Independent retailers	−0·3	+28·3	−9·7	+52·3
Multiples	−8·6	+58·0	+1·2	+135·0
Co-operative Societies	−43·6	+8·3	−48·8	+14·7

Source: *Census of Distribution 1971*

The percentage change shown in overall numbers of outlets between 1961 and 1971 differs slightly from the figure shown in the comparison above of 1961/71 trends between Scotland and Great Britain, due to the latter being based on registered traders enumerated for Census purposes rather than actual Census results. There are in addition, inevitably, a number of minor inconsistencies between the methods used for collecting data in the various censuses. These are explained in the footnotes to the main table on the 1971 Census in Appendix 2.

Self-Service and Supermarkets

Although full up-to-date analysis of Scottish retailing must await publication of the regional results of the 1971 Census, certain forms of trading—fortunately those which are of most general interest—can be studied without the benefit of Census results, thanks to the availability of substantial information from private and trade sources.

The Census, indeed, takes no account of the actual trading methods by which retailers operate and does not distinguish either self-service or supermarket outlets.

The growth of these forms of trading is perhaps the subject of the greatest interest, and is generally taken as a measure of progressiveness of a market in retailing terms. Scotland was a late developer in supermarketing. In 1962 Scottish supermarkets

GROWTH OF SUPERMARKETS IN U.K. AND SCOTLAND 1962-72

		Scotland	U.K.	Scotland as % of U.K.
1962	(No.)	41	996	4·2
1967	(No.)	237	2,803	8·5
Per cent change 1962/1967		+578	+281	+202
1972	(No.)	437	4,203	10·4
Per cent change 1967/1972		+184	+150	+122

Source: Survey and Directory of Self-Service Stores and Supermarkets 1962–1972

numbered 41 and accounted for 4·2 per cent of the national (United Kingdom) total. By 1967 the number had grown to 237 and the proportion to 8·4 per cent—within 1 per cent of Scotland's equivalent population base. By 1972, supermarket growth in Scotland had advanced to reach 10·4 per cent of the national total—itself still climbing steeply—to give 437 outlets of this type. The trend is shown in the table on page 176.

The actual situation (current as of 1972) regarding supermarket and self-service trading in Scotland relative to the nation is as follows:

	No.	Per cent of U.K.
Supermarkets	437	10·4
Self-service	1,498	10·6
Self-service and Supermarkets combined	1,935	10·5

The figures in this and the preceding table should be regarded as best available estimates rather than having census accuracy. The source from which they are taken is believed to cover 85 per cent of all supermarkets in the British Isles and 60 per cent of all self-service stores, and the estimates thus, if anything, understate the true position.

A word is also necessary concerning definitions. A supermarket is defined as a store of at least 2,000 square feet sales area (185 sq.m.) operated mainly on self-service lines, whose range of merchandise comprises all food groups including fresh meat, fruit and vegetables, plus basic household requisites (i.e. soaps and cleaning materials). A self-service store falls below this size definition and is categorised as one which presents the majority of its goods for selection by the customer without the intervention of staff and in which payment is made at a check-out.

The definition of a supermarket more widely accepted on the Continent is a store with a minimum sales area of 400 sq.m. or approximately 4,300 sq. ft. In practice, the average size of British supermarkets exceeds this Continental definition, being 4,632 sq. ft. in 1972 (430 sq.m.) and about 44 per cent of the total are larger than 4,000 sq. ft. (372 sq.m.). The terms 'hypermarket' and 'super store' are used to describe stores with sales area of at least 25,000 sq. ft. (2,320 sq.m.), either wholly or mainly operated on self-service lines, with at least 50 per cent of display area devoted to non-food items. Britain has lagged behind in the development of these very large stores, with a 1971 total of only 16 compared to, for instance, 370 in West Germany, 145 in France and 46 in Belgium. However the number is expected to double by 1975 and the pace of development and degree of interest have intensified lately.

The majority of supermarket outlets are operated by multiple groups (i.e. those having 10 or more branches). Nationally, almost two-thirds (64·3 per cent) of supermarkets are multiple-operated, and the percentage is slightly higher for Scotland. The remainder of the pattern differs sharply, though, with cooperatives, as expected, controlling a much-above average share of supermarkets in Scotland, and independents correspondingly fewer.

STRUCTURE OF SUPERMARKET TRADING BY CLASS OF OPERATOR
Scotland and U.K. 1972.

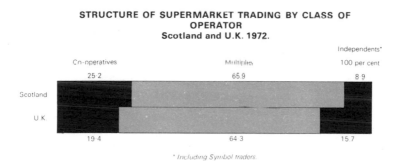

* *Including Symbol traders.*

In terms of both numbers of outlets and trade volume the situation is a constantly moving one, as is apparent from the Census results quoted earlier. Supermarkets themselves are now estimated to account for 38 per cent of national grocery turnover and self-service stores for a further 31 per cent. The operating structure of the supermarket trade, however, differs sharply from that of other self-service stores as shown by the data overleaf relating to Scotland.

Excluding supermarkets, which are assumed to stock a wide range of food and non-food commodities, larger proportions of self-service stores in Scotland tend to carry non-food goods such as health and beauty products, or alcoholic drinks, than the average nationally. Fewer sell fresh meat (unlike Scottish grocers as a whole), but the great majority —upwards of 70 per cent—sell fresh

OPERATING STRUCTURE OF SELF-SERVICE AND
SUPERMARKET OUTLETS IN SCOTLAND 1972

	Self-service stores %	Supermarkets %
Multiples	34·6	65·9
Independents	30·3	8·9
Co-operatives	35·1	25·2
Total (equals 100 per cent)	1,498	437

Source: Survey and Directory of Self-Service Stores and Supermarkets 1962

fruit and vegetables or bakery goods, and in this respect Scottish self-service stores are similar to those elsewhere. For historical reasons, though, Scottish grocers in general are more likely than elsewhere to sell fresh meat and produce, and alcoholic drinks (which generate sales from allied products such as cigarettes and tobacco, soft drinks etc.) The result is a larger than average share of the entire domestic food and drink trade.

Supermarket development in Scotland continues apace. Seventeen new stores were opened in 1971, twice the average for the two previous years and the pace shows no sign of slackening. Scotland is in the midst of a surge in multiple grocery trading, in which the largest retailing groups from England are playing a growing and often new part. This phenomenon is dealt with below. However the Scottish approach to the development of super store or hypermarket trading is also of interest.

Retail trade associations in Scotland, and individual retail groups, have trodden warily in this direction, both because of the recognised need for such developments—especially out of town shopping centres or 'free standing' super stores—to be integrated with local planning in a broad sense, and due to the nature of the Scottish market itself.

On the planning side, it has been urged in a study by the Economic Development Committee for the Distributive Trades* that on the one hand the Department of the Environment should lay down guidelines stating criteria for the acceptance of such

* The future pattern of shopping—Distributive Trades E.D.C.—HMSO 1971.

centres and on the other hand that the setting up of a body comparable to the Institute for Centre Planning in Denmark should be seriously considered. In the meantime the Scottish Retail Federation—uneasily conscious of its neo-Luddite role—has on occasion backed objections to hypermarket schemes because of lack of information on planning implications, and such developments as have taken place remain uniquely the responsibility of the enterprise concerned.

Scotland, it must be said, in theory offers few ideal hyper-market sites. A store of 40,000 sq. ft. (3,716 sq.m.) is generally assumed to require a population of some 200,000 within 8 or 9 miles radius. Till the present, emigration—especially amongst younger people—has formed an added disincentive among the risk and cost factors of opening very large stores, along with marginally lower per capita incomes. Local allegiances further-more mean that 'out of town' developments must be very care-fully sited even where a catchment area of sufficient density is offered, or 'out of town' may in fact become 'next county'.

For this reason, *edge* of town developments, which avoid such pitfalls, have tended to be favoured and some highly successful examples exist, enjoying a productivity which is noticeably above average. As already indicated, Scots have traditionally been accustomed to buying a wider range of goods through grocery stores than their English neighbours, and food stores account for a higher proportion of total trade—while Scots are by instinct highly price conscious.

Thus Fine Fare, which is the largest operator of actual super-markets in Scotland, with 69 stores in the category, points to an average sales per sq. ft. 6 per cent higher than their own national average, despite an average value per transaction 5 per cent lower. Fine Fare's 40,000sq. ft. supermarket at Bridge of Dee, outside Aberdeen, alone accounts for 10 per cent of the group's Scottish supermarket business—while Fine Fare's five supermarkets in Aberdeen itself continue to trade successfully. Fine Fare has two other smaller outlets ranking as super stores, at Kilmarnock (15,000 sq. ft.) and Airdrie (20,000 sq. ft.).

The first 40,000 sq. ft. super store opened by ASDA (Associated Dairies) outside Edinburgh in 1972 has had similar success, and this group—pioneer of hypermarkets in Britain—plans other

Scottish stores. Woolco (Woolworths) will open its first Scottish super store at Cumbernauld in late 1973.

Scotland is in fact becoming increasingly a focus for large store development, to the extent that planning constraints will allow. Particular importance naturally attaches to the question of adequate parking space, and a minimum of 500 car spaces is considered vital. Something like three-quarters of Scottish super store customers visit the store by car. Research conducted by Fine Fare in connection with their Aberdeen super store provides a useful commentary on customer motivations. Customers interviewed mentioned the following as particular attractions.

	Per cent mentioning
Location at edge of town	35
Parking facilities	65
Opening hours	40
Variety of departments	68
Food Hall	54
General atmosphere and service	28
Free bus service	10

Multiple Retailing Organisations

The distinctiveness of the Scottish retail scene—largely dominated by fascias unknown in the south—has till recently been due (apart from differences in actual trading patterns and special factors such as the greater significance of cooperative trading) to the strength of native Scottish chains and the reluctance of English multiple groups to expand into unknown territory. A massive change has taken place during the last few years as major operators such as Fine Fare, Tesco and Safeway bustle into Scotland.

Safeway began Scottish development in 1965 and Tesco, more cautiously, in 1971—incidentally bringing Green Shield Trading Stamps to Scotland for the first time. Tesco's first two stores are in Greenock and Perth, and both have surprised the group with their success. Both Tesco and Safeway (which already has 12 Scottish supermarkets) have new stores under way at Kirkcaldy and Ayr.

Page 183 shows in tabular form the operations of the leading multiple grocery organisations in Scotland. The largest Scottish

MAJOR MULTIPLE GROCERY ORGANISATIONS, SCOTLAND, DECEMBER 1972

	Counter Service	Self-Service	Supermarkets	Branches with Off-Licences	Total Branches
Galbraith Cochrane	—	208	43	48	251
Massey Lipton	22	102	46	63	170
Templetons	—	51	45	43	96
Total Allied Suppliers	22	361	134	154	517
Hay & Co. (Edinburgh)	10	34	19	35	63
Coopers Fine Fare/ Fine Fare	—	26	60*	62	95
Kibby's (Laws)	4	38	8	11	50
Wm. Jamieson	12	6	1	7	19
Wm. Low	—	10	33	38	43
John Curley	31	8	—	—	39
Johnstons Stores	4	10	1	14	15
Andrew Sloan	5	12	2	1	19
Safeway	—	—	12	8	12
Tesco	—	—	2	2	2

Source: *Trade Sources.*

* includes 3 super stores and 2 Buywell discount stores.

retail group is Allied Suppliers, trading under the Galbraith, Cochrane, Massey, Lipton, and Templeton names and with a total of 517 outlets, mainly self-service. Allied Suppliers was acquired by Cavenham Foods Ltd. in early 1972 and Hay & Co. (Edinburgh), a former subsidiary of Moores Stores Ltd., was acquired by Cavenham in 1971 as part of its acquisition of Wrights Biscuits. Adding Hay to the Allied Suppliers outlets gives Cavenham a total of 580 Scottish grocery outlets.

Among the other names shown it is of interest to note that Kibby's was sold by its parent Unigate to the Gateshead, Co. Durham group, Law's Stores Ltd., giving Law's its first venture into Scottish retailing which Law's now intend to expand. Andrew Sloan, formerly trading as Sloan's Dairies (Shops) Ltd., was acquired by Express Dairy as part of a deal involving its parent company, but the retail interests have now bought themselves out and recommenced trading under the Andrew Sloan name. The former Ross's Dairies group with over 100 branches was also acquired several years ago by Express Dairy but has since been disposed of in the form of single units or small groups, with some branches being closed down.

Co-operative Societies

The foregoing will have made it clear that the Co-operative movement occupies a special place in Scottish retailing. This continues to be the case in spite of the gradual decline in the relative importance of the co-operative in relation to retail trade as a whole. In 1961, Co-operative outlets in Scotland accounted for 11 per cent* of all retail shops, compared with 5 per cent over the whole country and took 19 per cent of retail turnover as against a national 11 per cent.

Exact comparison for later years is not yet possible, but according to A. C. Nielsen Company data, Co-operatives accounted for 12 per cent of grocery outlets in Scotland in 1971, taking 24 per cent of grocery turnover, national figures being 8 per cent and 15 per cent respectively.

* 1961 data based on the Central Scotland ITV area, comprising 82 per cent of all Scottish outlets.

Co-operative membership still numbers about 1 in every 4 Scots, although the total has slowly fallen from 1·42 million in 1964 to 1·27 million in 1971. More drastic falls have taken place in the numbers of retail societies—from 162 in 1964 to 87 in 1971, primarily the result of mergers between small neighbouring societies often with an overlap in membership. This trend has been encouraged as a vital and integral part of the movement's struggle to retain its competitive position. A further 10 mergers took place in 1972.

Retail Co-operative Societies were originally formed by consumers in order to purchase their requirements from an organisation in whose ownership they themselves participated, to be run as economically as possible, and returning to the members any trading surplus in the form of a dividend. The Scottish Co-operative Wholesale Society (SCWS) was formed over 100 years ago by the Federation of then existing retail societies to manufacture and supply goods for sale by member societies. The SCWS became, and remains, the most powerful single Scottish-owned retail business. (It still remains true that retail societies are under no obligation to buy supplies only from the SCWS, and this places the wholesale as well as the retail part of the movement in a directly competitive situation with other suppliers. In practice, though, the links are very strong, with the SCWS playing a role in buying, warehousing, production, retailing, and general advisory services as well as in supply.)

Total Co-operative sales in Scotland have fluctuated uneasily around the £160 million mark annually for the past decade, implying both a falling real sales volume and market share. Approximately 70 per cent of this business comes from grocery departments, including tobacco and alcoholic drinks. A breakdown of this grocery business for 1970 is as follows:

	Per cent
Grocery, bread, confectionery, tobacco and cigarettes	79·8
Butchery	10·2
Greengrocery, fruit and fish	1·0
Dairy products	9·0

These groups constitute about the same proportion of total business as the national average. Other principal cooperative departments are concerned with clothing and footwear, pharmacy, and fuel. SCWS activities extend to garages, banking and funerals. The SCWS has about 1,300 retail outlets which sell food.

Much has been done to overhaul the structure of the Co-operative movement in Scotland as elsewhere, and the process continues. The SCWS has needed not only to absorb new retailing methods, such as self-service and trading stamps (in this case 'dividend stamps' in place of the traditional cash dividend), but also to face up to a vastly changed competitive situation, as non-cooperative retailing has become concentrated in fewer hands able to build more of the larger, more attractive stores to which public preference has swung.

As part of the process of strengthening individual societies, as well as promoting mergers, the SCWS has entered into direct participation in retailing through Scottish Co-operative Retail Services (SCRS) a subsidiary which provides management services and capital. A Cash & Carry warehouse at Shieldhall in Glasgow, operating under the name of Compass Cash & Carry, is open to other retailers as well as Co-operatives. Studies have been carried out of the most suitable sites for hypermarkets. Much public goodwill—and demand from private trade sources—has been attracted by the Co-operatives' own 'Clan' label, applied to Co-op manufactured lines. Significantly, Co-operative promotions now include national as well as house brands, and the SCWS has become a major advertiser throughout Scotland, making extensive use of television as well as the national and local press.

The intensive self-analysis of SCWS activities came to a head in 1972 with the formulation of a far-reaching plan to combine the activities of the SCWS and SCRS into a single new body, the Scottish Co-operative Society Ltd. (SCS). The change was implemented as of 21st January 1973 and is seen as an opportunity for the Scottish Co-operative Movement to take advantage of its vertical structure, increase its market-orientation, and improve communication with the retail side of the movement—as well as increasing its confidence. There are in fact signs that the Co-operatives' falling share of grocery markets has already been stabilised and hopes run high that it may now even increase. Even more recently a full merger has been initiated between the SCS and the national Manchester based Co-operative Wholesale Society. The catalyst for this move, previously strongly opposed by Scottish Co-operative interests, was the plight of the SCS banking department after difficulties encountered in dealing with sterling certificates of deposit. The merger—voted through in May 1973, but with the St. Cuthberts Society of Edinburgh remaining independent—will create a single national co-operative organisation with sales in excess of £700 million.

Other Retailing Developments

As a comparison of Census data shows, there has been a gradual decline in the importance of the independent sector in food retailing—from 53 per cent of grocery trading in 1961 to 42 per cent in 1971. This decline would undoubtedly have been far greater but for the emergence of voluntary group trading which permits the retailer to retain his independence while giving him the advantages of buying at bulk rates and the benefit of progressive advice on merchandising, promotion, store layout and so forth.

From its beginnings in the mid-fifties group trading, which is a form of franchising, has come to exert a very considerable influence on the independent grocery trade and has fundamentally altered its shape. Retailers trading under voluntary group 'symbols' increased their national share of grocery business during the 1960s from 13 per cent to 22 per cent. During the same period the share taken by non-symbol independent grocers halved from 40 per cent to 20 per cent. Symbol grocers now do 53 per cent of business in the independent sector, and surveys have shown that the average symbol shop achieves about three times the turnover of the unaffiliated private trader.

Most of the large voluntary groups are wholesaler-sponsored and, with symbols increasingly appearing as private label brand names as well as on retail fascias, have become household names. Total retail strength numbers some 30,000 traders affiliated to 23 organisations, and with more than half belonging to the seven largest groups. Those which operate in Scotland are shown overleaf with their national and regional strengths (the figures are inevitably approximate).

VOLUNTARY GROUP TRADING, 1972

| | National | | Scotland | |
	Wholesalers	Retailers	Wholesalers	Retailers
Mace	26	4,800	4	300
Spar	20	3,035	1	195
Vivo	18	1,242	2	160
Centra	8	1,620	4	400
Four Star				
(Danish Bacon)	41	3,750	2	250
VG	9	2,715	1	192
Pinnacle	—	—	1	400

Source: Named Groups and Trade Sources.

Having come to dominate the independent grocery trade in Scotland as elsewhere, the voluntary groups now face problems in further growth and in holding their own against the multiples. Their share of trade has even slipped back a little. With the more progressive elements among the independents long converted to group trading, there is little scope for increases in membership, and stepping up turnover through existing outlets has become the main preoccupation.

Competition between groups—for members as well as business —has become intense.

Reversion to a more active role by the wholesaler has already resulted. Promotion at national and local level has been used to build corporate identity and boost trade. Partnerships between wholesale and retail elements are one way of extending voluntary group trade into large stores. Centra (Scotland) for instance envisages stores of up to 20,000 sq. ft. (1,858 sq.m.) run by individual retail members. Much of the present hesitancy stems from sheer economics, with retailers able to buy more cheaply from Cash & Carry warehouses than through their affiliated wholesalers. (Cash & Carry warehouses offer precisely the service the name implies and have become increasingly the only economic method by which wholesalers can continue to service the smaller retailer.

The average size is 17,707 sq. ft. (1,645 sq.m.)* and 21 per cent are larger than 25,000 sq. ft. (2,323 sq.m.)

Nationally, figures from the A. C. Nielsen Company show that 77 per cent of independent grocers (70 per cent of them 'heavy users') now use Cash & Carry warehouses and 68 per cent of symbol grocers—one-quarter of them being heavy users buying most of their requirements in this way. According to Nielsen, Britain now has 617 Cash & Carry depots* with an annual turnover of £707 million—more than double the 1969 figure and nearly one-fifth total grocery business at *retail* prices. Cash & Carry trading is by no means confined to groceries, though, as the following breakdown shows:

PROPORTION OF CASH & CARRY DEPOTS STOCKING:

	%
Frozen foods	83
Hardware	71
Electrical appliances	64
Textiles	63
With special catering sections	86

Source: A. C. Nielsen Co.

The above relates to May 1972. Since then, according to Neilsen, virtually all new cash and carries opened have stocked all the items listed above.

The latest count of cash and carry warehouses in Scotland gives a total of 75, grouped as follows:

Alliance	9
Big N	8
ICCG	9
Keen Cost	2
Newga	1
Trademarkets	8
Value Centres	4
Rando	6
Other groups (one each)	28

Source: The Grocer Directory 1972 and trade sources.

*Nielsen Census of Grocery Cash & Carry Warehouses, May 1972.

These numbers are on the increase, with new or planned Cash & Carry depots in Scotland running into double figures and English operators to the fore in what amounts to a virtual 'invasion'.

Lately, there has been a growth in Cash & Carry usage by symbol retailers, and the involvement of their wholesale sponsors in this form of trading has consequently deepened. Nationally, Nielsen's 1972 census shows 57 per cent of Cash & Carry depots as belonging to one of the eight largest symbol groups. Among the Scottish Cash & Carries, Trademarkets are operated by Watson & Phillip Ltd. of Dundee, who are sole operators of the VG franchise in Scotland, and Value Centres are operated by Spar (Britain) Ltd. Alliance Cash & Carry depots are operated by the Alliance group, a voluntary group sponsor but without retail members in Scotland.

With Cash & Carry facilities open to symbol traders as well as to unaffiliated retailers, Co-op Cash & Carries, and the likelihood of larger stores under symbol fascias, the lines of demarcation even between the newer forms of retailing are becoming blurred. Cash & Carry depots themselves do not only service retailers. According to Nielsen, 86 per cent have special catering sections and one group, Alliance, reports that caterers form 51 per cent of its customers—though grocers spend more per head.

One multiple retailer has announced its entry to the Cash & Carry field, and the line between Cash & Carry and discount trading is wearing thin. With margins pared to the bone and an increasingly price conscious public, food retailing in Scotland as elsewhere is moving towards a survival of the fittest in which those that remain will come increasingly to resemble each other. Other retailers such as chemists and confectioners will progressively move towards the same methods of trading.

Retailers' Associations throughout Britain have already to some degree anticipated these trends by broadening and merging their spheres of interest, recognising at the same time the common problems facing most retail sectors (difficulties in maintaining advantageous trading sites in the face of mounting property values, for instance). The formation in October 1972 of the Scottish Retail Federation, which parallels the Retail Consortium south of the border, has considerably rationalised the structure of retail representation in Scotland, in tune with the recommendations of the

Bolton committee* in 1971 and anticipating the report of the Devlin Commission, published in November 1972.†

The SRF admits three classes of members: Trade Associations fully prepared to conduct their operations within the structure of the Federation, Affiliated Bodies prepared to lend their support in a looser sense, and Direct Members consisting of substantial retail blocs such as the Co-operative Union. Members of the SRF so far are:

Co-operative Union Ltd. (Scottish Section)
Scottish Grocers Federation
Scottish Retail Drapers Association
Scottish Council, National Federation of Retail Newsagents,
    Booksellers and Stationers
Retail Distributors Association
Scottish House Furnishers Federation
Scottish Association of Watchmakers and Jewellers
Scottish Radio Retailers Association
Scottish Retail Credit Association
Scottish Tobacco Trade Federation
Scottish Licensed Grocers and Wine Merchants Association

Only the first two of these are full members, but this category is expected to spread as the aims of the Federation are more widely appreciated. Full and affiliated membership already covers 70 per cent of Scottish retail turnover with between 25,000 and 30,000 retail outlets represented.

Provision of a cohesive central organisation to represent Scottish retailing interests is the main objective of the new Federation, expressed through concerns respectively with trade practices, parliamentary matters where a common 'voice' is needed, and services to individual members. These extend to management services, stationery and equipment, shop fitting, training, insurance, and publications and are claimed by the Federation to add up to the widest range of services available to retailers anywhere in the U.K.

* 'The Small Unit in the Distributive Trades.' Bolton Committee of Enquiry on Small Firms.
† Commission of Inquiry into Industrial and Commercial Representation, sponsored by the Confederation of British Industry and the Association of British Chambers of Commerce.

Formation of the SRF also simplifies and strengthens Scottish representation amongst international retail bodies. The Federation is a member of the International Federation of Grocers Associations, which covers 17 countries and, within this, of the separate Council of EEC members which has now been formed. Scotland's traditional direct relationship with Europe is given full rein in this important body and Scotland will be host to the next IFGA Congress in 1974.

Scottish trade, like that of other regions, also incidentally receives a direct boost in terms of international links from the international structure of leading voluntary groups such as Spar Vivo. This organisation has established a new company called BV Intergroup Trading, in Amsterdam, which will take advantage of Spar Vivo's substantial power in both purchasing and distribution to improve efficiency at the multi-national level. British wholesalers are among the shareholders, and the new company will also offer European outlets to British manufacturers wishing to take advantage of the opportunities.

The Licensed Trade

In England and Wales, the sale of alcoholic drinks through retail outlets other than the specialist 'off-licence' (that is, a licence to sell drinks only for consumption off the premises) is a fairly recent innovation and liquor sales through grocery shops have only assumed importance during the last decade or so. In Scotland, alcoholic drinks have by tradition—stemming from ancient ties with France—been more widely available through conventional retail outlets.

The licensed grocer still forms an important element in the sale of alcoholic drink in Scotland and the majority of Scottish 'off licences' are grocers. The growth of liquor sales through supermarkets in the rest of the country, coupled with the later development of supermarkets in Scotland, means that Scotland is now only slightly ahead in this respect, with 39·1 per cent of supermarkets licensed to sell liquor compared with a national 36·7 per cent, and some other regions considerably higher.*

* Survey and Directory of Self Service Stores and Supermarkets 1962—1972.

A slightly lower proportion of Scottish non-supermarket self-service stores are now licensed than the national average (19 per cent against 20 per cent), the proportion having actually fallen during the last five years; however, this is a trend common to certain other regions, as this trade, no longer subject to price mainten-ance, is increasingly taken over by supermarkets. Over the whole of the grocery trade, though, the proportion of outlets licensed to sell alcoholic drink is still very nearly double the national average, and the difference is particularly marked in the independent sector.

RATIO OF LICENSED GROCERS TO ALL GROCERS
Scotland and Great Britain, 1972

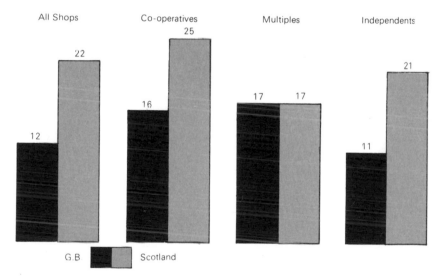

From its former distinctive position, Scotland is now conforming increasingly to the national pattern. The 'grocer's certificate' has now become an 'off sales certificate' and the specialist wine store—once considered an English import—handles a growing proportion of the trade, as well as supermarkets. The proportion of 'off' sales made through public houses and other primarily 'on' licence outlets is also increasing.

As regards the structure of the 'on' trade—that is, where alcohol may be consumed on the premises—important distinctions remain between the Scottish and English systems. The overall structure of the Scottish licensed trade is as follows:

LICENCES FOR SALE OF EXCISABLE LIQUOR BY TYPE OF PREMISES IN SCOTLAND 1972

Hotels	2,609
Restricted Hotels	250
Public Houses	4,176
Restaurants	406
Off-Sales	3,819
Clubs	2,125
Total	13,385

Source: Scottish Home & Health Department.

Overall, the number of licensed premises has tended to increase, having risen by over 10 percent within the last five years. Numerically, the largest rise has been in licensed clubs (544 more than in 1968), but in percentage terms the largest gain has been in licensed restaurants, which have more than doubled in the same period. Even so, the figures considerably understate the number of restaurants in Scotland, since many still operate under a public house licence, and hotel restaurants are of considerable importance.

Restricted hotels are a new category, introduced in 1962. They have no bar, and non-residents cannot obtain alcoholic refreshment without taking a meal. Incidentally, although most ordinary pubs have six-day licences, the fiction of the *'bona fide* traveller' requiring a journey of more than three miles to obtain a drink on Sunday is long dead.

Scottish licensing hours are still in general more restricted than in England, although off-sales can be made at any time between 8a.m. and 10p.m. Although Scotland is subject to the same Weights & Measures Act (1963) as England, a choice of spirit measure sizes is available to the Scottish publican, the most common size being one-fifth gill or one fluid ounce (about 2·8 centilitres) compared with the standard English one-sixth gill.

The whole question of the Scottish licensing system, like that of England and Wales, has been under review, with a separate committee under Dr. Christopher Clayson performing for Scotland the same task as the Erroll Committee south of the border. The Erroll Committee report, published in December 1972, proposed a general easing of present restrictions, and in particular advocated the opening of pubs at any times between 10 a.m. and midnight any day of the year, a lowering of the drinking age from 18 to 17, and the admission of young people from the age of 14 upwards to licensed premises.

The Clayson report has not at the time of writing been published, but close liaison took place between the two committees and the main recommendations for Scotland are expected to be similar, though with regard to existing differences between the Scottish and English systems. The report offers an opportunity for reform in matters such as Sunday opening and anomalies concerning after-hours drinking. However, the Erroll Committee recommendations on the lowering of the drinking age are less likely to be echoed in Scotland.

Reform is in any case far from imminent, since parliamentary discussion and legislation will first be needed, and a body of opinion in Parliament as well as among the public favours retention of the existing system. There is as yet no sign of amendments to the licensing laws entering the parliamentary timetable, however anomalous some aspects of the present situation may seem. In Scotland, although temperance polls (in which the public have under certain circumstances power to reverse the decisions of local magistrates regarding the granting of licences) are becoming rarer, the threat remains, and a few districts are still 'dry'. Temperance is still a strong force in parts of west Scotland, where opposition to Sunday opening, for instance, is firmly entrenched.

In some respects the Scottish licensing system has already provided pointers for changes in England. In Scotland the licence is held by the publican personally, instead of jointly by brewer and publican. Historically, the Scottish publican has been a good deal freer than his English counterpart in that the 'tied house' system, under which the licensee (usually in England a tenant of the brewery) must order all supplies through the brewery, is less widespread in Scotland, and the free trade correspondingly more important. This arises from the old custom of brewers lending money for purchase or improvement of premises without exacting a formal 'tie' in return.

As rationalisation proceeds on a national scale amongst the brewers (Scottish & Newcastle remains the only major brewery group under Scottish ownership) the Scottish way of doing things is gradually changing. Managed pubs (where the licensee is an employee of the brewery) have become increasingly common during the last ten years, especially in new housing estates. Branches of the Association of Licensed House Managers are being formed in the main Scottish centres. A tenancy system resembling the English one is taking shape in the previously 'free' sector of the trade.

Partly in consequence of these changes—though also due to social change and higher living standards—tremendous improvements in Scottish pubs have taken place in the last few years. Food and comfortable dining facilities are more widely available and surroundings vastly more salubrious. Discotheques—some with go-go dancers—are found in modernised pubs in the cities. The Scottish pub is no longer the preserve of the male. All this—though opposed by some—adds up to a social revolution which is the more remarkable by its suddenness.

8 The Scottish consumer

A VOLUME OF THIS scale cannot hope to depict in complete detail the progress of the average Scottish consumer from pay packet or salary cheque to supermarket check-out, and information concerning almost every aspect of consumer behaviour is nowadays available—or obtainable—for those requiring specific information in depth from market research sources or official statistics.

The aim of the present chapter is to describe in broad outline those essential circumstances of the Scot and of the Scottish household which can usefully contribute to a basic character portrait and give helpful pointers to the nature of Scotland as a market for consumer goods and services. The chapter following deals separately with the means of actually reaching the Scottish consumer in terms of marketing communications.

Personal Incomes

Incomes are, of course, when adjusted for direct taxes and savings, the basis of all spending power. Scottish incomes are a little lower than the average for the whole country—not surprisingly since it has already been noted (in Chapter 3) that the level of earnings in Scotland is below the national figure. The difference in both cases is about 3 per cent.

Incomes can also be compared in terms of size groupings, and on this basis it is found that a larger proportion of Scottish incomes are in the lower size groupings (42·6 per cent of Scottish incomes for the fiscal year 1969/70 were below £1,000, compared with 39·8 per cent nationally). Although Scotland has in proportion fewer incomes between £1,000 and £1,750, it has a higher proportion between £1,750 and £2,500 and the difference in structure taking all incomes above £1,750 is marginal—0·2 per cent. Thus Scotland shows a tendency to make up ground at the upper end of the scale.

PERSONAL INCOMES (before tax) SCOTLAND AND THE U.K. 1969-70

	Total amount (£ million)	Total No. of cases (000)	Average Income per case (£)
Scotland	2,458·7	1,877·4	1,310
United Kingdom	29,343·9	21,735·0	1,350
Scotland as per cent of U.K.	8·4	8·6	97·0

Source: Inland Revenue, Survey of Personal Incomes 1969/70.

SIZE DISTRIBUTION OF INCOMES BY NUMBER IN SCOTLAND AND THE U.K., 1969-70

Range of Income £	Scotland		United Kingdom	
	No. of Incomes 000	% of total	No. of Incomes 000	% of total
Below 500	194·1	10·3	1,978	9·1
500–999	606·3	32·3	6,671	30·7
1,000–1,749	694·1	37·0	8,689	40·0
1,750–2,499	278·3	14·8	3,085	14·2
2,500–3,999	72·8	3·9	895	4·1
4,000—and over	31·8	1·7	416	1·9
Total all Ranges	1,877·4	100·0	21,734	100·0

Source: Inland Revenue, Survey of Personal Incomes 1969/70.

Earnings from employment form easily the largest part of total incomes, about three-quarters. The proportion is a little lower for Scotland (72·1 per cent compared with a national 74·9 per cent for 1969/70), but it is higher in the Glasgow area—the Central Clydeside Conurbation—because of its heavily industrialised nature. Lower proportions of income in the Conurbation come from profits and professional earnings and from investment income—although the proportion of all income earned in Scotland coming from profits and professional earnings is a little higher than the national average (8·1 per cent against 7·5 per cent).

A further aspect of this question brought out in the table on page 200 is that a slightly lower proportion of total before-tax income is 'lost' in the form of taxation in Scotland—this phenomenon deriving, of course, from the lower average size of pre-tax incomes. The difference amounts to less than one per cent before-tax income, but becomes more significant when it is considered that the tax bill *per income* is 5 per cent lower in Scotland than it is for Great Britain as a whole. Taking the Glasgow Conurbation alone the difference is 7·4 per cent. This goes some way towards restoring the discrepancy in pre-tax incomes.

These figures—based on Inland Revenue sample surveys— enable a number of other useful comparisons to be made. The net amount of after-tax income in Scotland for 1969/70 (still the latest period available) was £2,048 million—that is, the amount of money received by the Scottish population for savings and personal expenditure purposes. This represented 8·6 per cent of the total for Great Britain—one per cent short of Scotland's population base of 9·6 per cent.

From the above, it is clear that *per capita* incomes in Scotland are significantly lower than the national average, and historically higher unemployment levels and slightly larger families—especi- ally in Central Scotland—tend to heighten this effect whereas, as has been shown above, the average size of actual incomes is only marginally down.

GROWTH OF PER CAPITA INCOMES BETWEEN 1964-65 AND 1969-70 SCOTLAND AND U.K.

	1964/65 £	1969/70 £	Per cent growth
Scotland	321	472	+47·0
U.K.	390	572	+46·7
Scotland as per cent of U.K.	82·3	82·5	+ 0·2

Source: Derived from Inland Revenue Surveys.

COMPONENT ANALYSIS OF PERSONAL INCOMES SHOWING TAXATION, 1969-70

	Scotland		Central Clydeside Conurbation		Great Britain	
	£000	% of total net income	£000	% of total net income	£000	% of total net income
Profits and professional earnings	199,800	8·1	46,500	5·4	2,145,000	7·5
Income from employment	1,773,200	72·1	672,200	78·5	21,536,700	74·9
Pensions, wife's earnings and family allowances	375,500	15·3	123,600	14·4	4,164,400	14·5
Deductions from earned income	49,800	2·0	17,700	2·1	958,500	3·3
Net earned income	2,298,100	93·5	824,600	96·2	26,887,600	93·5
Investment and other unearned income (less tax and deductions at source)	160,600	6·5	32,250	3·8	1,884,100	6·5
Total Net Income[1]	2,458,700	100·0	856,850	100·0	28,771,700	100·0
Total Tax	410,900	16·7	139,400	16·3	5,064,400	17·6
Net Income after Tax	2,047,800	83·3	717,450	83·7	23,707,300	82·4

Source: Inland Revenue: Survey of Personal Incomes 1969/70.

[1] Taxable income from all sources, after certain deductions, but before reliefs and allowances for tax.

During the five year interval between these two surveys, Scottish *per capita* incomes have grown fractionally—though not significantly—faster than those of the U.K. as a whole. The principal reason for this is Scotland's lack of population growth, whereas during the period in question the U.K. population grew by 2·7 per cent. Reviewing the Scottish result against the national average, the upward 'pull' of London and the South East must also be taken into account, and *per capita* incomes in Scotland compare favourably with some other regions.

Within Scotland itself, the distribution of incomes follows the distribution of population fairly closely, although certain regions—notably Edinburgh and the Borders—have above average 'shares' of the Scottish income cake.

	Per cent of Income	*Per cent of Population*
Glasgow	48·3	48·0
Falkirk/Stirling	4·9	4·8
Edinburgh	21·2	20·0
Tayside	7·9	8·6
Borders	2·1	1·9
South West	2·6	2·9
North East	8·3	8·6
Highlands	4·7	5·3

The present Planning Region boundaries will, of course, be superseded by those relating to the new regional local government structure during the next few years (see Chapter 2); however, there is no doubt either of the concentration of income in the Glasgow area or of the higher incomes in the other areas already mentioned.

Savings and Wealth

There is no single accurate measure of the amount of incomes saved, since a great diversity of savings exist, not all of which can be fully analysed and compared. Unfortunately the comprehensive Family Expenditure Survey published annually by the Department of Employment and which is used as the basis for assessing the spending patterns of Scottish households later in this chapter, cannot be used for this purpose since the aggregate of expenditure tends to exceed the amount of disposable income after deduction of tax and National Security payments.

Even within the relatively broad confines of the National Savings movement, a full comparison of savings levels between Scotland and the country as a whole cannot be made since data on savings *withdrawals* in Scotland are incomplete, being only published for the two Savings Bank groups, the Trustee Savings Banks and the National Savings Bank (formerly Post Office Savings Bank). If deposits alone are taken, Scottish savings *per capita* are shown to be substantially greater than the national average.

	1968 £	1969 £	1970 £	1971 £	1972 £
Scotland	67·5	72·3	79·9	98·1	115·1
Great Britain	62·4	62·2	64·9	75·6	84·1

However, this record takes no account of withdrawals, and thus the trend in savings balances cannot be assessed except for the Savings Banking media. A five year analysis is shown in the table on page 203 which includes *per capita* comparisons with the whole country. It will be seen that in the realm of the Trustee Savings Banks, Scottish balances run at a *per capita* rate nearly double the average, even though the rate of increase is now running behind the whole-country total. The Trustee Savings Banks have long been the traditional Scottish repository for savings, and indeed provide considerable local competition to the Clearing Banks.

In contrast, new deposits *per capita* in the National Savings Bank run at well under half the national rate, and Scottish purchases of Savings Bonds and Certificates are also below par. Although Scots save about as much as other Britons through the medium of National Savings Certificates, the Scottish saver has always looked askance at Premium Bonds, and the relatively new British Savings Bonds have not yet achieved the popularity in Scotland which they have elsewhere.

Balances held in recognised savings media are only one measure of accumulated assets, and various attempts have been made by economists to compute the total wealth held in Scotland. Although many of the necessary statistics are simply not available, some estimates were quite recently compiled based on the number and

NATIONAL SAVINGS DEPOSITS AND WITHDRAWALS, SCOTLAND AND GREAT BRITAIN 1968-1972

		1968	1969	1970	1971	1972
A. *Trustee Savings Banks*						
Deposits	£m	296·8	322·6	362·4	429·5	516·2
Withdrawals	£m	300·8	336·8	364·5	418·4	490·1
Balance outstanding[1]	£m	442·5	448·4	468·4	505·9	562·1
Balance outstanding *per capita* Scotland	£	85·1	86·1	89·8	97·0	107·7[2]
Great Britain	£	43·8	44·6	46·9	51·8	58·2[2]
B. *National Savings Bank*						
Deposits	£m	19·8	19·1	21·1	21·9	26·9
Deposits *per capita*						
Scotland	£	3·8	3·7	4·0	4·2	5·2[2]
Great Britain	£	10·4	9·5	10·2	10·4	13·1[2]
Withdrawals	£m	19·2	18·3	19·1	18·4	20·5
C. *Other Savings Purchased*						
National Savings Certificates	£m	21·0	21·5	23·7	44.6	34·4
Premium Savings Bonds	£m	5·7	5·8	4·7	7·6	7·3
British Savings Bonds	£m	4·7	7·8	5·1	8·4	13·7
Total other savings purchased	£m	34·4	35·1	33·0	60·6	55·4
Other savings purchased *per capita*						
Scotland	£	6·6	6·7	6·3	11·6	10·6[2]
Great Britain	£	8·1	8·1	7·9	13·4	12·8[2]

Source: National Savings Committee for Scotland Department for National Savings.
[1] Includes both Ordinary and Special Investment Departments.
[2] Approximate.

value of estates assessed for death duty purposes, with the aid of sample figures for estates below the death duty exemption limit of £5,000.* These estimates showed a markedly uneven distribution of assets, with Scotland in 1965 producing 11 per cent of the national total of estates valued at £40,000 or more—a result, so it seems, of profits made from the land or from heavy industry in the pre-1914 era.

* L. C. Wright, 'Some Fiscal Problems of Devolution in Scotland' in J. N. Wolfe (ed.), 'Government and Nationalism in Scotland', Edinburgh, 1969.

The same study concluded that *individual* holdings of assets were, on average, higher than for the whole of Great Britain (although the total amount of such assets held in Scotland on a population basis was lower)—evidence to support the legend of the thrifty Scot, albeit in a small minority. The table below compares Scottish and British holdings on a per-'wealth holder' basis.

ESTIMATED HOLDINGS OF SELECTED ASSETS PER WEALTH-HOLDER, SCOTLAND AND GREAT BRITAIN 1960 AND 1965

	1960		1965	
	Scotland £	Great Britain £	Scotland £	Great Britain £
National Savings Bonds, T.R.C's	565	396	632	406
Deposit Accounts	623	711	770	953
Building Society Deposits	1,449	1,386	1,906	1,628
Equities	5,319	5,430	9,479	5,367

Source: L.C. Wright, op. cit.

In terms of absolute wealth, evidence of a Scottish emphasis on financial assets can be demonstrated, stemming almost entirely from lower levels of house ownership; this also furnishes one reason for the relatively slow growth of aggregate wealth in Scotland since 1945—property having been the fastest growing asset of all. The study referred to above calculated that net wealth held in Scotland in 1965 amounted to £5,754 million, or 7·9 per cent of the U.K. total. 76·3 per cent of this was held in the form of financial assets compared with 65·2 per cent with the whole U.K. (Scotland's population in 1965 being 9·6 per cent of the U.K. total).

Housing Costs

It has already been established that Scottish incomes are a little below the British average, and we have seen above that it has been harder historically to hold wealth through property. Important differences in the structure of housing arrangements, and hence of housing costs, must be dealt with before the disposal of the remainder of Scottish incomes can be described in the proper context.

Despite a massive new housing programme (Chapter 1 gives details of actual house building) nearly three-quarters of unfurnished private rented property in Scotland dates from the last century—one reason for the lower level of Scottish rents. Historically, a lower rate of home ownership has prevailed in Scotland than elsewhere, and the overall level of mortgage payments is little over one-third of the U.K. average. Scottish local authority housing is more heavily subsidised than in England and Wales, due to a contribution from local rates as well as from the Exchequer. The proportion of identifiable public expenditure in Scotland going into housing is significantly higher than in other parts of the country.

The differences in the housing patterns between Scotland and the U.K. as a whole are clearly illustrated below.

TYPES OF ACCOMMODATION 1970-71

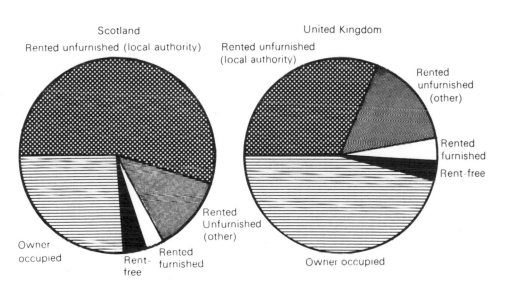

Source: *Family Expenditure Survey.*

In the privately-owned sector the Scottish home buyer has in the past not always benefitted from lower property prices. The Nationwide Building Society—one of the largest in Britain— carries out regular surveys of properties mortgaged to the Society and the following trend is shown.

AVERAGE PRICES OF HOUSES MORTGAGED TO THE NATIONWIDE BUILDING SOCIETY IN SCOTLAND AND GREAT BRITAIN, FOURTH QUARTERS 1966 AND 1971

| | 1966 (4th Quarter) | | 1971 (4th Quarter) | |
	New Houses £	Existing Houses[1] £	New Houses £	Existing Houses £
Scotland	4,459	4,531	5,922	6,134
Great Britain	4,067	4,449	6,218	6,852

Source: Nationwide Building Society.

[1] Of modern design and standards.

Thus in 1966 the average Scottish house cost more than the national average, and this position has now been reversed by a smaller rise in Scottish property values (33 per cent for new houses compared with a national 53 per cent and a massive hike of 72 per cent in London and the South East). In the mid-60s the demand for housing caused modern existing house prices in most regions to overtake the price of new houses; this was the case in Scotland and has remained so. At the time of the later set of figures shown, Scottish house prices were between 5 and 10 per cent below the national average. Severe housing bottlenecks have built up in those parts of Scotland where the oil industry is active, and Scottish house prices have advanced rapidly in consequence.

Given the much lower incidence of home ownership in Scotland the net result of all this remains, however, significantly lower housing costs for the Scottish public, amounting in 1970/71 to 13·4 per cent of total expenditure by Scottish households compared with a U.K. average of 17·8 per cent. In sterling terms the difference amounted to £1·67 weekly.

Household Expenditure (see footnote at end of section on expenditure)

Until recently, lower housing costs meant that despite slightly lower incomes (and ignoring the question of possible differences in overall savings levels) the spending power available to Scottish households was actually higher than the average. Average household expenditure for the U.K. is now, according to the Family Expenditure Survey, a little higher on non-housing items than for Scottish households. The difference is, however, less than 2 per cent.

AVERAGE WEEKLY EXPENDITURE BY SCOTTISH AND U.K. HOUSEHOLDS, 1965–67 and 1970–71

| | 1965/67 | | 1970/71 | |
	Scotland £	U.K. £	Scotland £	U.K. £
Total expenditure	22·41	23·06	29·09	30·73
Housing (including mortgages, alterations, etc.)	1·97	3·33	3·50	4·66
Other items	20·44	19·73	25·59	26·07

Source: *Family Expenditure Survey*
(Department of Employment)

The main reason for the change is a sharper increase in housing costs for Scotland, and these costs have increased still further recently, especially following rises in local authority rents. However, Scottish expenditure has gone up more slowly in a number of categories as shown in the table on page 208. Despite this, Scottish expenditure is well above the national average in several important fields (all expenditures are in terms of current prices).

The composition of household expenditure for Scotland is shown schematically overleaf alongside that for the U.K., with changes recorded in this case over a longer period for the sake of clarity.

Food

Scottish expenditure on food remains marginally ahead of the whole-country average (by an amount of 10p per household

GROWTH OF HOUSEHOLD EXPENDITURE BY
CATEGORIES IN SCOTLAND AND U.K., 1965-67 TO 1970-71

	Percentage growth between 1965/67 and 1970/71		Scotland as per- cent of U.K. 1970/71
	Scotland	U.K.	
Housing (incl. mortgages)	+ 77·7	+39·9	75·1
Fuel, light and power	+ 26·7	+30·0	104·4
Food	+ 22·6	+24·6	101·3
Alcoholic drink	+ 47·5	+48·9	108·8
Tobacco	− 1·9	+ 7·3	115·8
Clothing and footwear	+ 25·8	+32·5	105·5
Durable household goods	+ 7·8	+35·7	92·3
Other goods	+ 50·0	+41·1	91·5
Transport and vehicles	+ 43·3	+50·4	86·6
Services	+ 18·0	+30·3	90·5
Miscellaneous	+ 10·0	+25·0	110·0
Total Expenditure	+ 29·8	+33·3	94·7
(Minus housing	+ 25·2	+32·1	98·2)

Source: Family Expenditure Survey.
(Department of Employment).

weekly), and it is in the filling of the grocery shopping basket that some of the most significant traditional differences—occasionally difficult for the marketer of consumer goods to comprehend— remain between the Scottish and English ways of life (not that England and Wales form a single homogeneous market by any means, as can be clearly demonstrated in market research and sociological terms).*

A reasonably comprehensive account of food expenditure by product category is given in the Family Expenditure Survey and in view of the general importance of food in household expenditure this is reproduced on pages 210 and 211.

It is well known that the Scots are above average eaters of bread and flour confectionery, and expenditure on biscuits etc. is over half as much again as the U.K. figure (several of Britain's best known biscuit manufacturers are Scottish firms). Scottish families

* 'British Tastes', D. Elliston Allen. Hutchinson, 1968.

COMPONENTS OF HOUSEHOLD EXPENDITURE, SCOTLAND AND U.K.—1961-63 AND 1970-71

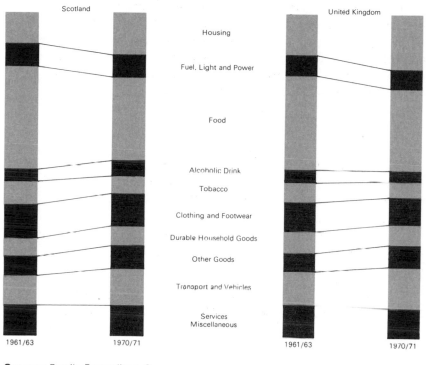

Scotland

United Kingdom

Housing

Fuel, Light and Power

Food

Alcoholic Drink

Tobacco

Clothing and Footwear

Durable Household Goods

Other Goods

Transport and Vehicles

Services
Miscellaneous

1961/63   1970/71   1961/63   1970/71

Source: *Family Expenditure Survey
(Department of Employment).*

continue to eat much more beef, in the best tradition, but correspondingly less mutton and pork with an overall expenditure on meat virtually identical to the national level. They buy exactly average quantities of butter, but more margarine and less of other fats.

Dairy products, vegetables and fruit are sectors where Scottish expenditure is below average, potatoes being an exception, and Scottish families appear to be especially fond of potato crisps etc. Preserves and sweet spreads are above average markets in Scotland, and soft drinks are another Scottish favourite with carbonated drinks being preferred sweeter and heavier than south of the border. The classic instance of Scottish food-buying distinguishing itself from the national pattern, though, is in soups where expenditure on canned and packeted varieties is nearly double the average.

Scotland as a market for food products thus differs widely in certain sectors from the 'norm' suggested by the population base. Some illustrations of these divergences are available from a compilation by the A.C. Nielsen Company. This includes some specific product categories not listed above and some non-food items generally available through grocery stores.

	% of G.B. Market		% of G.B. Market
Tinned cat foods	3	Yogurt	7
Facial tissues	8	Frozen peas	2
Paper towels	7	Tea-bags	13
Squashes and cordials	7	Instant potato	9
Jams	15	Coffee	6
Packaged flour	$5\frac{1}{2}$	Canned soup	18

AVERAGE WEEKLY EXPENDITURE BY SCOTTISH HOUSEHOLDS ON FOOD PRODUCTS BY CATEGORY 1970-71

	Scotland pence	U.K. pence	Scotland Index (U.K. = 100)
Bread, rolls etc.	49	41	120
Flour	2	3	67
Biscuits, shortbreads, wafers etc.	29	19	153
Cakes, buns etc.	27	22	123
Breakfast and other cereals	12	12	100
Beef and veal	64	46	139
Mutton and lamb	13	24	54
Pork	8	15	53
Bacon and ham (uncooked)	22	24	92
Ham, cooked (incl. canned)	7	8	88
Poultry, other and undefined meat	69	65	106
Fish	19	19	100
Fish and chips	4	6	67

AVERAGE WEEKLY EXPENDITURE BY SCOTTISH HOUSEHOLDS ON FOOD PRODUCTS BY CATEGORY 1970-71 — Continued

	Scotland pence	U.K. pence	Scotland Index (U.K. = 100)
Butter	20	20	100
Margarine	8	7	114
Lard, cooking and other fats	5	6	83
Milk, fresh	56	62	90
Milk, dried, canned; cream etc.	7	8	88
Cheese	13	14	93
Eggs	24	22	109
Potatoes	18	17	106
Potato products, incl. chips, crisps	9	7	129
Other and undefined vegetables	34	44	77
Fruit	36	39	92
Sugar	10	11	91
Syrup, honey, jam, marmalade etc.	6	5	120
Sweets and chocolates	26	26	100
Tea	14	15	93
Coffee	6	8	75
Cocoa, drinking chocolate and other food drinks	1	2	50
Soft drinks	19	15	127
Ice cream	6	6	100
Soups (canned and packaged)	11	6	183
Other food, foods not defined	21	23	91
Meals bought away from home	106	106	100
Total	781	771	101

Source: Family Expenditure Survey

All these figures are, of course, based on current prices and do not take into account slight differences in regional price levels which may exist. A more exhaustive analysis of Scottish food consumption and expenditure appears in the National Food Survey* published each year and which permits differences in real

*Household Food Consumption and Expenditure, Ministry of Agriculture, Fisheries and Food (H.M.S.O.).

consumption levels to be measured as well as nutritional trends and so forth. The Family Expenditure Survey itself enables estimates of market sizes in Scotland to be calculated if the figures given are multiplied first by 52 to give annual totals and then by the number of private households in Scotland (about 1·7 million).

Alcoholic Drink

The distinctive—and often difficult—nature of the licensed trade in Scotland has already been described. This does not inhibit Scots from spending above average amounts on alcoholic beverages— 8·8 per cent more per household than the national figure in 1970/71.

In this sector, along with tobacco, there is a tendency for survey respondents to understate the true quantities purchased by as much as half it is thought. Nevertheless this result is born out by successive recent surveys and must be considered correct at least in relative terms (some surveys in the early sixties recorded a below average Scottish expenditure in the category, but this is presumed to reflect an understatement, later corrected, rather than a dramatic increase in consumption of alcohol).

Scottish drinking follows its own characteristic pattern, as the table below shows

AVERAGE WEEKLY EXPENDITURE BY SCOTTISH HOUSEHOLDS ON ALCOHOLIC DRINKS, 1970-71

	Scotland pence	U.K. pence	Scotland Index (U.K.=100)
Beer, cider etc.	75	89	84
Wines (incl. tips)	10	15	67
Spirits, liqueurs etc. (incl. tips)	60*	28	214
Drinks not defined	4	5	80
Total	149	137	109

Source: Family Expenditure Survey.

* Figure subject to large standard error.

Even allowing for sampling error, it is clear that spirit consumption is a great deal higher than average. This is principally due to the drinking of larger quantities of the fabled native Scottish life-water. Research* has identified 53·5 per cent of adult Scots as whisky drinkers compared with 47·6 per cent over the whole of Great Britain. When it comes to regular whisky drinking (once a week or more) Scotland shows the rest of the country a much cleaner pair of heels with 19·4 per cent of all adults against a national 10·6 per cent.

Scotland is also noted, however, for a much higher *per capita* consumption of Vodka—always the favourite white spirit in Scotland—whereas Gin has never been particularly popular nor, to a lesser extent, has rum.

As a race the Scots are not great wine drinkers (though connoisseurship lingers from the 'auld alliance' with France) and have modest appetites for vermouths and ports—although including an above average portion of sherry drinkers. Scottish beer consumption on a *per capita* (or per household) basis is down from the national figure, but again has its own particular pattern. Scottish beer is stronger and has something in common with the local brews of Belgium and Northern France. The old Scots habit of chasing down a whisky with a glass of lager means, not unnaturally, that more lager is drunk in Scotland—about half the total quantity brewed in Britain—and traditional Scottish lager is of unusual strength. Canned beer is a good deal more widely drunk in Scotland, reflecting the importance of home drinking and off-licence sales.

Other Expenditure

The Scot has been reluctant to abandon the smoking habit despite the massive evidence of links with disease. 49 per cent of Scottish adults are cigarette smokers, compared with a national 42 per cent* and 18 per cent are heavy smokers (20 a day or more) against a national 15 per cent. Overall Scottish spending on tobacco products has been falling in relation to the U.K. average but is still 16 per cent higher per household.

*Target Group Index © BMRB, 1972.

AVERAGE WEEKLY EXPENDITURE BY SCOTTISH HOUSEHOLDS ON TOBACCO, 1970-71

	Scotland pence	U.K. pence	Scotland Index (U.K. = 100)
Cigarettes	145	122	119
Pipe tobacco	7	8	88
Cigars and snuff	3	4	75
Total	154	133	116

Source: Family Expenditure Survey.

As the above shows, the difference lies in a heavier cigarette consumption, and fewer Scots are pipe or cigar smokers. Scots people have taken to the current fad for cigarillos, however, as keenly as others.

Scottish family expenditure on toiletries and cosmetics runs some 12 per cent down from the U.K. average and, although fashions change fast, some underlying differences persist. Scotswomen take as much care of their faces (in terms of product usage) as other British women but use fewer specific make-up products such as powder, rouge and lipstick. They have tended to be more cautious in the adoption of new eye make-up products. Shampoos and hair sprays are slightly more widely used by Scotswomen, as are some hand care products. In general the emphasis is on the practical rather than the esoteric or up-to-the-minute.

Although traces of erstwhile Scottish attitudes to fashion can still be found—for instance in women dressing with an eye to each other rather than to their menfolk, or husbands delegating clothes-buying to their wives, and in a generally less fashion-conscious outlook—the levelling influences of the budget chain store and more recently of the 'boutique' have made themselves felt here as elsewhere. Winter clothes have a longer selling season, and there is more emphasis on the tweeds and woollens for which Scotland is famous, but fashion sense in Scotland has caught up rapidly during the last few years and the gap continues to close.

The clothing and footwear market as a whole receives an above average share of family budgets in Scotland, to the extent of about 5 per cent. The only clothing sectors where Scottish expenditure falls below average are women's outerwear and underclothing (including hosiery). However, fashion accessories such as hats and gloves are more important items to the Scots woman, and made-to-measure or home dressmaking earns a market 22 per cent above the national per household figure in materials and making-up charges.

The Scottish mother's purse is at its most free when buying for her children. This indulgence in clothes for the young is stimulated and catered for by relatively large numbers of good-class specialist retailers. Altogether this market is 23 per cent higher than the national equivalent, and the emphasis is particularly marked in the case of girl's clothing.

Household Goods

Family expenditure on household goods is lower in Scotland than the national figure, and this applies to furniture, soft furnishings and household textiles—though not to floor coverings, where Scottish households spend nearly a quarter more than the British average—as well as to durable goods and appliances.

In the case of furniture especially, this result stems from the particular circumstances of Scotland during the past decade. At the beginning of the sixties, Scottish expenditure in this sector was well below the U.K. figure. Later, redevelopment schemes, new towns and rising incomes contributed to what amounted to a huge spending spree on furnishings, and in 1967 Scotland represented a market over half as large again as the national average on a per family basis. Growth has now reverted for the present to a sub-average rate, with the already noted exception of floor coverings—where Scottish tastes make themselves felt in entirely different colours and a devotion to richly patterned carpets.

In the case of domestic appliances, Scottish ownership levels are simply lower than in regions with a recent record of greater prosperity—with the exception of washing machines, where overall ownership is fractionally above par, thanks to a greater incidence of twin-tub machines. The following table shows the position for the main appliances and systems.

P

OWNERSHIP LEVELS OF HOUSEHOLD APPLIANCES, SCOTLAND[1] AND GREAT BRITAIN 1971-72[2]

Percentage of households owning:	Scotland	Great Britain
Electric cooker	56·1	41·6
Gas cooker	37·1	54·2
Refrigerator	57·7	72·7
Deep-freeze	3·2	4·9
Dishwasher	0·8	1·3
Automatic washing machine (front loading)	8·4	9·1
Washing machine (twin-tub)	29·8	26·3
Washing machine (any other kind)	17·4	19·8
Spin-dryer (separate)	13·9	25·0
Vacuum cleaner	82·4	83·9
Central heating	21·1	32·2

Source: *Target Group Index* © *BMRB 1972.*

[1] Fieldwork south of the Caledonian Canal only.
[2] Fieldwork period April 1971—March 1972.

The Scottish preference for cooking by electricity rather than gas (the reverse of the national pattern) is long-standing, and perpetuated by on the one hand the habit of staying with the same fuel when moving house (in the face of the blandishments of the respective fuel authorities) and on the other hand the emphasis on apartment buildings in Scottish redevelopment projects.

Note : These comparisons of Scottish levels of expenditure are based on a single year, and it should be recognised that comparatively small variations from year to year can lead to large differences in distinctions drawn between Scottish and National average expenditures. Nevertheless the comparisons shown reflect, in the main, well-established characteristics and variations from the National mean G.M.

Other Characteristics and Behaviour

A number of other pointers to the nature of the Scottish consumer can briefly be given, and to provide a standardised base of reference the Target Group Index already referred to is a convenient source.

The lower level of appliance ownership by Scottish households extends into the motoring sector with 44·8 per cent of Scottish households possessing a car compared with a national (Great Britain) 54·7 per cent. Two or more car households are correspondingly less common in Scotland, and 43·8 per cent of Scottish adults hold a car driving licence against a national 50·1 per cent. There are some differences in the pattern of annual mileage driven, with Scottish motorists showing a slight tendency to be either occasional motorists (less than 5,000 miles a year) or long distance drivers (over 20,000 miles).

	Scotland %	Great Britain %
Below 5,000 miles	43·4	40·0
5,000—9,999 miles	29·6	29·6
10,000—19,999 miles	19·7	24·5
20,000 miles or over	7·3	5·9

Whether by car or not, slightly fewer Scottish adults than the average (59·7 per cent against 63·1 per cent) were found by the 1971/72 TGI survey to have taken a holiday away from home in the previous twelve months. Fewer Scots, too, are gardeners and fewer visit pubs.

However, a greater Scottish following of pastimes such as Bingo, dancing and betting on horse races make up for these deficiencies, and among sports, golf and the winter thrills of skating and skiing (this last practised increasingly on Scots' home ground) have a high relative popularity. Tennis, water sports and riding have fewer Scottish devotees. When it comes to spectator sports, watching football is the top Scottish pastime, with an attendance rate 30 per cent higher than for the whole of Britain. Rugby League, Motor Racing and Cricket are three diverse sports having in common a scant level of Scottish interest.

To conclude this examination on a more serious note, and to recall the financial basis underlying this chapter, all major forms of life insurance are much more widely held by Scots, and Scots are more likely to be holders of bank savings or deposit accounts than current accounts—the reverse of the national pattern. As already discussed, they are less likely to be participants in the various parts of the National Savings schemes with the exception of the Trustee Savings Bank.

A summary tabulation of the research findings from which the above description is compiled is given below

	Scotland %	Great Britain %
Adults taking a holiday away from home in last 12 months	59·7	63·1
Adults responsible for upkeep of a garden	61·5	66·6
Adults visiting pubs	52·1	62·5
More than once a week	15·1	19·7
More than once a month, but at most once a week	19·8	20·0
Once a month or less	17·1	22·8
Adults ever taking part these days in:		
Bingo	14·0	13·1
Dancing	25·3	21·4
Ten-pin bowling	3·7	4·7
Football pools	32·8	32·7
Betting on horse-racing	12·5	10·9
Fishing	7·8	7·9
Riding	1·3	2·4
Sailing	1·6	2·0
Skiing	1·7	0·8
Water-skiing	0·5	0·6
Squash	1·7	1·6
Skating	3·1	2·6
Swimming	18·1	19·8
Golf	7·8	4·4
Lawn Tennis	3·8	6·1
Paid attendance in last 12 months at:		
Association Football	27·8	21·4
Cricket	1·3	5·5
Greyhound racing	3·9	3·2
Horse racing	5·2	5·9
Motor racing	3·3	5·1
Rugby League	1·4	2·7

Adults holding:

Life Insurance (payable on death only)	44·2	39·1
Life Insurance (payable on death or maturity of policy)	43·6	41·8
Savings in Building Societies	11·0	22·3
Savings in Unit Trusts	5·0	5·9
Stocks and Shares	6·0	6·0
Premium Bonds	31·2	40·9
Savings in National Savings Bank	16·8	23·9
Savings in S.A.Y.E.[1] scheme	4·0	4·2
Banks[2]: Savings account	34·7	22·3
Banks: Current account	26·8	41·5
Banks: Deposit account	23·8	21·4

Source: *Target Group Index* © *BMRB 1972.*

[1] Save-As-You-Earn.
[2] Includes Trustee Savings Banks.

9 Advertising and media

THIS CHAPTER CONTINUES THE previous chapter's discussion of the Scottish consumer in the specific direction of his or her patronage of information and entertainment media and consequent 'exposure' to advertising and related methods of promotion of goods and services. The opportunity is taken to give a brief account of the Scottish advertising industry and relevant sectors of the publishing business.

Marketing campaigns will frequently employ a combination of advertising media, and the advertising agency in question will normally be concerned with the establishment of media schedules consistent with the advertiser's budget and the nature of the product and its market. Technical data, rates, and detailed information on readership, viewership etc., can generally be obtained through advertising agencies or media proprietors. For this reason, and because such data are subject to periodic changes, only a general review is offered in this volume.

Newspapers and Readership

Britain's national newspapers, of course, circulate in Scotland, but with a readership pattern somewhat different from that in England and Wales on account of the existence of local Scottish media and variations in regional printing arrangements. In two cases specifically Scottish editions of national papers are produced locally—the *Scottish Daily Express* and the *Daily Record* which is the Scottish equivalent of the *Daily Mirror*. Both of these are mass-selling papers, and between them are read by the majority of Scottish adults.

A lower rate of readership amongst Scottish women is evident from the table overleaf. This may partly be explained by a greater interest in more indigenous media, readily available in the main

READERSHIP OF DAILY MORNING NEWSPAPERS IN SCOTLAND, 1971
(National readership figures in brackets)

	All Adults %		Men %	Women %
Daily Mirror	3	(33)	3	2
Daily Express	48	(23)	55	43
Sun	—	(21)	—	—
Daily Mail	4	(12)	6	3
Daily Telegraph	2	(9)	2	1
Daily Record	43	(4)	50	37
The Guardian	1	(3)	1	1
The Times	1	(3)	1	1
Financial Times	1	(2)	1	—

Source: *National Readership Survey 1971.*

population centres. The main reason for the low penetration of the English 'quality' papers such as the *Times* and *Guardian* into Scotland is the existence of two excellent Scottish daily papers, the *Scotsman* published in Edinburgh by the Thomson Organisation and the *Glasgow Herald,* published by George Outram & Co. which is indirectly part of the House of Fraser. Although the circulation of these papers is relatively small (about 78,000 for the *Scotsman* and 85,000 for the *Glasgow Herald*[1]) their influence is high, and both include daily business news sections. The *Scotsman* in particular has the reputation of a mouthpiece for Scotland south of the border.

The readership of Sunday newspapers in Scotland follows a pattern uniquely its own. An analysis appears on page 223.

In this case the great siphoner-off of readers from the most popular English papers is the *Sunday Post*, published in Dundee by D. C. Thomson & Co. (which has no connection with the Thomson Organisation). The *Sunday Post* is not only read almost universally throughout Scotland but with its one million-plus circulation has a unique status as an informative and emotional link for Scots the world over.

The *Sunday Mail*, the Scottish equivalent of the *Sunday Mirror* (and no relation to the English *Daily Mail*) has a substantially

[1] Circulation figures taken from BRAD and quoted in round figures.

READERSHIP OF NATIONAL SUNDAY NEWSPAPERS IN SCOTLAND, 1971
(National readership figures in brackets)

	All Adults %		Men %	Women %
News of the World	24	(38)	26	21
People	19	(35)	23	16
Sunday Mirror	8	(33)	10	7
Sunday Express	25	(25)	26	24
Sunday Post	79	(11)	79	79
Sunday Times	8	(9)	9	8
Observer	5	(6)	6	5
Sunday Mail	52	(6)	55	50
Sunday Telegraph	2	(5)	2	2

Source: National Readership Survey 1971.

larger readership in proportion than the *Sunday Mirror* does nationally, and the same is true to a lesser extent of the week day *Daily Record*.

The *Scottish Daily Express*, as shown in the first table, enjoys in proportion a far greater sale than its English twin.

The *Sunday Post* and *Sunday Mail* are the only major Sunday newspapers published in Scotland. Several other important daily newspapers of regional significance are published, however. These include the *Press & Journal* in Aberdeen (circulation about 106,000), the *Dundee Courier* (123,000), the *Greenock Telegraph* (24,000) and *Paisley Daily Express* (18,000).

Scotland's four cities are also served by evening papers which have an overall readership amongst Scottish adults of 39 per cent. Glasgow has the distinction, rare today amongst British cities, of two 'evenings' the *Evening Times* (circulation 172,000) and *Evening Citizen* (160,000). These titles are evidence of the considerable degree of concentration which has penetrated the ranks of Scottish newspaper proprietors. In relation to this it is noteworthy that the principal newspapers in Scotland are published in pairs. Thus Outrams have the *Glasgow Herald* and *Evening Times*, and also own the *Paisley Daily Express*, in the west, while in Edinburgh the Thomson Organisation publishes the *Scotsman* and the *Evening News* (circulation 146,000).

The Thomson Organisation also own the Aberdeen *Press & Journal* and its evening sibling the *Evening Express* (74,000). In Dundee D. C. Thomson publishes both the *Courier & Advertiser* and the *Evening Telegraph* (circulations 124,000 and 62,000) as well as, of course, the *Sunday Post*. The *Daily Record* and *Scottish Daily Express* are products of the Scottish stables of the International Publishing Corporation and Beaverbrook Newspapers respectively. Beaverbrook also publish the Glasgow *Evening Citizen*. Only the small *Greenock Telegraph*, remaining in the hands of its original Scottish proprietors Orr, Pollock & Co., has no evening or Sunday sister paper.

Apart from this 'pairing', one interesting point to emerge from the above is the greater circulations achieved by the Aberdeen and Dundee morning papers, and by the evening papers in Glasgow and Edinburgh, than by the quasi-national *Glasgow Herald* and *Scotsman*. The present ownership mix of Scottish newspapers leaves considerable scope for further rationalisation, and the pattern cannot be considered stable.

Although both the *Glasgow Herald* and *Scotsman* have succeeded in modestly increasing their circulation, there must be some doubt whether in the long run there is room for both. Both Glasgow evening papers have lost circulation during the last few years, and some believe that a reduction to one is inevitable.

Among the two most widely-read morning papers, the *Daily Record* and *Scottish Daily Express*, the former has been gaining circulation, following a move to a new, highly automated web-offset plant—at the expense of the latter. An agreement amongst the leading newspaper proprietors to rationalise their Scottish interests is well within the bounds of possibility.

The local press in smaller towns and country districts in Scotland is confined to weekly or bi-weekly newspapers, and here too there has been some degree of concentration, although only a handful of major groups—all Scottish-owned—have emerged. In the absence of any joint advertising sales organisation, there are still upwards of 150 'buying points' for local press advertising in Scotland. The industry is now in a relatively healthy position after a period when widespread closures seemed likely, and very few titles have been lost during the last few years.

Principally for this reason (and also because other media are usually available) the development of 'national' advertising through the Scottish weekly press has been slow, and for instance campaigns where blocks are supplied with space for addition of local dealers' names are the exception.

As strictly local advertising media, however, the Scottish weeklies fulfil a unique role. The local paper is considered a vital supplement to the perhaps more authoritative but less parochial daily, and is almost certainly more thoroughly read. In some areas it is the *only* significant press advertising medium, and in districts which are beyond the reach of ITV transmitters it *is* the only medium apart from posters, the cinema or direct transmission of advertising material to people's homes. None of the daily newspapers makes really substantial inroads into the mainstay of Scottish local press advertising, the classified columns. These remain a major growth area and represent a microcosm of local life.

In districts where the oil industry has already made itself felt, the local press has been able to perform a valuable service in advertising jobs and facilities such as transport and warehousing. The effects are now spreading downwards along the east coast into Kincardineshire, Angus and Fife, and similar consequences will give a boost to papers in northern Scottish counties.

Big improvements are noticeable in the layout of many papers, and there have been some substantial gains in readership figures, especially in the west. Web-offset installations are becoming more common, and at least 21 papers are now printed by this method. The resultant increase in use of colour has helped to make the papers concerned more faithful and hence more popular reflectors of community life. The switch to web-offset has also created spare capacity, since the new plant must be more intensively used, and some useful printing contracts from continental as well as British publishers have been secured.

In the field of general printing, Scotland offers a number of first-class book and general jobbing printers with every technical facility, and Scottish printers attract much business from English publishers. Much of the Scottish publishing industry is now controlled outwith Scotland, though independent concerns of international stature still survive and prosper.

Television

The organisation of the television industry in Scotland has already been described (Chapter 5). Scottish Television and its neighbour Grampian Television (the two being associated for time sales purposes in the joint company STAGS) reach between them a potential audience of 4·5 million in 1·4 million homes. This is about 87 per cent of Scotland's population.

The extension of the BBC charter and the television act until 1981, has done something to increase the industry's confidence and promote stability. The structure of ITV is unlikely to change before 1976 but there is no automatic security of tenure for the exisiting programme contractors thereafter. There is also to be a technical review of television broadcasting in the regions, which may lead to a more rapid extension of UHF transmitter areas resulting in increased availability of colour and the ability to bring a television signal to sparsely populated areas of the U.K.

The total number of television receiving licences in Scotland in February 1973 was 1,527,663, excluding the old people's homes and demonstration licences. The breakdown of this figure is shown below, with a comparison for the U.K.

TELEVISION LICENCES CURRENT IN SCOTLAND AND UNITED KINGDOM, FEBRUARY 1973

	Monochrome	Colour	Total	Per cent
Scotland No.	1,317,445	210,218	1,527,663	13·8
Per 000 pop.	253	40	293	—
United Kingdom				
No.	13,884,927	3,173,583	17,058,510	18·6
Per 000 pop.	250	57	307	—

Source: The Post Office (Television Licensing Organisation).

The lower proportion of colour licences in Scotland is due to a later start in transmissions than some regions and to gaps in the present coverage of colour transmitters on account of topography. Although in *per capita* terms Scotland has slightly fewer television licences than the national average, the difference is made up by

Scotland's slightly larger average households, and within the over-all area covered by STAGS ITV transmissions are seen by 95 per cent of all individuals.

An outline of television coverage in Scotland in audience terms is as follows:

SIZE OF THE T.V. AUDIENCE IN SCOTLAND, JANUARY 1973 (Figures in thousands)

	Total	With ITV	ITV Households Total	Receiving BBC 2
A. *Households*				
Central Scotland	1,357	1,270	1,195	884
N.E. Scotland	386	361	295	176
STAGS	1,565	1,456	1,420	1,013
B. *Individuals*				
Central Scotland	4,144	4,003	3,813	2,980
N.E. Scotland	1,176	1,125	939	568
STAGS	4,790	4,601	4,532	3,390

Source: *JICTAR Establishment Survey 1973.*

Within the areas of coverage, homes receiving ITV (that is, with multi-channel sets) amount to 91 per cent of the total and the pro-portion is as high as 95 per cent of individuals. Reception of BBC2 requires either a dual-standard set (VHF 405 lines and UHF 625 lines) or an all-UHF set, and altogether 1,157,000 Scottish ITV homes have sets capable of receiving UHF transmissions, of which 12 per cent cannot actually receive BBC2 (i.e. are out of range), leaving the 'net' total of 1,013,000 BBC2 homes shown in the above table.

Overall, 47 per cent of TV sets in Scottish homes are rented, and the more modern the set the more likely it is to be rented. This applies to 54 per cent of UHF-only sets and popularity of the rental system, especially since credit controls were largely abolished in July 1971, has been a major reason for the rapid growth of colour reception throughout Great Britain.

INDICES OF ITV VIEWING IN THE CENTRAL SCOTLAND ITV AREA

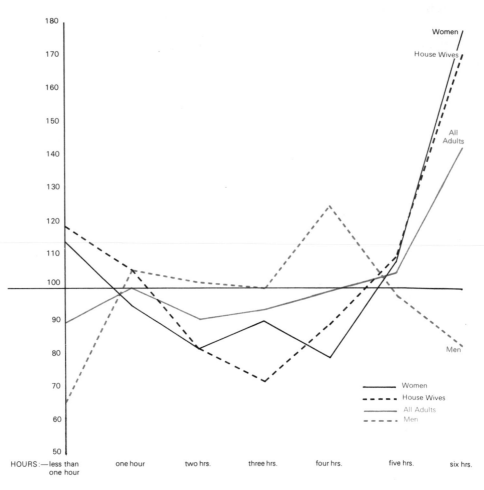

100 = National average figure for each daily length of viewing time.

Source: Derived from Target Group Index © BMRB 1972.

Source: Derived from Target Group Index © BMRB 1972.

ITV households tend to be a little larger than average, and are hence more likely to include children. The average age of the audience is thus also younger. Most studies of television viewing tend, for obvious reasons, to concentrate on the ITV channel. Over the whole country, sets in homes which can receive both BBC and ITV are switched on for an average of 4·7 hours per day, with an average ITV share of the total audience of 54 per cent.*

The Scottish audience tends to show a slight preference for viewing BBC rather than ITV programmes by comparison with the network as a whole, with an ITV rating two to three points below the average. Except during the summer months, however, according to industry surveys the ITV channel tends to have the larger viewing audience in Scotland as elsewhere. Research also shows that Scots are on balance slightly lighter viewers than the average. A profile of the Scottish viewer is shown graphically on page 228, and it is evident from this that Scots *women* are more prone to be heavy viewers (upwards of 5 hours per day) than the average, and are also more likely to be very light viewers; this applies especially to Scottish housewives. Scottish men, by contrast, are more likely to view for between 1 and 4 hours daily than the network average.

A detailed analysis of the TV audience and of viewing patterns can, of course, be obtained from either of the two ITV programme companies or from STAGS. Of the total audience some 10 percent are in the 'overlap' area between the transmitters belonging respectively to the Central Scotland and North East Scotland stations, and advertisers may reach either audience separately as well as the combined STAGS coverage. Scottish ITV coverage is unique in mainland Britain in that it includes virtually no overlap with other stations—a mere 0·1 percent of the audience amounting to 2,000 homes—and thus offers an 'isolation' which is ideal for purposes such as the measurement of campaign results or test marketing.

A variety of services related to television advertising are provided by the STAGS organisation under their 'Six Point Service Plan'. This includes retail sales and merchandising activities, direct mail advertising, and retail and consumer research facilities.

---

* **Source:** IBA period year ended 31st August 1972.

Cinema

It was noted in Chapter 5 that the Scots go more frequently to the cinema than is now the average attendance rate for the whole country. The same chapter gave an outline review of Scottish cinemas and their seating capacity (page 134). The relatively high rate of Scottish cinema patronage makes the big screen a useful way of reaching local audiences with advertisement material both for local small budget advertisers and as a component of co-ordinated national or regional campaigns.

The prime cinemagoing audience is one of young people and within the STAGS area (92 per cent of Scotland's population) 86 per cent of 15–24 year-olds are cinemagoers, averaging 14 visits to the cinema each year.* The total number of admissions annually in Scotland is about 20 million. This is equivalent to 11·1 per cent of all cinema admissions in Great Britain.

CINEMAGOING IN THE STAGS ITV AREA

	Visit Cinema in course of one year %	Average number of Cinema visits %
All Adults STAGS	48·4	9·51
All Adults G.B.	48·1	7·97
15-24 year old STAGS	85·7	14·02
15-24 year old G.B.	83·3	13·10

Source: Screen Advertising Association.

Sales of cinema advertising are handled by several contracting organisations of which the two largest, The Advertising Films Division of the Rank Organisation, and Pearl & Dean operate on a large scale nationally and provide a complete service including production of films. The Rank Organisation is naturally concerned with its own cinemas, and the ABC, Classic and Star circuits and certain other groups are handled by Pearl & Dean.

* *Source:* Screen Advertising Association.

Radio

Commercial radio of local origin will come to Scotland for the first time in 1974, when transmissions begin from the new Radio Clyde. Nine minutes of advertising per hour will be permitted, in the form of 'spot' advertisements, with sponsorship of programmes on the American pattern not permitted. The station will cover the Greater Glasgow area, and will be joined later by a similar station which will cover the Edinburgh area.

Radio listening in Britain—to the BBC—has until now been running at a rate of some 9 hours per head per week, little over half the North American level. One of the main objectives of the new commercial broadcasters will be to increase this total and to win a major share of the present audience away from the BBC so as to offer the largest possible audience to advertisers.

Since the demise of the off-shore 'pirate' radio stations— which included a so-styled 'Radio Scotland'—in 1967 the only commercial radio station whose broadcasts have been available to Scottish listeners is Radio Luxembourg. Scottish listening levels to the English-language broadcasts of Radio Luxembourg have always been among the highest in Britain, undeterred by the greater distance from the transmitter. Radio Luxembourg is primarily a youth advertising medium, with half its audience aged under 25. Its popularity in Scotland is a good augury for the success of home-grown commercial radio, and important local interests such as department stores are likely to find the new medium particularly helpful.

Posters

Outdoor advertising media are naturally available in Scotland as elsewhere, and provide a wide variety of possibilities for putting advertising messages before the Scottish public on either a full regional or strictly local basis. Indications concerning outdoor media are always less precise than for others, due to fluctuations in site availability resulting from property re-development, Local Authority activity and so forth. The poster advertising industry in Britain has also undergone major reorganisation since the break-up of the former Cosales consortium in 1971.

Rationalisation has consolidated itself at the national level with

Q

the emergence of two large contracting groups, British Posters and Independent Poster Sales, with the former having an estimated 75 per cent of all sites. The largest member of British Posters is Mills & Allen, which includes the former Scottish and north-eastern contractor General Poster. Independent Poster Sales includes several contractors operating in Scotland and the existence of these consortia greatly simplifies the use of outdoor sites. Another facility is the Advertising Agency Poster Bureau of 42 Kingsway London WC2 which buys, plans and handles campaigns for its members on a non-profit-making basis.

As a result of these developments, very few individual media-owners of importance remain in outdoor advertising in Scotland as elsewhere. However, the availability of bus sides and other forms of transport advertising in Scottish cities is a significant part of the outdoor advertising scene, and a related development has been the more systematic use of bus shelters, through a new consortium 'Adshel', a development which has resulted in improved municipal amenities as well as more outdoor advertising space.

A tremendous increase in sophistication of the service available to outdoor advertisers has also resulted, even at the loss of some flexibility. British Posters in particular have made a feature of pre-selected campaigns based on computerised site information, and organised primarily on a basis corresponding to ITV area boundaries. Advertisers can select the sites more likely to be seen by individual target groups such as housewives or men.

Historically, an absence of firm research data has been a draw-back of outdoor advertising, but a great deal of original work has been done during the past decade and one firm Outdoor Research Surveys Ltd. has specialised in the subject, devising an operational research model which can assist advertisers in selecting the opti-mum campaign to reach the required population segment in a particular area.

Advertising and Public Relations

A long-established native advertising industry exists within Scotland, and there is a Scottish branch of the Institute of Practitioners in Advertising (which includes Newcastle-upon-Tyne). It is estimated that about £10 million-worth of advertising business is placed each year through agencies located in Scotland, and although this is a small fraction of total British advertising business (perhaps 2 percent) the industry derives positive benefit from its distance from the London centre of the British advertising world and from its close identification with the Scottish market.

Scottish agencies are by their nature small, although the highest billing is now in excess of £2 million. The bulk of their expenditure is placed with Scottish media and most of their clients are Scottish. In a Scottish context this local business attains a significant level; Scottish agencies for instance bill some £3 million annually with Scottish daily newspapers and £750,000 with Scottish weekly newspapers. They also generate £1 million for the ITV network.

Rationalisation has not been felt to the same extent as in London, although some groupings which are significant by local standards have taken place. Several Glasgow agencies have recently been acquired by the Rex Stewart Group (including D. C. Cuthbertson, McMurtrie and McInnes Thomson) and Woolward Royds also represents a recent grouping of several Scottish agency interests. Glasgow is the principal advertising centre, followed by Edinburgh, but there are flourishing agencies in Aberdeen and other centres, and some Scottish agencies have offices in two or more locations.

Scottish agencies commonly draw (though to varying extents) on the creative base offered by London, and it is clearly impracticable for them to support in-house research and marketing facilities. There is an almost complete absence of Scottish-based research facilities in particular, although this may be expected to change in the future.

Within the context described, really large advertising accounts amongst Scottish agencies are rare, and inevitably much business goes south of the border. There is no doubt that the use of a London-based agency suits many Scottish advertisers very well. For national advertisers it gives the feeling of more intimate contact both with ancillary marketing services and with the central media-buying process. However, when it comes to handling advertising business in Scotland, and above all in local Scottish media, the Scottish agency has built-in advantages which more than compensate for the lack of a full range of services.

Although the Scottish people form an integral part of the British public, and behavioural variations are nowadays essentially minor, marketing strategies, as will be apparent from even a casual study of this book, to succeed must often differ in ways which the non-Scottish agency is—all other things being equal—less well placed to be aware of and respond to. One answer to this problem in sectors where differences are significant—for instance food and drink—is the use by national advertisers of separate agencies for England and Scotland.

Scottish agencies are thus in the unfortunate position where Scottish advertisers, beyond a certain size, tend to seek the 'umbrella' of a London agency because of its ostensibly stronger creative/marketing/media base, and English and foreign advertisers or agencies frequently fail to appreciate the extent of minor but significant differences in marketing and promotional strategy required to succeed in Scotland.

There are signs that this is changing. Scottish agencies presently are benefitting from a faster growth in business than the industry as a whole, stemming largely from local Scottish sources—from new business established in Scotland and from advertising by local and central Government institutions. Scottish advertising interests are confident that this growth can be sustained. With this acquired strength and confidence, some Scottish agencies are now in a better position to compete for Scottish business in the London market, and better equipped to compete with non-Scottish agencies on their home ground. On a small scale, Scotland has seen several promising new agency openings.

The growth prospects now seem to lie before the region, coupled with this new strength in Scottish agency management, have been reflected in a return of control of some Scottish-based accounts back to Scotland and consequently to Scottish agencies. One of the largest London agencies (Ogilvy, Benson & Mather) has already opened a Glasgow office in response. It is too early to say whether this is the start of a trend and southern-based agencies cannot, of course, immediately assume a Scottish identity by virtue of their presence; such newcomers in any case pose more of a threat to Scottish business held by other London agencies than to existing Scottish agencies. Other well-known agency names established in Scotland include Charles Barker, The Brunning Group, Austin Knight, R. & W. Advertising, and G. Street.

Scottish Public Relations activity has also shown rapid growth, after a cautious beginning. The Scottish area group of the Institute of Public Relations has over 80 members, but it is estimated that several times that number are involved with Public Relations activity in Scotland, and total Scottish expenditure on PR activities may be as high as £6 million.

The arrival of new industry, the tendency for control of Scottish firms to return to Scottish hands, the oil exploration boom and increasing sophistication in Scottish business itself have all created an environment favourable to PR activity. Public Relations have played an important part in the work of the various promotional and development bodies whose task has been to attract industry, tourists and population to Scotland. As the Scottish economy has matured in a modern sense, the growth of PR activity on behalf of services, institutions and government have been proportionately even greater than that for industry.

For interests concerned with oil, especially, PR has proved a rapid, sensitive management communications tool, and growth is foreseen in this form of indirect communication rather than in advertising itself. Its use is likely to increase dramatically as oil companies, service organisations and authorities concerned with the infrastructure alike find a growing need to acquaint the public and each other with the implications of their activities and objectives.

Appendix 1: Directory

GOVERNMENT ORGANISATIONS

Scottish Office, St Andrew's House, Edinburgh EH1 3DQ   Tel. 031-556 8501   Telex 72202.

Department of Employment, Stuart House, 30 Semple Street, Edinburgh EH3 8YX   Tel. 031-229 2433.

Scottish Industrial Development Office, Department of Trade & Industry, 314 St Vincent Street, Glasgow C3   Tel. 041-248 2855.

Regional Development Grants Office, Magnet House, Waterloo Street, Glasgow G2 7PB   Tel. 041-221 9833.

Export Credits Guarantee Department, 108 George Street, Edinburgh EH2 4LN   Tel. 031-225 3004   Telex 72170.

Department of Health and Social Security, Argyle House, 3 Lady Lawson Street, Edinburgh EH3 9SH   Tel. 031-229 3501.

Inland Revenue, Press and Information Office, Somerset House, London WC2   Tel. 01-836 2407.

Customs & Excise, King's Beam House, Mark Lane, London EC3 Tel. 01-626 1515.

Meteorological Office, 26 Palmerston Place, Edinburgh EH12 5AN Tel. 031-225 6561.

Scottish Special Housing Association, 15 Palmerston Place, Edinburgh EH12 5AJ   Tel. 031-225 1281.

Her Majesty's Stationery Office, 13a Castle Street, Edinburgh EH2 3AR Tel. 031-225 6333.

National Engineering Laboratory, East Kilbride, Lanarkshire   Tel. 0355-2 20222.

FUEL AND POWER AUTHORITIES

The Scottish Gas Board, Granton House, West Granton Road, Edinburgh Tel. 031-552 6271.

South of Scotland Electricity Board, Inverlair Avenue, Glasgow G43 2HS Tel. 041-637 7177.

North of Scotland Hydro-Electric Board, 16 Rothesay Terrace, Edinburgh 3   Tel. 031-225 1361.

236

National Coal Board (Scottish Division), Lauriston House, 80 Lauriston Place, Edinburgh 3 Tel. 031-229 2515.

TRANSPORT AND SHIPPING ORGANISATIONS

Freightliners Ltd., 227 Ingram Street, Glasgow G1 1DA Tel. 041-332 9876.

British Rail, Buchanan House, 58 Port Dundas Road, Glasgow G4 0HG Tel. 041-332 9811.

British Road Services (Scottish Division), 11 Bothwell Street, Glasgow G2 6NA Tel. 041-248 4411.

Road Haulage Association, Scottish Area Office, 17 Woodside Crescent, Charing Cross, Glasgow G3 7UL Tel. 041-332 9201.

Scottish Transport Group, Carron House, 114-116 George Street, Edinburgh EH2 4LX Tel. 031-226·7491.

British European Airways, Scottish Airways Division, Glasgow Airport, Abbotsinch, Paisley, Renfrewshire PA3 2SD Tel. 041-887 1111.

British Caledonian Airways Ltd., London Airport-Gatwick, Horley, Surrey RH6 0LT Tel. 01-283 8755.

Aberdeen Harbour Board, Harbour Office, 16 Regent Quay, Aberdeen Tel. 0224 52571.

Clyde Port Authority, 16 Robertson Street, Glasgow G2 8DS Tel. 041 221 8733.

Dundee Harbour Trust, Harbour Chambers, Dundee Tel. 0382 24121.

Forth Ports Authority, Tower Place, Leith, Edinburgh 6 Tel. 031 554 6473.

REGIONAL DEVELOPMENT AUTHORITIES

Highlands and Islands Development Board, Bridge House, Bank Street, Inverness Tel. 0463 34171 Telex 7567.

North East Scotland Development Authority, 15 Union Terrace, Aberdeen AB1 1NJ Tel. 0224 55971.

Eastern Borders Development Authority, 1 Quay Walk, Berwick-upon-Tweed Tel. 0289 6749.

South West Scotland Development Authority, Dumfries County Buildings, Dumfries Tel. 0387 3141.

Central Borders, Selkirk County Offices, Melrose Road, Galashiels Tel. 0896 3177.

Scotland West Industrial Promotion Group, 21 Bothwell Street, Glasgow G2 6NJ Tel. 041-221 4296.

South East Scotland Development Authority, 36 Palmerston Place, Edinburgh EH12 5AJ Tel. 031-226 4767

Tayside Development Authority, City Chambers, Albert Square, Dundee
Tel. 0382 23141.

NEW TOWNS

Cumbernauld Development Corporation, Cumbernauld House,
Cumbernauld   Tel. 023-67 21155

Glenrothes Development Corporation, Glenrothes House, Glenrothes,
Fife   Tel. 059-275 4343.

Livingston Development Corporation, Livingston, West Lothian   Tel.
58 31177.

East Kilbride Development Corporation, Norfolk House, East Kilbride
Tel. 035-52 28788.

Irvine Development Corporation, Perceton House, Irvine, Ayrshire
Tel. 029-47 4100.

INDUSTRIAL, PROFESSIONAL AND COMMERCIAL ORGANISATIONS

Scottish Council, Development and Industry, 1 Castle Street, Edinburgh EH2 3AJ   Tel. 031-225 7911   Telex 72349.

Confederation of British Industry, 5 Claremont Terrace, Glasgow C3
Tel. 041-332 8661.

Scottish Trades Union Congress, 12 Woodlands Terrace, Glasgow C3
Tel. 041-332 4946.

Scottish Industrial Estates Corporation, 3 Woodside Place, Glasgow
C3   Tel. 041-332 6651.

Scottish Tourist Board, 23 Ravelston Terrace, Edinburgh
Tel. 031-332 2433.

The Law Society of Scotland, 26 Drumsheugh Gardens, Edinburgh
EH3 7YR   Tel. 031-226 7411.

Aberdeen Chamber of Commerce, 15 Union Terrace, Aberdeen AB9 1HF
Tel. 0224 29222.

Dundee Chamber of Commerce, Chamber of Commerce Buildings,
Panmure Street, Dundee DD1 1ED   Tel. 0382 22122.

Edinburgh Chamber of Commerce, 20 Hanover Street, Edinburgh EH2
2EN   Tel. 031-225 5851.

Glasgow Chamber of Commerce, 30 George Square, Glasgow G2 1EQ
Tel. 041-221 8583.

The Scottish Stock Exchange, Stock Exchange House, 69 St. George's
Place, Glasgow G2 1BU   Tel. 041-221 7060.

The Institute of Bankers in Scotland, 62 George Street, Edinburgh
EH2 2LY   Tel. 031-225 7076.

Scottish Retail Federation, 7 Eglinton Crescent, Edinburgh 12   Tel. 031-225 3214.

ADVERTISING AND MEDIA ORGANISATIONS

Bureau of British Television Advertising, Knighton House, Mortimer Street, London W1   Tel. 01-636 6866.

Scottish Newspaper Proprietors' Association, 10 York Place, Edinburgh 1   Tel. 031-928 6787.

Scottish Daily Newspaper Society, 90 Mitchell Street, Glasgow C1 Tel. 041-221 9741.

Screen Advertising Association, 11 Hill Street, London W1A 4NE Tel. 01-499 6353.

Advertising Agency Poster Bureau, 42 Kingsway, London WC2 Tel. 01-242 7848.

Institute of Practitioners in Advertising, Scottish and N.E. Branch, c/o L. C. Young Esq., R. & W. Advertising Ltd., 18 Rutland Square, Edinburgh EH1 2BH   Tel. 031-229 7493.

Institute of Public Relations, Scottish Area Group, c/o W. H. Hemp-Hamilton Esq., J.P., F.I.P.R., Anchor Line, 16 Royal Exchange Square, Glasgow G1 3AB.

A comprehensive listing of press, television, outdoor and other advertising media, including rates and technical data, appears in the following monthly publication:

British Rate & Data, 30 Old Burlington Street, London W1X 2AE Tel. 01-437 0644.

Appendix 2

1. Retail Shops by Kind of Business 1961, 1971 (a)

	1961		1971	
Kind of business	*Shops (No.)*	*Turnover (£000)*	*Shops (No.)*	*Turnover (£000)*
TOTAL RETAIL SHOPS (b)	542,301	8,828,111	485,346	15,217,963
Grocers and provision dealers	146,777	2,350,711	107,563	3,992,806
Other food retailers	114,655	1,727,896	94,281	2,606,110
Dairymen	6,573	363,739	4,245	563,293
Butchers	42,419	625,156	33,888	879,903
Fishmongers, poulterers	6,330	75,838	4,838	83,538
Greengrocers, fruiterers (including those selling fish)	33,073	289,598	24,149	377,935
Bread and flour confectioners	17,260	233,025	17,370	335,939
Off-licences	9,000	140,539	9,791	365,502
Confectioners, tobacconists, newsagents	70,108	797,832	54,024	1,297,239
Clothing and footwear shops	86,555	1,366,737	81,139	2,247,644
Footwear shops	14,104	219,621	12,647	337,235
Men's and boys' wear shops	13,577	270,022	14,339	469,489
Women's and girls' wear, household textiles and general clothing shops	58,874	877,094	54,153	1,440,920
Household goods shops	60,343	948,335	73,664	1,939,381
Furniture and allied shops	16,498	371,346	23,125	676,639
Radio and electrical goods shops (excluding hire)	16,517	269,942	18,893	566,790
Radio and television hire shops	2,225	71,350	3,316	179,901
Hardware, china, wallpaper and paint shops	25,103	235,696	28,330	516,051

240

Kind of business	1961		1971	
	Shops (No.)	Turnover (£000)	Shops (No.)	Turnover (£000)
TOTAL RETAIL SHOPS (b)	542,301	8,828,111	485,346	15,217,963
Other non-food retailers	60,113	706,913	70,371	1,572,825
Bookshops and stationers	5,967	83,721	8,196	208,374
Chemists and photographic dealers	18,097	346,504	16,884	736,889
Cycle and perambulator shops	5,630	38,509	3,037	42,174
Jewellery, leather and sports goods shops	17,506	162,745	22,600	397,950
Other non-food shops	12,913	75,433	19,654	187,438
General stores	3,750	929,687	4,304	1,561,956
Department stores	784	545,421	914	937,955
Variety and general household stores	2,966	384,266	3,390	624,002

(a) Including estimates for non-response.
(b) Including fixed lockable premises in permanent markets but excluding other market stalls and mobile shops.

2. Retail Shops by Form of Organisation and Kind of Business (Food and Non-Food) 1961, 1971 (a) (b)

Form of organisation and kind of business	1961		1971	
	Shops (No.)	Turnover (£000)	Shops (No.)	Turnover (£000)
TOTAL RETAIL SHOPS	542,301	8,828,111	485,346	15,217,963
Co-operative societies	29,396	959,339	15,053	1,100,644
Multiples	66,701	2,578,898	67,479	6,061,363
Independents	446,204	5,289,875	402,814	8,055,955
Food shops	261,432	4,078,607	201,844	6,598,916
Co-operative societies	23,440	729,368	11,734	803,850
Multiples	31,845	1,032,576	27,220	2,548,491
Independents	206,147	2,316,664	162,890	3,246,575
Non-food shops (including general shops)	280,869	4,749,504	283,502	8,619,046
Co-operative societies	5,956	229,971	3,319	296,794
Multiples	34,856	1,546,322	40,259	3,512,872
Independents	240,057	2,973,211	239,924	4,809,381

(a) Including estimates for non-response.
(b) Including fixed lockable premises in permanent markets but excluding other market stalls and mobile shops.

3. Retail Shops by Form of Organisation and Kind of Business 1971 (a) (b)

Kind of business	All retail shops		Co-operative societies		Multiples		Independents	
	Shops (No.)	Turnover (£000)	Shops (No.)	Turnover (£000)	Shops (No.)	Turnover (£000)	Shops (No.)	Turnover (£000)
TOTAL RETAIL SHOPS	485,346	15,217,963	15,053	1,100,644	67,479	6,061,363	402,814	8,055,955
Grocers and provision dealers	107,563	3,992,806	7,730	559,931	10,839	1,724,356	88,994	1,708,520
Other food retailers	94,281	2,606,110	4,004	243,920	16,381	824,135	73,896	1,538,055
Dairymen	4,245	563,293	417	167,006	539	262,165	3,289	134,122
Butchers	33,888	879,903	2,551	43,948	4,193	160,300	27,144	675,655
Fishmongers, poulterers	4,838	83,538	48	697	117	3,859	4,673	78,983
Greengrocers, fruiterers (including those selling fish)	24,149	377,935	527	8,980	963	38,077	22,659	330,878
Bread and flour confectioners	17,370	335,939	252	12,526	5,846	135,677	11,272	187,736
Off-licences	9,791	365,502	209	10,763	4,723	224,058	4,859	130,681
Confectioners, tobacconists, newsagents	54,024	1,297,239	71	3,772	6,022	205,251	47,931	1,088,216
Clothing and footwear shops	81,139	2,247,644	1,229	37,938	16,511	1,289,697	63,399	920,010
Footwear shops	12,647	337,235	304	6,970	6,214	229,797	6,129	100,468
Men's and boys' wear shops	14,339	469,489	205	6,379	4,410	238,726	9,724	224,384
Women's and girls' wear, household textiles and general clothing shops	54,153	1,440,920	720	24,588	5,887	821,174	47,546	595,158

3. Retail Shops by Form of Organisation and Kind of Business 1971 (a) (b)

Kind of business	All retail shops Shops (No.)	Turnover (£000)	Co-operative societies Shops (No.)	Turnover (£000)	Multiples Shops (No.)	Turnover (£000)	Independents Shops (No.)	Turnover (£000)
TOTAL RETAIL SHOPS	485,346	15,217,963	15,053	1,100,644	67,479	6,061,363	402,814	8,055,955
Household goods shops	73,664	1,939,381	607	29,360	10,640	636,983	62,417	1,273,038
Furniture and allied shops	23,125	676,639	254	15,507	2,013	182,943	20,858	478,189
Radio and electrical goods shops (excluding hire)	18,893	566,790	185	9,004	3,298	206,923	15,410	350,862
Radio and television hire shops	3,316	179,901	8	750	2,808	163,291	500	15,860
Hardware, china, wallpaper and paint shops	28,330	516,051	160	4,098	2,521	83,827	25,649	428,126
Other non-food retailers	70,371	1,572,825	713	25,289	4,751	449,557	64,907	1,097,980
Bookshops and stationers	8,196	208,374	5	282	547	55,375	7,644	152,717
Chemists and photographic dealers	16,884	736,889	632	21,339	2,572	312,095	13,680	403,455
Cycle and perambulator shops	3,037	42,174	9	392	9	409	3,019	41,373
Jewellery, leather and sports goods shops	22,600	397,950	37	2,790	1,305	72,954	21,258	322,206
Other non-food shops	19,654	187,438	30	485	318	8,723	19,306	178,229
General stores	4,304	1,561,956	699	200,435	2,335	931,384	1,270	430,138
Department stores	914	937,955	249	156,523	296	423,939	369	357,492
Variety and general household stores	3,390	624,002	450	43,912	2,039	507,445	901	72,645

(a) Including estimates for non-response.
(b) Including fixed locable premises in permanent markets but excluding other market stalls and mobile shops.

FOOD AND OTHER RETAIL OUTLETS BY COUNTY IN SCOTLAND, 1971

(BUSINESSES ENUMERATED FOR THE 1971 CENSUS OF DISTRIBUTION)

Country and County	Total retail shops	Grocers and provision dealers	Other food retailers	Confectioners, tobacconists, newsagents
Scotland	44,561	10,869	9,261	4,902
Aberdeen	2,825	599	638	311
Angus	2,557	569	554	328
Argyll	801	246	111	75
Ayr	3,176	743	639	314
Banff	557	147	109	49
Berwick	239	65	50	30
Bute	303	73	55	45
Caithness	315	99	54	22
Clackmannan	411	119	87	39
Dumfries	811	210	127	83
Dunbarton	1,371	364	309	152
East Lothian	578	151	119	56
Fife	3,004	771	633	316
Inverness	813	246	108	60
Kincardine	261	79	51	19
Kinross	80	22	16	10
Kirkudbright	292	85	44	24
Lanark	11,475	2,735	2,587	1,318
Midlothian	5,297	1,055	1,194	646
Moray	561	135	108	44
Nairn	116	28	18	10
Orkney	234	94	37	15
Peebles	147	32	25	19
Perth	1,396	314	229	170
Renfrew	2,434	597	553	304
Ross and Cromarty	578	188	94	48
Roxburgh	525	116	119	48
Selkirk	273	64	48	24
Stirling	1,601	436	287	175
Sutherland	186	61	22	18
West Lothian	795	237	148	80
Wigtown	333	89	49	39
Zetland	216	100	39	11

Appendix 3

RETAIL TRADE CATEGORIES: DEFINITIONS

Grocers and Provision Dealers: including delicatessens, health food shops and 'general stores' selling both food and non-food items.

Dairymen: including depots from which roundsmen operate.

Bread and Flour Confectioners: including depots from which roundsmen operate.

Off-Licences: excluding those attached to public houses and those in establishments classified as grocers.

Confectioners, Tobacconists and Newsagents: establishments specialising in the sale of these products.

Footwear Shops: excluding those specialising in repairs.

Men's and Boys' Wear Shops: including retail bespoke tailors.

Women's and Girls' Wear, Household Textile and General Clothing Shops: including drapers, needlework and second-hand clothing shops and clothing hire and repair shops.

Furniture and Allied Shops: including furniture repair shops, antique and art dealers, and second-hand furniture shops.

Radio and Electrical Goods: excluding hire.

Radio and T.V. Hire Shops: excluding wired relay sets.

Hardware, China, Wallpaper and Paint Shops: including do-it-yourself shops and glasswear dealers.

Booksellers and Stationers: including establishments selling artists supplies, maps, second-hand books, and circulating libraries.

Chemists and Photographic Dealers: including those selling cosmetics etc. and photographic film and accessories.

Cycle and Perambulator Shops: including those selling motor and cycle accessories.

Jewellery, Leather and Sports Goods Shops: including those repairing jewellery and those selling watches, travel and fancy goods, toys and camping equipment.

Other Non-Food Shops: including florists, pet-food shops, general second-hand dealers, sub-post-offices, pawnbrokers, handicraft shops and those selling scientific, medical and surgical goods.

Department Stores: those having 25 or more persons engaged selling a wide range of commodities including clothing and household goods.

Scottish Retail Federation
Scottish Stock Exchange
Scottish Television Ltd.
Scottish Tourist Board
Scottish Transport Group
South of Scotland Electricity Board
Tayside Development Authority
The Glasgow Herald
The Rank Organisation (Advertising Films Division)
University of Strathclyde (Department of Urban Studies)
West Central Scotland Plan Steering Committee

Index